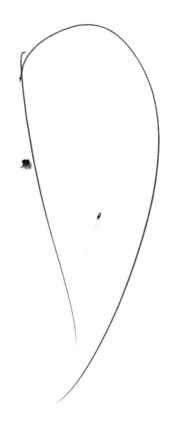

IN SEARCH OF ISRAEL

IN
SEARCH
OF
ISRAEL

THE HISTORY OF AN IDEA

MICHAEL BRENNER

PRINCETON UNIVERSITY PRESS

This edition is a substantially revised translation of *Israel: Traum und Wirklichkeit des Jüdischen Staates* by Michael Brenner, © Verlag C.H. Beck oHG, Munchen 2016

Published by Princeton University Press,
41 William Street, Princeton, New Jersey 08540

In the United Kingdom: Princeton University Press,
6 Oxford Street, Woodstock, Oxfordshire OX20 1TR

press.princeton.edu

Jacket image: Western wall (Wailing Wall). Jerusalem, Israel. Roman Sigaev / Alamy Stock Photo

Library of Congress Cataloguing-in-Publication Data

Names: Brenner, Michael, 1964– author.
Title: In Search of Israel : the history of an idea/Michael Brenner.
Other titles: Israel. English
Description: Princeton : Princeton University Press, 2018. | Includes bibliographical references and index.
Identifiers: LCCN 2017037393 | ISBN 9780691179285 (hardcover : alk. paper)
Subjects: LCSH: Israel. | Israel—History. | Judaism—Israel.
Classification: LCC DS125.5 .B7413 2018 | DDC 956.9405—dc23 LC record available at https://lccn.loc.gov/2017037393

British Library Cataloging-in-Publication Data is available

This book has been composed in Sabon Next and Gotham

Printed on acid-free paper. ∞

Printed in the United States of America

10 9 8 7 6 5 4 3 2 1

To my daughter Simone,
who helped me explore new sides of Israel

CONTENTS

ILLUSTRATIONS AND MAPS

All maps have been prepared for this book, and are copyright © Peter Palm, Berlin/Germany

ACKNOWLEDGMENTS

Living in two countries and writing about a third encourages continuous reflection on the specific characteristics of different societies. I am grateful to my German publisher, C. H. Beck, and especially to Wolfgang Beck and Ulrich Nolte, for insisting that I write an earlier version of this book despite my initial hesitations, and I am just as grateful to Princeton University's Brigitta van Rheinberg for insisting that I write a substantially different book for an English-reading audience. It has been a real pleasure to work with Princeton University Press once again, where Amanda Peery and Debbie Tegarden have assisted me in various stages of turning my manuscript into a book. My copyeditor Eva Jaunzems made invaluable contributions to improve the final shape of this book.

My colleagues both at Ludwig Maximilian University in Munich and at American University in Washington, DC, have provided substantial input from the early stages of the German edition to the last stages of the English edition. Directing two quite different centers for Israel Studies in Munich and Washington, and serving on the board of yet two other academic centers in Israel have taught me to view the Jewish state from a variety of angles both from inside and outside. In Washington, I am indebted to my colleagues Pamela Nadell, Max Paul Friedman, Lisa Leff, and Guy Ziv, who have commented on various parts of my project and have been supportive in so many other ways. Lillian Abensohn has been the kindest and most generous donor any holder of a named chair can imagine, and her insight as an academic herself into Israeli society and Jewish literature have helped me gain new perspectives into my subject matter.

A new initiative of American University's College of Arts and Sciences supported the last stage of this book manuscript by providing me with a "book incubator." Thanks to Dean Peter Starr's and Associate Dean U. J. Sofia's support, I was able to gather some of my most esteemed colleagues for an intensive and extremely stimulating meeting, which helped to shape the final form of the manuscript. Alon Confino, Arie Dubnow, Yoav Gelber, James Loeffler, Yoram Peri, Derek Penslar, and Daniel Schwartz were extremely generous with their time and their comments, reading the whole manuscript critically and discussing it for an entire day in the most pleasant critical spirit.

In Munich, my colleagues Noam Zadoff, Mirjam Zadoff, Daniel Mahla, and Philipp Lenhard, as well as our visiting professors from Israel, Shlomo Ben-Ami and Natan Sznaider, all provided valuable suggestions to improve the original German edition of the book. I am grateful for having been invited as a visiting professor to the University of Haifa at an earlier stage and for continuing to serve on various committees in different institutions. My special thanks go to Eli Salzberger and Fania Oz-Salzberger from the University of Haifa and to Yfaat Weiss from the Hebrew University in Jerusalem. My long conversations with them have left their imprint in this book as well. Dimitry Shumsky in Jerusalem has read and commented on the manuscript extensively, as has John Efron in Berkeley and Michael Meyer in Cincinnati.

I would also like to thank three graduate students who provided indispensable help in the search for sources and with the editing of the text: Dominik Peters and Julia Schneidawind in Munich, and Omer Kaufman in Washington. Librarian Ann Brener never despaired of finding new and ever more obscure pamphlets in the bottomless treasure chambers of the Library of Congress, in whose beautiful reading rooms a good part of this book was written.

As always, my most profound thanks go to my family. My daughter Simone, to whom this book is dedicated, shares with me an inside and an outside perspective on Israel, and showed me parts of Tel Aviv I would have been too old to explore by myself. My wife, Michelle Engert, took me on many imaginary walks through endless versions of this manuscript, inspired me to write yet another version, and made sure that I kept in mind the readers of the book. Many ideas in the book were born in our real walks, during which I gained a totally new appreciation for Clio, the muse of history.

IN SEARCH OF ISRAEL

A STATE (UN)LIKE ANY OTHER STATE

"Now appoint for us a king to judge us like all the nations."

SAMUEL 8:5

The eminent Oxford philosopher Isaiah Berlin took great pleasure in telling the story of a party he attended in the 1930s where the later president of the State of Israel, Chaim Weizmann, then the leader of the World Zionist Organization, was asked by an aristocratic British lady admirer, "Dr. Weizmann, I do not understand. You are a member of the most cultured, civilized, brilliant and cosmopolitan people in history and you want to give it all up to become—Albania?" According to Isaiah Berlin, Weizmann pondered thoughtfully and slowly on the question, then his face lit up like a light bulb. "Yes!" he exclaimed: "Albania! Albania!"

To become a people like any other people! That was the idea that many Zionists had in mind when they set out to realize their project to create a Jewish state. The Declaration of Independence of the State of Israel internalized this notion in a central passage that stresses "the natural right of the Jewish people to be masters of their own fate, like all other nations, in their own sovereign State." Jews, so their argument went, had always been the archetypal "other" in history. Only by ending the "abnormal" situation of their dispersion in a worldwide diaspora and by reestablishing their own state after two millennia would "normality" be regained in the form of a small Jewish state. Thus, the Jews would become "a nation like all other nations" and their state a state like all other states—an imagined Albania.[1]

Over two millennia Jews had received attention way beyond their numerical strength, as historian David Nirenberg observed: "For several thousand years people have been thinking about Judaism. Ancient Egyptians spent a good deal of papyrus on the Hebrews; early (and not so early) Christians filled pages attempting to distinguish between Judaism and Christianity, the New Israel and the Old; Muhammad's followers pondered their Prophet's relation to Jews and 'Sons of Israel'; medieval Europeans invoked Jews to explain topics as diverse as famine, plague, and the tax policies of their princes. And in the vast archives that survive from Early Modern and Modern Europe and its cultural colonies, it is easy enough to demonstrate that words like 'Jew,' 'Hebrew,' 'Semite,' 'Israelite,' and 'Israel,' appear with a frequency stunningly disproportionate to any populations of living Jews in these societies."[2]

The sociologist Zygmunt Bauman called this phenomenon "allosemitism." In contrast to the negative "antisemitism" and the positive "philosemitism," "allosemitism," which is based on the Greek word for "other," simply refers "to the practice of setting the Jews apart as people radically different from all the others, needing separate concepts to describe and comprehend them and special treatment in all or most social intercourse. . . . It does not unambiguously designate either hatred or love of Jews, but contains the seeds of both, and assures that whichever of the two appears, is intense and extreme."[3] Allosemitism was endemic to Europe and beyond due in large part to the legacy of the Christian church, which put the Jews "in the role of ambivalence incarnate." They were beloved as the people of Jesus but hated as Christ-killers; they were held in esteem for the Old Testament, but despised for not accepting its prophecies as interpreted by the New Testament. In modernity, Jews became the most mobile of all pariahs and parvenus. "They were the epitome of incongruity: a non-national nation, and so cast a shadow on the fundamental principle of modern European order: that nationhood is the essence of human destiny." [4]

The image of the Jews as the "other" was of course used by Jews themselves as well, and this from earliest times. It originates with the biblical notion of a "chosen people" and is repeated in various forms throughout the books of the Bible and later in rabbinical literature and Jewish liturgy. The daily *Alenu* prayer contains the passage, "For God did not make us like the nations of other lands, and did not make us the same as other families of the Earth. God did not place us in the same situations as others, and our destiny is not the same as anyone else's." Otherness is already cited in ancient Jewish sources as the cause for anti-Jewish hatred. According to the biblical book of Esther, Haman, the advisor to the Persian king, claimed:

> There is a certain people dispersed among the peoples in all the provinces of your kingdom who keep themselves separate. Their customs are different from those of all other people, and they do not obey the king's laws; it is not in the king's best interest to tolerate them. If it pleases the king, let a decree be issued to destroy them. (Esther 3:8–9).

While the modern Jewish Reform movement tried to eliminate some of the self-distinctions in liturgy and practice, the notion that the Jews remained different was shared by many Jews and non-Jews alike in the twentieth century. Israel

Mattuck, the most prominent Liberal rabbi in England in the first half of the twentieth century, wrote in 1939: "The Jews are anomalous because they do not fit into any of the three normal categories for the classification of human groups. . . . Though the Jews are not a race, they are a separate group; though they are not a nation, they have from remote times memories of a national life; though they are dispersed, they are unified. The unity of the Jews is psychological, produced by their religion, history, and experience. The Jews are unique."[5]

Zionism aimed to overcome this sense of otherness by forcing the Jews to fit into categories valid in the nineteenth and twentieth centuries. Once they were universally regarded as a nation and had their own state, they would no longer be vulnerable to assaults against their alleged uniqueness and cease to be victims of antisemitic attacks. The Zionist Joseph Heller summarized this attitude when he wrote shortly before the State of Israel was founded: "A nation, like an individual, is normal and healthy only when it is able to use *all* forms of innate gifts and harmoniously to unfold *all* forms of economic and cultural creativeness. For this purpose the nation needs political freedom and the right to utilize the natural resources of the soil as the basis of its economic growth. The task of normalization means for the Jews a real 'transvaluation of values,' because of the unquestioned hegemony of the spirit throughout Diaspora history. . . . Above all, the nation must 'return to the soil' not only in the physical sense but also in the psychological."[6]

Seventy years after the establishment of the State of Israel, Israel has achieved many goals of the Zionist movement, but the plan to become a state "like any other" has not been fulfilled. If the Jews were the archetypical "other" in history, ironically, Israel—which so much wanted to avoid the stamp of otherness—has become the Jew among the nations. The Jewish state is rarely conceived as just a state like any other state, but rather as unique and exceptional: it is seen either as a model state or as a pariah state.

Israel ranks as 148th of the 196 independent states in terms of geographical area, and as 97th in terms of population, which is somewhere between Belize and Djibouti. However, the international attention it attracts is exponentially greater than that of Belize or Djibouti, or for that matter Albania. Considering only the volume of media attention it attracts, one might reasonably assume that the Jewish state is in the same league as the United States, Russia, and China. In the United States, for the last three decades, Israel has figured more prominently than almost any other country in foreign policy debates; in polls across Europe, Israel is considered to be the greatest danger to world peace; and in Islamic societies it has become routine to burn Israeli flags and argue for Israel's demise. No other country has been the subject of as many UN resolutions as Israel. At the same time, many people around the world credit Israel with a unique role in the future course of world history. Evangelical Christians regard the Jewish state as a major player in their eschatological model of the world. Their convictions have influenced US policies in the Middle East and the opinions of some political leaders in other parts of the world. Following Zygmunt Bauman's concept, one might speak today of a phenomenon called allo-Zionism.

The idea of exceptionalism exists, of course, in many other national narratives as well. The Greeks regarded all other nations as barbarians, and the French believed in their *mission civilisatrise*. Over decades, historians have had heated discussions over the thesis of a peculiar path of German history.[7] And, as C. Vann Woodward reminded us, American historians have always been accused of laying "excessive claims to distinctiveness and uniqueness in their national experience."[8] "American Exceptionalism" has been characterized by values such as freedom, egalitarianism, and laissez-faire principles.[9] The United States of America also shares with Israel the notion of being a "chosen nation," as Todd Gitlin and Liel Leibovitz have noted: "Amid an epic history of claims to heaven-sent entitlement, only two nation-states stand out for the fundamental, continuous, and enduring quality of their convictions, and the intense seriousness (and hostility) with which others take their claims: the United States and Israel."[10] What distinguishes the case of Israel from other exceptionalisms is the fact that it is regarded as an exceptional state not only by itself, but by much of the rest of the world as well. Based on the accounts in the foundational texts of both Christianity and Islam, where the Jews were often viewed as the prototypical other, the Jewish state became the collective expression of "the other state." Even in scholarship, both in Israel and outside the Jewish state, it seems almost normal to point to the *abnormal* character of Israel's history. Historians, sociologists, and political scientists provide many different interpretations of Israel, but they seem to agree on its uniqueness. To cite a few random contemporary examples: Daniel Elazar's study of Israel's society begins with the sentence, "The State of Israel is, in many respects, sui generis."[11] Uri Bialer opens his analysis of Israel's foreign policy as follows: "Among the nations of the world Israel is unique."[12] Todd Gitlin and Liel Leibovitz claim: "Why not inter the Zionist movement in the history books and turn to the governance of an ordinary state in a world of states? The answer is obvious. Israel is not, has never been, and can never be an ordinary state."[13] Law professor Yedidia Stern takes a clear position when he states: "The State of Israel cannot be satisfied with a 'normal' democratic existence and should not divest itself of its Jewish uniqueness."[14] Michael Barnett writes in his study on Israel's alleged singularity: "Israel slips through the cracks because it is perceived as existing outside or blurring most conceptual boundaries and categories."[15] And to provide one last example among many, Jerold Auerbach states: "Israel remains a historic anomaly."[16]

Authors critical of Israel, or even hostile toward it, often share this perception of Israel's anomaly, though coming at it from the opposite point of view. American-Palestinian literary scholar and political activist Edward Said, for example, has claimed: "A Jewish state is on national, religious, cultural, juridical, and political grounds different from any other state." In his view, the Jewish search for normality results in the abnormal situation of the Palestinians: "If, in a Jewish state, normality is defined by Jewishness, abnormality is the normal condition of the non-Jew."[17] Referring to Said's model, Northeastern University economist M. Shahid Alam, who denies Israel's right of existence, suggests: "A deeper irony surrounded the Zionist project. It proposed to end Jewish 'abnormalcy' in Europe by creating an 'abnormal' Jewish state in Palestine. . . . Clearly, the Zionists were proposing to trade one 'abnormalcy' for a greater, more ominous one."[18] Zionists and anti-Zionists, Israelis, and opponents of the Jewish state seem to agree on one thing: Israel is different from other states.

The ultimate irony is that the term "normalization," so often employed by Zionists in order to correct the path of Jewish history, has in the twenty-first century received a meaning turned against Israel. Resistance against the normalization of relations with a Jewish state has characterized those who identify Israel as a settler-colonialist state. It has become a frequent slogan in the BDS (Boycott, Divest, and Sanction) campaign. Normalization stands for them as a "colonization of the mind." As one activist website puts it: "The normalization of Israel—normalizing the abnormal—is a malicious and subversive process that works to cover up injustice and colonize the most intimate parts of the oppressed: their mind."[19] In the eyes of the opponents of Israel's normalization, Israel should be treated differently from other states and ultimately become what the Jews have always been: the other, the abnormal. Thus, the use of the concept of normalization, launched by the Zionist movement in the late nineteenth century as a response to antisemitism has gone full circle. Used in its negative sense, it now serves the opponents of Israel to delegitimize the existence of the Jewish state.

There are numerous reasons why many people perceive the tiny State of Israel as unique and ascribe to it a meaning of universal significance. To start with, it was probably naïve to assume that the centuries-old stereotype of the Jew as the classical outsider would simply disappear with the advent of the Zionist movement. Stereotypes and opinions of the Jews have been etched so deeply into the minds of so many people across the world that an indifferent position toward a Jewish state is almost impossible. As if this were not enough, Israel's birth was directly connected to a genocide unique in modern history. Moreover, in contrast to other modern states, most of Israel's first-generation citizens did not originate in the territory that would later become their state. Neither did their immediate ancestors. Israel has the unique distinction of being what we might call an almost completely "imported nation."

A closer look will show that there is an additional element in Zionist history that runs counter to Weizmann's desire to become just another Albania, a desire that will be explored in greater depth in this book. While he and other Zionist thinkers and Israeli statesmen claimed to strive simply for a state "like all other states," they themselves were in reality not satisfied with such a concept. They aspired to more, namely to create a model state and thus to fulfill the goal of the ancient prophets that Israel become "a light unto the nations."[20] It was this internal contradiction between an aspired normality and a claimed uniqueness that constituted and continues to constitute an enormous challenge for the self-definition of the Jewish state.

Beginning with the founder of political Zionism, Theodor Herzl, there existed always a very strong conviction among Zionists that a Jewish state must be a model society for all humankind. David Ben-Gurion, the most important political leader in Palestine from the 1930s and the first prime minister of Israel, repeatedly called for the establishment of a state that would fulfill the biblical vision of the Jews as a "light unto the nations." This demand is reiterated by a long line of Israeli leaders, all the way up to Prime Minister Benjamin Netanyahu. In an address at the Herzliya Conference in 2010, for example, he called the Jewish people "a proud people with a magnificent country and one which always aspires to serve as 'a light unto the nations.'"[21] His education minister, Gideon Sa'ar, declared that the task of the country's education system should be turning the country into "a light unto the nations."[22] Official Israel continues to display this ideal in many variations and on many different levels. Thus, visitors arriving at Ben-Gurion Airport today (2017) are confronted in an exhibition on Zionist and Israeli history with Theodor Herzl's words: "Zionism encompasses not only the hope of a legally secured homeland for our people . . . but also the aspiration to reach moral and spiritual perfection."[23]

Concepts like "normality" and "uniqueness" cannot be measured scientifically. They are a matter of subjective perception.[24] Israel's exceptionalism might well be a myth, but like every well-cultivated myth it has become a reality in the imagination of many people. This book does not try to substantiate or demystify the question of whether Israel is a unique state or a "state like any other state." It describes rather a discourse over exactly this question, which runs like a scarlet thread through the text. It will serve us as a key for addressing the most important questions for accessing the very nature of this first Jewish state in modern history. Is it a state based on a common ethnicity or religion? Should it be a state where Jews from the whole world can find a safe haven but continue to live their lives just as they did before in their old homes, or should it be a Jewish state in which they will cleave to new values, different from those of their countries of origin? What are the borders of this state? And what is the role of non-Jews in a Jewish state?

This book traces the tensions between particularistic and universal elements in the idea of a Jewish state by recounting how Zionist visionaries imagined such a state and how Israeli leaders implemented these ideas over the course of a century. It is not a history of Israel's wars and its politics, but concentrates instead on the essential question of the meaning of this state and its transformation.[25] It tells the story of a state as it emerges in the minds of its own leaders and in the imagination of the larger world. It is the story of the real and the imagined Israel, of Israel as a state and as an idea.

The history of Israel has always been a global history, for the very reason that the Jewish people were spread around the globe. Political Zionism has its roots in various parts of Europe, it spread to America, and it has affected the Jewish communities in the Middle East and North Africa. Histories of Zionism and of Israel often neglect to show, however, the context in which their main protagonists acted. Thus, it is almost forgotten today that the Zionist movement was just one of several paths European Jews sought to take in order to "normalize" their peculiar situation. That is why this book opens with a chapter on a crucial year in Jewish history, 1897. It was a watershed year for modern Jewish history, and not only because the First Zionist Congress convened that year. Within a few months, four distinct new paths for a projected "normalization" of Jewish history were publicly proposed: Radical assimilationism, diaspora Autonomism, socialist Bundism, and political Zionism. As the first chapter of this book will show, the emergence of Zionism as a political movement has to be seen in the larger context of competing Jewish responses to the challenges of the new century.

The second chapter traces the *Kulturkampf* within the Zionist movement between the concepts of a state of the Jews and a Jewish state. One model was Theodor Herzl's New Society, which projected not only a refuge for persecuted Jews, but also an exemplary society for all humankind. This society was to be Jewish mostly in the sense that the majority of its members would be Jews. However, they would neither speak Hebrew (nor Yiddish), nor would Jewish culture or religion play any significant role in their foundational concepts. Herzl's Seven-Hour-Land, based on the idea of a seven-hour working day, would be a cosmopolitan model state, emphasizing social improvement and technological innovation. He portrayed it as a tolerant society, embracing Jews and non-Jews, and denying membership only to those who aspired to establish an exclusive theocracy at the expense of others. His model competed with more particularistic paradigms. Cultural Zionists strove for the renewal of the Hebrew language and the creation of a distinct secular Jewish culture, while socialist Zionists aimed at creating an ideal "New Jew," who would work the soil in a collectivist settlement (*kibbutz*), and religious Zionists envisioned a society based on *halakha*, the principles of Jewish religious law. For all of them, Herzl's model meant simply imitating bourgeois European culture and transporting a Western European society to the Middle East, or in other words, assimilation on a collective scale. While Herzl wanted to save the Jews from antisemitism, other Zionists wanted to save Judaism and Jewish culture from complete assimilation.

Chapter 3 discusses the road to statehood in the wake of the Balfour Declaration of 1917 that had promised the Jews "a national home in Palestine," but without defining what exactly was meant by this vague term. The Zionists, too, remained unclear for a long time about the meaning of Jewish sovereignty. Based on recent scholarship, I will suggest that for the mainstream General Zionists led by Chaim Weizmann and for the socialist Zionists led by David Ben-Gurion, far-reaching autonomy under British or international rule seemed a more realistic option than full independence until World War II. Even the nationalist Revisionists around Vladimir Ze'ev Jabotinsky, who fought for a Jewish state on both sides of the Jordan River, proposed concepts quite different from what would eventually become the State of Israel. In Jabotinsky's vision of a greater Palestine on both sides of the Jordan River, Arabs would not only enjoy full equality, they would be represented at the highest echelons of power.

This chapter looks at the different blueprints for a future Jewish national home, both inside and outside of Palestine. The various concepts of a future Jewish society *in Palestine* were part of a broader global struggle to establish a place for Jewish self-determination. During the 1920s and 30s the rise of right-wing antisemitic regimes in Europe increased the sense of urgency for a Jewish place of refuge anywhere in the world. In contrast to the Zionists who envisioned Jews settling in their historical homeland, the Territorialists advocated for the creation of a Jewish territory either in Australia, East Africa, or South America, places where they supposedly would not encounter opposition. By relinquishing the idea of connecting this territory with their ancient past, they also relinquished to a large degree the notion of uniqueness that came with that past. And it was precisely the lack of this historic notion that made the idea unpopular among most Jews. A Jewish state in East Africa or South America might have seemed pragmatic at the time and, in retrospect, it might well have saved many lives, but it lacked the emotional attraction of the Zionists' plan tied to the Jews' ancestral land.

As mentioned above, the Declaration of Independence of the State of Israel internalized the notion of the "normalization" of Jewish history in a central passage that stresses "the natural right of the Jewish people to be masters of their own fate, like all other nations, in their own sovereign State. Jews, so the argument went, had always been the archetypal "other" in history. Only by ending the "abnormal" situation of their dispersion in a worldwide diaspora and by reestablishing their own small Jewish state after two millennia would normality be regained. But their idea was not to create a state "like any other state," for the founders maintained that a Jewish state arising from a catastrophe, which they viewed as the culmination of a long history of suffering, was obligated to play a unique role: It should become the materialization of the biblical mission of the Jews as "a light unto the nations." The rejection of the state's existence by its Arab neighbors only strengthened its need for legitimacy.

Chapter 4 explains what Ben-Gurion and Israel's first governments envisioned in striving to become a model society for all humankind—and what the idea of a Jewish state meant after the State of Israel was established. It follows also the repeated attempts to define who is Jewish in a Jewish state. The Law of Return of 1950 stated that every Jew had the right to "return" to Israel and would be granted Israeli citizenship—but it left the legal definition of who was a Jew open. In an unprecedented action, Ben-Gurion sent out a letter to fifty of the most respected Jewish intellectuals all over the world asking them to provide their definition on the question of who is a Jew—and thus qualified to become an Israeli citizen. Several times, Israel's Supreme Court and Israel's parliament, the Knesset, uttered their own verdicts on this question. Their broad and inclusive definitions reflected the secular nature of the Jewish state during the first decades of its existence.

In 1967, Israel experienced its second founding. With its triumphant victory in the Six-Day War, Israel stood once again in the spotlight of the entire world. It emerged as a regional power and became identified with the biblical Goliath rather than with its traditional image of David, the underdog. In addition, with newly conquered territories in the Golan Heights, the West Bank of the Jordan River, East Jerusalem, the Gaza Strip, and the Sinai Peninsula, Israel came to govern over a much larger Arab population. The political climate within the country became increasingly nationalistic, and the triumph of right-wing parties under Menachem Begin in the

1977 elections was regarded as a revolution in Israeli politics. Perhaps the most significant transformation of Israel's society is to be found during this decade.

As told in chapter 5, the short-lived reality of a small and modest state was now replaced by the lavish vision of a Greater Israel, often interpreted as a fulfillment of Israel's divine mission and the unique role the Jewish state has to play in history. Combined with the political and religious radicalization of the Palestinian population, this not only led to new conflicts, such as the two Palestinian uprisings, but also to a precipitous decline in popularity of the secular and socialist models of the state's early leaders. Instead, more nationalistic and more religious definitions of the uniqueness of the Jewish state gained ground. The settler ideal began to replace the kibbutz ideal, the idea of the holy land superseded that of the secular state.

This process was briefly interrupted in the 1990s, when an alternative vision of Israel as part of a new Middle East emerged. Under Prime Minister Yitzhak Rabin, and with the participation and encouragement of the United States, Israel signed a peace agreement with the Jordanians in 1994. (A similar understanding had been reached with Egypt already in 1978.) The Oslo Accords, reached in 1993 and then 1995 with the Palestinians, signaled a new approach of reconciliation—and normalization. Rabin's long-time associate (and rival) Shimon Peres imagined a region in which Israel and the Arab states would be united in their aspirations for a common economic market and for political stability. Ultimately, they failed in their attempts to create normality for the Jewish state as an integral part of the Middle East.

The assassination of Rabin by a Jewish extremist, the following wave of violence, and the inflexibility of the Palestinian leadership brought the peace process to a standstill. But

Israeli society continued its process of transformation. In economic terms, it was transformed into a first-world country, a fact formally recognized by its joining the OECD in 2010. The Israel of the twenty-first century has been dubbed "the Start-Up Nation," and has one of the world's most successful high-tech industries. There was a price to pay, however. The state that once was proud of the relative equality in the lifestyle of its citizens has become a society with a wide gap between rich and poor.

Global Israel is far more than a phenomenon of the economic market. While most of Israel's new immigrants at the turn of the millennium came from the former Soviet Union, there are also "new Jews" knocking at Israel's doors. Millions of people in Africa and Asia who define themselves as descendants of the so-called lost tribes of the biblical Israelites would be eligible for Israeli citizenship if they were recognized as Jews by Israel's Chief Rabbinate. Not only are today's new immigrants more global than ever before—but so are Israel's emigrants. Contrary to the original Zionist ideal which envisioned the gathering of the exiles as part of the normalization of the Jewish situation, the Jewish diaspora has not only remained in existence but has actually grown as the result of an Israeli diaspora. New York and Los Angeles, and more recently Berlin—of all places—have become popular destinations for Israelis leaving their homeland, either temporarily or permanently. As chapter 6 will show, "alternative Israels" have gained prominence in literary and artistic form as well, from Eshkol Nevo's utopian novel *Neuland* to Yael Bartana's video project "Europe Will Be Stunned" about an imaginary return of Israeli Jews to Poland. As I argue in this chapter, ironically, the longing for normality in their lives has led Israeli citizens to look for new homes abroad and Israeli writers and artists to embrace the diaspora that once was so much despised by Zionism.

The conclusion of the book points to the crossroads where Israel stands today. On the one hand, it is an economically flourishing start-up nation with a universalist tradition and cosmopolitan habits. On the other, it is a country very much caught in the conflicts within its own region. For over half a century Israel has controlled a territory of unclear political status and a people that rejects its rule. It is a deeply divided society, in which both the secular population and universalist values are declining, while religious and more particularistic elements gain ground. It is a country with enormous achievements and one that has suffered setbacks. It is a state constantly at the center of global attention and, for better or worse, anything but "another Albania."

THE FIVE SEASONS
OF 1897

SHAPING THE JEWISH FUTURE

The Jews have suffered from too much
history and not enough geography.

—SIR LEWIS NAMIER

For European Jews, the nineteenth century began with a myriad of promises and hopes. In Western Europe, enlightenment and emancipation promised to transform them from outsiders to insiders. Here, the century brought many improvements for Jews; they did well economically and culturally, and were in the process of becoming integrated into society. But as the century came to a close, obstacles to integration became more and more tangible. A new racially based antisemitism closed many doors in the West, while in the East, pogroms and anti-Jewish policies shattered any dreams of progress.

There were two traditional roads leading out of this dilemma: one was conversion, the other emigration. One led out of Judaism, the other out of Europe. By the end of the century, America had become the promised land for many European Jews. The majority, though, wanted to remain Jews *and* Europeans, if only they were allowed to do so. They looked for ways finally to achieve in the twentieth century what they considered the normalization of their millennia-long role as outsiders.

The year 1897 saw the emergence of a diversity of paths that might lead to such an imagined normalization. In Berlin, the future German foreign minister Walther Rathenau wrote a passionate essay arguing for the thorough assimilation of German Jews. In Vienna, the editor of the liberal newspaper the *New Free Press*, Theodor Herzl, planned the First Zionist Congress, which took place in Basel in the summer of that same year. It was followed by the first meeting of the new Jewish socialist movement, the *Bund*, in Vilna in the fall of 1897. In Odessa, Simon Dubnow, the leading Jewish historian of his time, formulated the theoretical foundation for the cultural autonomy of the Jews within the diaspora.

Thus, within a few months, the major concepts of Jewish modernity were laid out. Zionism was only one of these responses to modern antisemitism and delayed integration. It should be seen in the context of the emergence of other responses, such as radical assimilation, socialist Bundism, and diaspora nationalism. While these paths could not be more different, their ultimate goal was the same: that Jewish history should be normalized, and the Jews should cease to be singled out as a group.

WINTER IN BERLIN

For well-informed readers, it was not very hard to detect who was hiding behind an article that appeared in the respectable German journal *Die Zukunft* (The Future) in early 1897, under the title, "Hear, O Israel." They could easily guess that the pen name "W. Hartenau" was a thin disguise for Walther Rathenau, heir to one of Germany's most significant industries, the *AEG* (General Electricity Company). Rathenau was an aspiring intellectual, who would much later become German foreign minister and then the Weimar Republic's most prominent political victim, when he was assassinated by a right-wing extremist in 1922. In 1897, young Rathenau was in search of a radical solution to the "Jewish question."

Although German Jews had been granted formal legal equality in the 1871 constitution of the new German Empire and had almost unprecedented upward economic mobility, they were not yet considered "normal Germans." They were not appointed to government ministerial posts or made military officers, and very few entered positions as civil servants. Most remained socially excluded.[1]

Unlike most of his Jewish contemporaries, Rathenau blamed his fellow Jews for this situation. He suggested that a more radical assimilation was needed and deemed it necessary to begin his essay with the sentence, "I want to profess straight off that I am a Jew." Indeed, one might otherwise have surmised that the author of this pamphlet was an antisemite.[2] In an earlier version, Rathenau had actually asked: "Does it require an explanation if I tend toward antisemitism?"[3] While he cut this sentence from the final publication, he left in the following passage: "Strange sight! In the midst of German life [there is] an isolated, strange human tribe, resplendently and conspicuously adorned, hot-blooded and animated in its behavior. An Asian horde on the soil of Brandenburg [the region around Berlin] . . . . In close association with each other, strictly closed off from the outside—thus they live in a semivoluntary, invisible ghetto, not a living member of the people [*Volk*], but a foreign organism in its body." And the Berlin Jew Rathenau asked, "What must be done?"

Rathenau answered his own question. What was needed was "an event without historical precedent: the conscious self-education of a race to assimilate to outside demands. Assimilation not in the sense of Darwin's 'mimicry,' adopting the color of their surroundings, but assimilation in the sense that tribal qualities–regardless of whether they are good or bad–that are demonstrably hateful to fellow Germans [*Landesgenossen*] are cast off and replaced by more suitable ones . . . The goal of the processes should not be imitation Germans, but Jews who are German by nature and education."[4]

Rathenau's father, Emil, was part of Germany's business elite. The founder and director general of its leading electricity company, he was "the Bismarck of an industrial empire." Walther grew up nominally Jewish but did not practice the Jewish religion. In contrast to many of his fellow elite Jews, who sought to get an entry ticket into European society by converting to Christianity, baptism was no option for him. He considered such a step opportunistic, superficial, and hypocritical, and he knew, moreover, that in the end, it still would not open the doors closed to Jews, since "a baptized Jew is never the same as a baptized Christian."[5]

Rathenau recognized that growing up Jewish in Imperial Germany meant facing barriers, even for the wealthiest segments of society. As he later recalled: "There is a painful moment every young Jew experiences and never forgets for the rest of his life: when he first becomes fully aware that he is born a second class citizen and that no talent and no merit can free him from this situation."[6]

Nor was a return to their ancient homeland an option for Rathenau, who believed that "the majority of German Jews have only one national sense: the German. Like our ancestors, we want to live and die in Germany and for Germany. Others may establish a 'Reich' in Palestine—nothing draws *us* to Asia."[7] Rathenau was more radical than most Western European Jews in his adamant expression of patriotism and his desire for radical assimilation, but his rejection of Zionism

FIGURE 1. Walther Rathenau in the uniform of a Prussian cuirassier.

resonated with most of them. Their home was Europe. The Middle Eastern region of Palestine seemed nothing more than ancient history to them.

Rathenau was an extreme example of the Jewish urge for assimilation among German-speaking Jews at the turn of the twentieth century. He took the threat to Jewish existence seriously and looked for radical responses. This distinguished him from the majority, who considered themselves German or Austrian citizens of the Jewish faith and who were convinced that the barriers, old and new, preventing their total integration were nothing but a temporary burden imposed upon them by their success.[8] Rathenau was the mirror image of the founder of political Zionism, Theodor Herzl, and in order to fully understand the latter, one has to study the former.[9]

SPRING IN VIENNA

A holy spring awaited the city of Vienna. *Ver sacrum (Sacred Spring)*—that was what Gustav Klimt and the other avant-garde artists of the Vienna Secession, which was founded on April 3, 1897, called their new journal. The Secession promised to break with the style of previous generations and establish a new era of modern art. The architect Otto Wagner defined their task as adapting "the face of the city to contemporary humanity."[10] In the realm of literature, too, changes were underway. The old meeting place of the literary bohème, the Café Griensteidl, was demolished and replaced by the Café Central. The new rising star among provocative young Austrian writers was Karl Kraus, whose celebrated journal *Die Fackel* (The Torch) consisted almost exclusively of his own contributions.

Just one day after the foundation of the Vienna Secession, spring arrived also for the musical enthusiasts of Vienna. On April 4, Gustav Mahler signed a provisional contract as director of the Imperial Orchestra; he would return to Vienna from Hamburg, where he had been a celebrated musician. Before he would finalize his contract, however, he had to undergo a brief but significant procedure: he was baptized and became a member of the Catholic church. As he noted himself, without this step he would have had no hope of being hired. Karl

Kraus (who would convert to Catholicism over a decade later) praised Mahler's arrival in Vienna as the end of the *ancien régime* in the city's musical life.[11] The antisemitic press, however, continued to refer to Mahler as a Jew and to denounce him and his music in racial terms.

On April 5, spring-like emotions overwhelmed the Czech citizens of the Habsburg Monarchy when Prime Minister Count Badeni issued a (short-lived) ordinance that elevated Czech to an official language beside German, to be used for government business in Bohemia and Moravia. The supporters of the antisemitic Christian Social Party in Vienna saw the first signs of spring a few days later, when Emperor Franz Joseph appointed Karl Lueger as mayor on April 16. Lueger had been elected already three times in the last two years, but each time the emperor had declined to officially appoint him due to Lueger's populism and antisemitism. After his fourth election, the emperor could no longer refuse. When the city's Jews heard of Lueger's appointment they were in the middle of their preparations for Passover, which would begin that evening. Many of them did not feel like celebrating the exodus from slavery to freedom while their own freedom seemed endangered. They were certainly not among Lueger's supporters, but they constituted only 8 percent of the city's population. Among the remaining 92 percent one could gain popularity with antisemitic attitudes, and indeed Lueger's continued expressions of antisemitism did not hurt him. He was reelected several times and remained an extremely popular mayor until his death in 1910. The Viennese liked to call him "the God Almighty of Vienna."[12]

Lueger's election made some Viennese Jews doubt that they would ever be accepted as normal Austrian citizens, and one of these was the editor of the cultural section, the *Feuil-*

FIGURE 2. Karl Lueger, mayor of Vienna, around 1900.

leton, of the renowned *Neue Freie Presse* (New Free Press) newspaper. He recorded a coincidental encounter with Lueger: "Toward evening I went to the Landstrasse district. In front of the polling place a silent, tense crowd. Suddenly Dr. Lueger came out to the square. Enthusiastic cheers; women waved white kerchiefs from the windows. The police held the crowd back. A man next to me said with tender warmth but in a quiet tone of voice: 'That is our *Führer*!'"[13]

The man who would later become Germany's *Führer* lived also in Vienna at the time and thought that the encounter with Lueger had changed his life. He wrote in *Mein Kampf*: "Today I see in this man even more than previously the most powerful German mayor of all times." Adolf Hitler recorded that during this period his antisemitism crystallized, for this was "the most formative phase of my life."[14]

Springtime in Vienna: Karl Lueger rules the city hall, Gustav Mahler conducts the opera, Gustav Klimt exhibits in the Secession Gallery, Sigmund Freud begins his self-analysis in the Bergstrasse, Adolf Hitler's *Weltanschauung* takes shape, an enormous new Ferris wheel is dedicated in the Prater amusement park—and, in the offices of Vienna's most important newspaper, its cultural editor plans a congress. The editor is a well-known and highly respected person in the city. Stefan Zweig, himself to emerge as a literary star of Central Europe in later decades, remembers his first encounter with him when he entered the premises of the *New Free Press* in 1901: "This temple of progress preserved another sacred relic in the so-called *Feuilleton*; . . . He who appeared on the first page had hewn his name in marble, as far as Vienna was concerned." Younger authors almost never received the chance to publish in these sacred pages, but the young and still completely unknown Stefan Zweig had decided to appear at the offices personally in order to present the case for his writing: "The editor of the *Feuilleton* received visitors only once a week between two and three o'clock. . . . It was not without a beating heart that I walked up the iron circular staircase that led to his office and had myself announced. After a few moments the attendant returned and said that the *Feuilleton* editor would see me and I walked into the small narrow room. The *Feuilleton* editor of the *Neue Freie Presse* was Theodor Herzl, and he was the first man of world importance whom I encountered in my life—although I did not then know how great a change this person was destined to bring about in the fate of the Jewish people and in the history of our time."[15]

Herzl was not only known as an editor of the *New Free Press*, but also as an author of numerous plays performed on the stages of the best-known Viennese theaters. When Freud sent him his *Interpretation of Dreams*, hoping he would have it reviewed, Herzl did not respond. Herzl was a household name for Freud, while Freud was rather unknown to Herzl. The two quite different prophets lived a stone's throw from each other: Herzl in Berggasse 6, Freud in Berggasse 19. And yet, they met only in Freud's dreams.[16]

Freud was an attentive reader of Herzl, but like most Viennese Jews he had little sympathy for what Herzl proposed in his pamphlet *Der Judenstaat* (*The Jewish State*, or literally: The State of the Jews) in 1896. Indeed, Herzl's ideas of a Jewish state were met mainly with disbelief and scorn. The two Jewish publishers of his own newspaper refused the bare mention of Herzl's Zionist movement in the *New Free Press*, even though its founder was one of their most important editors. And Karl Kraus publicly ridiculed Herzl as the "King of Zion." There was no irony, though, in Stefan Zweig's description of Herzl's appearance as truly royal: "Theodor Herzl rose to greet me, and unwittingly I realized that the ironic witticism 'the king of the Jews' had some truth to it. He actually looked regal with his broad forehead, his clear features, his long, black, almost blue-black, priestly beard and his dark brown, melancholy eyes."[17]

This was the man who tried to relieve European Jews of their illusions that integration into their respective home countries might be possible. He had drawn a gloomy picture in *The Jewish State*: "We have honestly endeavored everywhere to merge ourselves in the social life of surrounding communities and to preserve the faith of our fathers. We are not permitted to do so. In vain are we loyal patriots, our loyalty in some places running to extremes; in vain do we make the same sacrifices of life and property as our fellow citizens; in vain do we strive to increase the fame of our native land in science and art, or her wealth by trade and commerce. In countries where we have lived for centuries we are still cried down as strangers. . . . We might perhaps be able to merge ourselves entirely into surrounding races, if these were to leave us in peace for a period of two generations. But they will not leave us in peace."[18]

Herzl had only recently come to the conclusion that he and his fellow Jews would not be left in peace. He had experienced antisemitic incidents during his childhood and youth in Budapest, but when at the age of eighteen he moved to Vienna with his parents, he was still a believer in integration and assimilation.[19] He did not want to be an outsider but part of German-speaking society and culture. While he was already working on his Zionist manifesto, he noted in his diary on July 5, 1895: "By the way, if there is one thing I should like to be, it is a member of the old Prussian nobility."[20]

Herzl's ties with Judaism were less pronounced. He neither had a circumcision nor a Bar Mitzvah for his son Hans. But the more he wanted to be just a "normal" member of mainstream society, the more others reminded him of his Jewishness. Shortly after his admission, his student fraternity "Albia" decided to welcome only new members who could prove their "Aryan" lineage. Herzl resigned in protest and started to think about radical measures "to solve the Jewish question." First he came up with the idea of leading all Viennese Jews into St. Stephen's Cathedral in a solemn act of mass conversion, only to realize that the new antisemitism was racially and not religiously motivated and thus would not spare baptized Jews. Another attempt to address the dilemma of antisemitism was self-criticism. In his play, *The New Ghetto,* he suggested, just as Walther Rathenau had, that the Jews must free themselves of the ghetto within themselves.

Had Austrian society welcomed Herzl and not reminded him constantly of his Jewishness, he would probably never have become a Zionist. Like Rathenau, Herzl too wanted Jews to live a "normal life." His diagnosis of the "Jewish question" was similar to Rathenau's, but he proposed a very different cure. Herzl was well aware of Rathenau's essay and respected his analysis: "If he is advising the Jews to adopt a different bone structure, I will happily accompany him to this future of selective breeding. I am not poking fun at it, as any typical Jew would, but wish to concur with him. It is just that I think that the Jews will only be able to absorb the phosphorus for these new bones from a single source, namely from their own."[21]

Herzl's stay in Paris as correspondent for his Vienna newspaper in the early and mid-1890s, during the Dreyfus Affair, was the last decisive link in a chain of events that turned him into an advocate for a much more radical solution. What worried Herzl was not so much the fact that the Jewish officer Alfred Dreyfus was falsely accused and convicted of high treason, but that *the Jews* were held responsible for the alleged actions of one person. If anti-Jewish slogans were popular in the motherland of Jewish emancipation—then Jews were not safe anywhere, Herzl concluded.

Not in Paris—and certainly not in Vienna, to which Herzl returned in 1895. He was now convinced that he had been chosen to find an answer for what contemporaries called the "Jewish question" and to save the Jewish people. On June 16, 1895, he wrote in his journal, "I believe that for me life has ended and world history has begun."[22] He felt a calling to show the Jews their future path, and his book *The Jewish State* would be their guide.

The main argument of the book was: If a Jew is refused a normal life in Paris or Vienna, then he or she has to create a path to normality elsewhere, and in a Jewish society—be it in Palestine or in Argentina. And if Jews are rejected as Germans or French, then they have to reclaim their own nationality. Like every nation, the Jewish nation needs a national home, a state of its own. This was the reasoning behind Herzl's *Jewish State*.

"We are a people, one people," was one of the most provocative statements in this pamphlet. German and French Jews in their vast majority identified themselves as German or French citizens of the Jewish faith. They felt they only belonged to the German or French nation. Their Jewishness remained in the religious sphere—this their representatives claimed, even though they knew all too well that many Jews were entirely secular. Stefan Zweig observed the same rejection of Herzl's ideas among Austrian Jews: "What foolishness is this that he has thought up and writes about? Why should we go to Palestine? Our language is German and not Hebrew, and beautiful Austria is our homeland."[23]

Karl Kraus was one of these voices. He sarcastically remarked that the Jews did not come to Europe many centuries ago "to stimulate tourism."[24] According to Kraus, absolutely nothing drew them to Palestine. When Herzl tried to sell his ideas to Vienna's Chief Rabbi, Moritz Güdemann, he initially sensed more interest and sympathy, but he observed how soon Güdemann cooled toward his ideas. Perhaps this was related to a visit Güdemann paid to Herzl's home in December of 1895. As he entered the living room, the rabbi witnessed Herzl

FIGURE 3. Theodor Herzl in the Austrian resort of Altaussee, August 1900.

lighting the candles on his Christmas tree. What is perhaps most astonishing from today's perspective is the fact that the future leader of the Zionist movement did not even sense how deeply upsetting this scene must have been to the rabbi. Herzl wrote in his diary, "I was just lighting the Christmas tree for my children when Güdemann arrived. He seemed upset by the 'Christian' custom. Well, I will not let myself be pressured! But I don't mind if they call it a Hanukah tree—or the winter solstice?"[25]

Herzl realized that he was not taken seriously and that respected members of society had begun to poke fun at him.[26] But his plans were rejected and ridiculed not only in Vienna. When he turned to Baron Rothschild and Baron Hirsch in Paris for support, they showed no interest. Most Orthodox Jews also flatly rejected Herzl's plan: Only the messiah should lead the Jews back to the holy land. Even if Herzl's appearance resembled their notions of the messiah, they were not waiting for a secular Jew to bring them back to their ancient home. None of these setbacks dissuaded Herzl from pursuing his plans. Maybe the Jewish leaders and intellectuals could brush him off—but the Jewish masses would follow him. Herzl would have not been Herzl if he had not made grand plans for the new state even before its establishment was anywhere on the horizon. He promised his friend, the famous playwright Arthur Schnitzler, the position of theater director in the new state.[27] And when Baron Maurice de Hirsch, the best-known Jewish philanthropist in Paris, after the Rothschilds, died unexpectedly in April of 1896, Herzl wrote full of self-confidence: "The Jews lost Hirsch, but they have me."[28] In June, he was received like the messiah in Sofia, and in July he was compared to Moses and Columbus while visiting London.

SUMMER IN BASEL

Herzl was not satisfied with building a theoretical state for the Jews. As soon as his book was published, he began preparing a Zionist congress. He chose Munich as its site and had already publicly announced the event, when, due to the protests of both the local Jewish community and the German Rabbinical Association (he would call them the "protest rabbis"), he had to abandon this location. German Jews did everything possible to avoid the impression that they might have dual loyalties. They needed to make it absolutely clear that they belonged to no other nation than the German and laid claim to no other territory than Germany.[29]

Herzl soon found a new place for the congress. In the Swiss city of Basel there was only a small Jewish community, most of them recent immigrants from Eastern Europe, and they would not intrude on his plans. Resistance came, however, from Jewish dignitaries all across Europe. The British Chief Rabbi, Herman Adler, spoke of a "tremendous mistake" and his Viennese counterpart Moritz Güdemann, who had caught Herzl lighting his Christmas tree, responded with the publication of an anti-Zionist pamphlet, in which he emphasized that Jews no longer clung to their own nationality, but only to their religion. He called on his fellow Jews to do everything in their power to advance integration and emancipation, while rejecting Herzl's plan as a premature capitulation to antisemitism. For Güdemann, it was the mission of the Jewish people to live scattered over the earth. Herzl responded pointedly: "This mission is talked about by all those who are doing well in their present places of residence—but only by them."[30]

Despite the manifold rejections Herzl also found his comrades-in-arms while planning the First Zionist Congress. Among his close friends was the architect Oskar Marmorek, who had just designed the popular "Venice in Vienna" feature at the local Prater amusement park, an international attraction, with its new Ferris wheel. Herzl regarded Marmorek primarily as "the first architect of the Jewish renaissance."[31] Lueger's election as mayor had triggered Oskar Marmorek and his brother Alexander to question the successful integration of Jews into Austrian society. "The architect described the virulent state of Anti-Semitism in Vienna. Things were getting worse and worse. He thought there was some relief in the fact that the City Council had been suspended. I explained to him the nature of such a suspension: it was a suspension of the Constitution. And after that? Either the Constitution is allowed to function normally again—in which case the common variety of anti-Semites will return with a lot of noise; and stronger than ever! Or the Constitution is suspended 'for good.' This would be done with a furtive loving glance in the direction of the anti-Semites." Oskar's brother Alexander immediately understood: "There will be no other course left but to assign us a state of our own!" Herzl rejoiced at so much understanding and noted in his diary: "I was inwardly delighted. I need such supporters at this point."[32]

One of the most popular cultural critics of the time, Max Nordau, was another big supporter of Herzl. Like Herzl he was born in Budapest, and although his father was a rabbi he favored Jewish assimilation. Since 1880 he had lived in Paris, where he produced numerous popular books, translated into fifteen languages, which mainly criticized the path of modern civilization. Among them was the best-selling *Degeneration* (1892), which introduced a term later misused by the Nazis in their attacks against "degenerate" art. Nordau was also the author of the play *Doctor Cohn*, which like Herzl's *The New Ghetto*, was a parody of the assimilated Jewish bourgeoisie of his time. Nordau was Herzl's man. The two writers had known each other already before Herzl became a Zionist. Nordau understood immediately what moved Herzl and sympathized with his ideas: "He showed me the way toward fulfilling my obligations towards my people."[33]

When Herzl opened the Zionist Congress in Basel on August 29, he knew, as a fellow dramatist, that Nordau was the one participant besides himself who would impress the two hundred or so delegates. He would use him to prove the respectability of the movement. Thus, Herzl was upset when Nordau showed up in a casual suit for the opening ceremony: "One of my first practical ideas, months ago, was that people should be made to attend the opening session in tails and white tie. This worked out splendidly. Formal dress makes most people stiff. This stiffness immediately gave rise to a sedate tone—one they might not have had in light-colored summer suits or travel clothes—and I did not fail to heighten this tone to the point of solemnity. Nordau had turned up on the first day in a frock coat and flatly refused to go home and change to a full-dress suit. I drew him aside and begged him to do it as a favor to me. I told him: today the presidium of the Zionist Congress is nothing at all, we still have to establish everything. People should get used to seeing the Congress as a most exalted and solemn thing. He allowed himself to be persuaded, and in return I hugged him gratefully. A quarter of an hour later he returned in formal dress."[34]

To most of the East European delegates, such niceties would have seemed marginal, but Herzl knew the importance of refinement. The new movement was so much ridiculed between Vienna and London, between Munich and Basel that it had to find a way to evoke respect. Thus, he changed the location of the meeting at the last minute from a smoky beer cellar to the most desired conference hall in town, the *Stadtcasino*. The world had to be shown that this was a respectable movement, not a gathering of the lunatic fringe.

What kind of Jewish society in Palestine did the Zionist Congress envision? Its delegates passed a resolution that stated:

"Zionism aims at establishing for the Jewish people a publicly and legally assured home in Palestine." From the beginning, Zionism's goals were rather vague. "A publicly and legally assured home" meant different things to different people. And what exactly were the borders of Palestine? Herzl had to heed the interests of the Turkish Sultan, who never would have agreed to an independent Jewish state within his Empire. The question of whether the "legally assured home" for the Jewish people should actually be an independent state or an autonomous province within the Ottoman Empire was deliberately left open by the formula of the Basel Congress. It allowed for the immediate purchase of large chunks of the territory known as Palestine or *Eretz Yisrael,* and it would serve as the basis for the Balfour Declaration two decades later, which used almost the same wording.[35]

Herzl's congress was an unequivocal response to his opponents. Not all of them started to take him seriously, but they could no longer ignore the fact that Herzl had many supporters among the masses of East European Jews. It was there that Jews were most plagued by economic misery and political repression. After the beginning of a wave of pogroms in 1881, an annual average of over twenty thousand Jews left the Czarist Empire for North America. The message of the Zionist Congress resonated among the deprived Jews who remained in the East. Sholem Rabinovich, who would become the most popular Yiddish writer under his pen name Sholem Aleichem, summarized the goals of Zionism in a pamphlet published right after the first congress. Elsewhere he made fun of the opponents of Zionism: "Some will say, 'So you've had a congress! Psha! Not worth a pinch of snuff! A lot of talk, speeches, speeches! That's where it all will end!' Others will make fun of the whole affair. 'What do you think about it? About those

FIGURE 4. Theodor Herzl addresses the Sixth Zionist Congress in Basel, 1903.

Zionists, that want to bring the messiah down!' And some will fly into a rage, as though someone had upset a good business deal for them. 'Atheists! Disbelievers! Want to hold back the Redemption!' So here we are, reckon it up, and draw your own conclusions." Sholem Aleichem himself did not agree with the skeptics. In 1898 he published another pamphlet, entitled "Why Do the Jews Need a Land of Their Own?" in which he answered the question in his own idiosyncratic way: "Some question! . . . It's as though they were asking you what do you want a home for? Naturally everyone should have a home. What else? Stay outside?"[36]

Herzl did not invent Zionism. For centuries and even millennia, Jewish religious sentiments had been directed toward the Land of Israel. Three times a day Jews prayed (and still pray) for a return to Zion. Every year on Passover, they utter their hope to meet next year in Jerusalem. But these yearnings were directed toward a heavenly Jerusalem and toward messianic times, in which a third Temple would be built. Only in the nineteenth century and in the context of the rise of nationalism was the heavenly Jerusalem transformed into a worldly Jerusalem. Nothing characterized this transformation better than a small pamphlet written in 1862 by the socialist Moses Hess, an early companion of Karl Marx. The title of his *Rome and Jerusalem* did not allude to the holy cities of Christianity and of Judaisim, but rather to the struggle of modern nations to establish their own states. "Rome" referred to the newly established Italian state rooted in the ancient Roman Empire, which gave Hess hope that Jews too would be able to rebuild their own state after two millennia of statelessness.[37]

In the borderlands between Western and Eastern Europe, religious Jews began, already in the middle of the nineteenth century, to see a common theme in the national struggles of the respective nations among whom they lived and the Jewish longing for their own homeland.Rabbi Zvi Hirsch Kalisher experienced the national struggles of Germans and Poles in the Prussian province of Posen, where he resided, while Rabbi Judah Alkalai was born in Bosnian Sarajevo and moved to Serbian Semlin—both areas that remained hotbeds for nationalists of all sorts. In their respective writings, both argued that Jews should return to the Land of Israel even before the arrival of the messiah. They were among the earliest examples combining secular European nationalism with traditional Jewish religious sentiments.[38]

These and successive publications by an East European enlightened Jewish elite, the *maskilim*, demonstrated early on that it was not possible easily to distinguish between a secular national movement for the Jews and a religiously inspired battle. Both the rabbis and the *maskilim* wrote in the language of the Bible, which was for the Jews so deeply embedded in their prayer and study that the religious and the political tended to interpenetrate. Religious elements thus entered into the Jewish national movement by way of language and through religious connotations inherent in the geography of the Land of Israel.[39]

Hebrew was a thoroughly familiar language to Leon Pinsker, a *maskil* from Odessa, whose father was a scholar and a teacher of Hebrew. When Pinsker published his pamphlet *Autoemancipation!* in 1882, as a reaction to the recent pogroms, he chose, however, to write it in German. And most of his articles, printed in the enlightened Jewish journals *Raszvet* and *Sion* were written in Russian. *Autoemancipation!* was in some respects a forerunner of Herzl's *Jewish State*, while in others it was quite different. Pinsker, who was a physician, regarded antisemitism as Judeophobia, an incurable disease. Like Herzl fourteen years later, he sought to raise the status of the Jews from their "abnormal" existence of homelessness: "Since the Jew is nowhere at home, nowhere regarded as a native, he remains an alien everywhere."[40] And in the fact "that the Jews are not considered an independent nation by other nations, rests in part the secret of their anomalous position and of their endless misery."[41] But unlike Herzl, who thought that their return to an idealized normality would result in the dissolution of the diaspora and that ultimately all Jews remaining in the diaspora would assimilate, Pinsker's "normality" envisioned the dual existence of a Jewish diaspora alongside a projected Jewish state. While some Jews would become residents of this new Jewish state, which (just as in

Herzl's pamphlet) was to be built either in Palestine or in Argentina, others—and this most likely meant the majority— would remain in the diaspora, where they should receive full cultural autonomy. As Dimitry Shumsky makes clear in his illuminating article on Pinsker, this attitude was consistent with his general struggle for a multinational citizenship within the Czarist Empire. "He sought to turn the Jew from a member of an obviously homeless people into a person with a dual home, like a Greek in Odessa, or a Ukrainian in Moscow."[42]

Herzl knew neither Hess's nor Pinsker's writings. He also had very little knowledge of the *Hovevei Zion* (Lovers of Zion) movement, founded after the first pogroms of 1881 and built into an international movement by Pinsker in 1884 with the goal of promoting Jewish immigration to Palestine. The various branches of the movement had gathered thousands of members before Herzl founded the Zionist movement, and they constituted the backbone of the first modern immigration wave (*Aliya*) to Palestine, but they lacked strong leadership and effective organization. This Herzl would provide. The Russian Zionist Menahem Ussishkin wrote in a letter to Herzl's early Zionist antagonist Ahad Ha'am: "[Herzl and his friends] have hope, but they have also a concrete plan; we have hope, but we don't know what to do with it."[43]

The Zionist Congress was a triumph for Herzl: "Were I to sum up the Basel Congress in a word—which I shall guard against pronouncing publicly—it would be this: At Basel I founded the Jewish State. If I said this out loud today, I would be answered by universal laughter. Perhaps in five years, and certainly in fifty, everyone will know it."[44] It was exactly fifty-and-a-half years later that David Ben-Gurion would proclaim the State of Israel under a giant portrait of Theodor Herzl.

FALL IN VILNA

Zionism was not the only Jewish mass movement that was established in 1897 with the aim to normalize the situation of the Jews and to find an answer to what was then called the Jewish question. Only a few weeks after the Basel Congress, on September 25th (October 7th according to the Gregorian calendar), a small group of East European Jewish socialists met in Lithuanian Vilna (Vilnius, then part of the Czarist Empire) in order to establish the *Algemeyner Yidisher Arbeter Bund in Poyln un Rusland* (the General Jewish Worker's Association in Poland and Russia), usually just referred to as the "Bund." For them, "the Jewish question" was less a political and much more a social and economic matter.[45] Their concrete goal was to unite all Jewish proletarians, who had begun organizing themselves into small groups in the late 1880s, in order to create better conditions for Jewish workers. The fact that the founding of the Bund took place over Rosh Hashanah, the Jewish New Year, which religious Jews spend praying in the synagogue, symbolized the anti-religious self-understanding of the Bundists. Their rejection of organized religion would remain characteristic of the movement, even though their fight for national Jewish minority rights took on momentum over time.

Like the Zionists, the Bundists also had recognized that the Jews had to walk on new terrain. For them, however, the future was not in Palestine but in Eastern Europe or North America, their language was not Hebrew but Yiddish, the political movement they sympathized with was Socialism and not Zionism, and the means to achieving their goals was class struggle rather than a national uprising. The Bund opposed the Zionists as bourgeois reactionaries. Zionism, in turn, denounced the Bundist ideology as blind to the dangers of Jewish life in the diaspora.[46]

While Zionism ultimately reached its goal and established a Jewish state, the Bund became a victim of the Holocaust and fell into oblivion in Jewish collective memory. In the Soviet Union, the party was outlawed, as were all political parties besides the Bolsheviks. In interwar Poland, however, Zionists and Bundists were equal rivals in the fight over leadership of Jewish communal life. The Bundists, like the Zionists, developed their own educational system, had their own sports associations, edited their own newspapers, and were militant in fighting back antisemitism. In the 1936 elections to the Jewish community boards, the Bund emerged as the strongest Jewish faction in most urban areas. About 40 percent of all Jewish voters in Poland's seven largest Jewish communities voted for the Bund.[47]

The establishment of the Bund was a rather modest affair, in striking contrast to the festive aura of the Basel Congress. Herzl wanted a publicly recognized grand affair and invited dignitaries. He moved the venue of the congress from a seedy beer-cellar to the respectable Casino. The founders of the Bund convened secretly and did everything in their power to avoid being discovered by the official authorities of the Czarist Empire. "This was to be a secret meeting of insiders, not a constituent assembly."[48]

Herzl convened the congress in Basel because he feared the resistance he would likely have encountered in a more established Jewish community. Vilna, by contrast, was known as the "Lithuanian Jerusalem" and was one of the most important centers of Jewish life in the world. The home of numerous Talmud scholars, it occupied a leading role in Jewish learning. In the late nineteenth century, the city also became a center of the *maskilic* movement, of the Hebrew and Yiddish press, and of the earliest socialist Jewish activities.

Only thirteen delegates—eleven men and two women—assembled in a small private home on the outskirts of Vilna. They represented five cities (six came from Vilna, three from Warsaw), two already established journals (*Arbeter shtime* and *Der yiddisher arbeter*), and their supporters numbered around 3,500 throughout the so-called Pale of Settlement, the territory in the western part of the Russian Empire in which Jews were restricted to live. The Bund constituted an early and significant part of the overall workers' movement in Russia. Three of the nine delegates who founded the Russian Social Democratic Party, the mother party of both Bolsheviks and Mensheviks, were Bundists.

In contrast to the spectacular event orchestrated by Herzl in Basel, the leading theorist of the Bund, Vladimir Medem, regarded the beginnings of the Bundist movement as part of an evolution: "The Bund! Founded? That is the wrong expression. It was not founded, but it was born, it developed, grew like every living organism develops and grows. . . . A movement of instinctive attraction of the worker for the worker provoked the agglomeration of grains of sand, of little human dust in a block of granite."[49]

In its early phase the Bund lacked a charismatic figure like Herzl. This was partially the result of the different tasks of the two organizations. In the interests of establishing a state, Herzl constantly looked to meet with the political leaders of the world. The Bundists, on the other hand, organized strikes to demand better conditions for workers. Led by Arkadi Kremer, a leader of one of Vilna's Marxist circles, they at first rejected any marks of sectarian character and aimed at unifying the diverse Jewish proletarian groups in order to lead them jointly

FIGURE 5. Bundists and other socialists in Vilna protest against the pogroms of October 1905.

into the Russian Social Democratic Labor Party.[50] This changed only at the Fourth Party Congress in Bialystok in 1901, when the Bund propagated the minority rights of Jews. They now demanded a federal structure for the Czarist Empire and autonomy rights for every national minority.[51] By then the Bund had grown into a mass movement with 34,000 members in 276 chapters.

The Bund now also represented Jewish workers in the New World. Another event of 1897 was of landmark importance for organizing the Jewish proletariat in America. On April 22nd, Abraham Cahan founded the most important institution devoted to promoting socialism among the Yiddish-speaking Jewish masses of New York, the Yiddish paper *Der Forverts* or the *Jewish Daily Forward* (JDF). Even its critics acknowledged its impact: "The JDF is much more than a paper. It is an institution which has the most powerful moral (or perhaps immoral) influence on the Jewish street. . . . The JDF is for the Jews what the church is for the Christians . . . the editor is their pope . . . the paper is their university."[52]

The *Forverts* registered the establishment of the new Zionist movement with little enthusiasm. Herzl was already used to being scorned in Vienna and Paris; now he also had to read sarcastic expressions about his leadership in the news from New York, where he was called "the new Moshe Rabenu [Moses] who will bring the Jews to their land of milk and honey."[53] The *Forverts* was not interested in a bourgeois Jewish state but aspired to establish a classless socialist International. Even though the Lower East Side of New York with its sweatshops and tenement houses was not exactly the *goldene medine* (the "golden land" many emigrants had envisioned), America still stood for the dream of freedom and promised opportunities that Europe could not offer. For the editors of the *Forverts* the new homeland was America and not Palestine.

Abraham Liessin, the *Forverts*' correspondent reporting from the Zionist Congress, questioned the very basis of Zionism, the assumption that the Jews constituted a nation. The discourse of the existence of a Jewish people plays into the hands of the antisemites, he argued. Zionism might be a matter of the heart for its adherents, but it opposes reason. Jews had no common language, no common tradition, and no common goals for the future—thus, he insisted, they should not be considered a nation.[54]

The anti-Zionist arguments of the *Forverts* were based on practical considerations. Palestine was not sufficiently developed to offer the miserable Jewish masses a new home. And even if two million Jews should settle there, that would still be far from a solution to the "Jewish question." The normalization of the Jews, according to the *Forverts*, could only become a reality in the New World.

WINTER IN ODESSA

Odessa was part of a new world as well. In 1897, the city was just one century old—founded by Catherine the Great in the territories Russia had conquered from the Ottoman Empire in the late eighteenth century. The modern cosmopolitan city, originally established as a military port on the Black Sea, counted 400,000 inhabitants. A third of them were Jews, others were Russians, Ukrainians, Rumanians, Greeks, Armenians, and Turks. Life in the city was "dominated by the grain trade rather than by scholarship or culture."[55] But beginning in the middle of the nineteenth century, the city became a haven for Jewish intellectuals from the whole of the empire. It was here that Leon Pinsker wrote his *Autoemancipation!* in 1881, and here that he presided over the Hibbat Zion (Love of Zion) movement, together with the *maskil* Moshe Leib Lilienblum; it was here where Asher Ginsberg, better known as Ahad Ha'am established his elitist Bnei Moshe circle; and it was here that the writers Sholem Yankev Abramovich (Mendele Moykher Sforim), Mordekhai Rabinovich (Ben Ami), and Hayim Nahman Bialik published their Yiddish and Hebrew novels, stories, and poems. Odessa was a "laboratory of modernity," and "only in Odessa could this particular symbiosis between Judaism and modernity" exist, as historian Steven Zipperstein observed.[56]

Odessa was also home to the historian Simon Dubnow, who argued that the year "1897 introduced a turn of events in the life of Russian Jews. The stagnation of society that had lasted around fifteen years, gave way to a movement of a national and social character."[57] One such movement was founded by Dubnow himself: the movement for national minority rights and Jewish autonomy for all Jews living in Eastern Europe.[58]

Dubnow was born in 1860, the same year as Theodor Herzl.[59] His family background could not have been more different, however. He grew up in a traditionally religious Jewish family in a small shtetl in Belarus. He distanced himself from religion already in his young years, taught himself languages and secular knowledge, and later became the most important Jewish historian of his generation. In search of a warmer climate and intellectual stimulation Dubnow settled in Odessa in 1890. The events taking place in far-away Basel in 1897 resonated also in the city on the Black Sea: "Odessa reverberated with the echoes of this first all-Jewish congress," writes Dubnow.[60]

In the winter of 1897, Jewish intellectual life in Odessa was clearly in ferment. Buoyed by news from the Basel Congress, a group of Jewish intellectuals with sympathies toward Zionism but skepticism toward Herzl began to meet weekly in the city. Among them were Dubnow, Ahad Ha'am, and the writer Mendele Moykher Sforim. In the luxurious villa of the president of the Society for Enlightenment, they discussed various options for a Jewish future. Dubnow wrote in his memoirs: "We sat in soft leather chairs and held discussions over a glass of tea. . . . The debates in our small circle, which met regularly until the spring of 1898, were extremely fertile. They spurred our thoughts, sharpened them and made them more profound. They gave Ahad Ha'am and me inspirations for the further development of our literary systems."[61]

When the First Zionist Congress was convened in Basel, Dubnow was in close vicinity. He vacationed in Switzerland. But he refused to attend the nearby congress, as he feared that his promotion of diaspora nationalism would provoke the delegates who were convinced that Jews should leave Europe and settle in their own country. In contrast to most other observers, Dubnow understood the close relationship between the seemingly secular movement and Jewish religious sentiments: "Among these messianists there was no place for me."[62] The Zionist Congress stimulated Dubnow to finalize his own vision for the normalization of the Jewish future. In October 1897, just after his return to Odessa, he published the first of his "Letters on Old and New Judaism" in the Russian-Jewish journal *Voskhod*. They served as the basis for his theories of Jewish diaspora nationalism and the foundation of the political party, which he established in 1906, the Jewish People's Party.

Like the Zionists, Dubnow too regarded the Jews as a nation; and like the Bundists, he envisioned the future of the Jews in the diaspora. His focus was the place where the vast majority of Jews lived, namely Eastern Europe, and the language, which most of them spoke, namely Yiddish. But Dubnow objected to the solutions offered by Zionism and Bundism, just as assimilationalism seemed both undesirable and unrealistic to him. He was shaped by the theories of national autonomy, as they had developed under the Habsburg Monarchy. In contrast to the Zionists, he refused to see the future of the entire Jewish population as lying in their own state in a far-way territory. Just as Czechs and Poles, Slovaks and Croats, Jews too should continue to live in the areas they inhabited and insist on their rights as a national minority with their own culture and language. He further objected to the socialist ideas that characterized the Bundist movement and favored liberal democratic concepts instead. And finally, he fiercely rejected the idea of the assimilationists that the Jews should so completely integrate into the societies in whose midst they lived as to forfeit their own traditions, their language, and their educational systems.[63]

Just as the Zionists were caught between a yearning for normality on the one hand and the temptation to regard their nation as a unique case on the other, Dubnow too was struggling between normalizing the situation of Jews as one national minority among many and pointing to their unique place. For him, the Jewish nation, after living for two millennia outside its original territory, had become the diaspora nation par excellence. It had internalized a nationalism free of violence or the need to suppress other people: "As a spiritual or historical-cultural nation, deprived of any possibility of aspiring to political triumphs, of seizing territory by force or of subjecting other nations to cultural domination . . . it is concerned with only one thing: protecting its national individuality and safeguarding its autonomous development in all states everywhere in the Diaspora."[64]

In other words, he argued that the Jews were the most obvious instance of a nation, so much so that they had by-passed the stage where they needed a territory. According to Dubnow, only the Jews had undergone all traditional phases of nationalism and thus constituted a spiritual-historical nation, a nation that did not require a territory in order to remain a nation. They did not need a geographical state, but as a national minority with their own rights they should constitute a "state within the state."[65] Dubnow did not only fight for these convictions as a politician, they were also manifest in his historical work. In his magisterial ten-volume *World History of the Jewish People*, he left no doubt that a history spread among the nations would continue to be the fate of the Jews well into his own time. For him, Jewish history had not a single center (Israel), but changing centers along the course of history (Israel, Babylonia, Spain, Eastern Europe). If anything characterized Jewish history, it was the dispersion of the Jews around the globe. Consequently, Dubnow's history was the history of a diaspora people.[66]

At the end of the nineteenth century, the future of the Jews seemed more confusing than ever before. Were they a nation or a religion? Should they integrate into the societies around them or set out on a distinctive path? Would socialism, autonomism, assimilation, or Zionism bring them closer to their goals? Nobody could foresee that the answer to all of these questions would largely be determined not by their own decisions but by the fate that befell them in the twentieth century. In 1897, the future of European Jewry was still wide open. It could lead to America or to Palestine or it might remain in Europe; it could be a road to freedom, redemption, or destruction.

THE SEVEN-HOUR-LAND

A LIGHT UNTO THE NATIONS

> Yes, we are strong enough to form a State,
> and, indeed, a model State.[1]
>
> **—THEODOR HERZL**

UTOPIAN IDEALS

Nowhere in Herzl's writings do we read of a State of Israel. In fact, not until 1948 did we know what a future Jewish state would be called.[2] Herzl himself referred to it by a name that has fallen into oblivion today: the Seven-Hour Land.[3] In his proposed society no one should work more than seven hours a day, which was a revolutionary suggestion for his own time, just as it remains today. For Herzl, this was by no means a small detail. The importance he attached to the seven-hour workday can be seen in the fact that Herzl drew the flag of the new state with seven stars, symbolizing the Seven-Hour-Land.

This flag would demonstrate to the whole world that Herzl's projected state was anything but just another state. His "experiment for the well-being of all humanity" should not only offer a safe haven for persecuted Jews; it was to become a model state for the improvement of people from all nations and religions.[4] He wrote in his diary: "At first we shall only work on and for ourselves in all secrecy. But the Jewish State

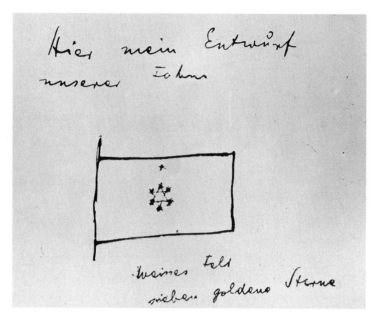

FIGURE 6. Herzl's drawing of the flag for the "Seven-Hour-Land."

will become something remarkable. The land of the seven-hour working day will be not only a model country for social experiments and a treasure-house for works of art, but a miracle country in all civilization. It will be a destination for the civilized world which will come to visit us the way it now visits Lourdes, Mecca, Sadagora."[5] And in his *Jewish State* he says: "We will seek to bestow the moral salvation of work on men of every age and of every class; and thus our people will find their strength again in the land of the seven-hour day."[6] Already at the outset he states, "Yes, we are strong enough to form a State, and, indeed, a model State."[7] Herzl's vision embodies a paradox that Zionism would never be able to solve: To turn the Jews into a nation like any other nation while at the same time entrusting them with a very special state, a model state.

The seven-hour-land, the miracle land, the model state: these were Herzl's visions of a future Jewish state. His model was profoundly universalist. Jewish elements had no major significance in his concept. To be sure, religion played a role in this state. This was the case especially when biblical provisions went hand in hand with social innovations. Herzl speaks also of the rebuilding of the temple, and of operas about the heroes of Jewish history. But all of this has merely symbolic meaning. In Herzl's vision, religion becomes an ornament. The temple he had in mind resembled his Vienna synagogue in Seitenstettengasse much more closely than the ancient Jerusalem temple on Mount Moriah. Of course, Herzl never thought to reintroduce animal sacrifice. In his sanitized version, the women pray in the gallery and the temple seats are sold according to the view they offer. On Friday evening, Shabbat songs like *Lekha Dodi* are chanted to the accompaniment of a lute rather than an organ.

Herzl had a clear plan also regarding the languages to be spoken in his Jewish state: "Every man can preserve the language in which his thoughts are at home." But he did not really mean *every* language. The languages spoken by most Jews, namely Yiddish in Eastern Europe and Ladino in southeastern Europe and Turkey, or the Judeo-Arabic spoken by the Jews of North Africa would not qualify: "We shall give up using those miserable stunted jargons, those Ghetto languages which we still employ, for these were the stealthy tongues of prisoners. Our national teachers will give due attention to this matter." And Hebrew? He rejected the language of the Bible as well: "We cannot converse with one another in Hebrew.

Who amongst us has a sufficient acquaintance with Hebrew to ask for a railway ticket in that language?"[8]

Herzl wanted to keep the rabbis in their synagogues and restrict the power of the generals by creating a small professional army. The major power in the new state was to be the "Jewish Company," which was "partly modelled on the lines of a great land-acquisition company. It might be called a Jewish Chartered Company, though it cannot exercise sovereign power, and has other than purely colonial tasks. The Jewish Company will be founded as a joint stock company subject to English jurisdiction, framed according to English laws, and under the protection of England."[9] Most of his treatise is dedicated to practical issues, such as immigration, workers' settlements, and the education of skilled workers.

Herzl thought that the preservation of what he called "little habits" would be especially important for the cohesion of the new society. He dedicated an entire chapter to these little habits, which were just another name for the comfortable living standard to which immigrants from Europe would be accustomed: "There are English hotels in Egypt and on the mountain-crest in Switzerland, Viennese cafes in South Africa, French theaters in Russia, German operas in America, and the best Bavarian beer in Paris. When we journey out of Egypt again we shall not leave the fleshpots behind. Every man will find his customs again in the local groups, but they will be better, more beautiful, and more agreeable than before."[10] Although Herzl was not free of colonialist fantasies, he flatly refused to be identified with colonialist concepts, as practiced for example in South Africa: "After all, we don't want a Boer state, but a Venice."[11]

There is much discussion among scholars about the role that the local Arab population would play in Herzl's Jewish state. While some interpretations focus on an early diary entry of June 12, 1895, in which Herzl seems to lay out the expropriation and perhaps even the expulsion of the local population, others point to his tolerant treatment of the local population in his published writings or to his naïveté, as when he simply cannot imagine the Arab population renouncing all the technological and cultural progress that the new state would provide.[12] One should keep in mind that at the time of his 1895 diary entry, Herzl did not even know if the future Jewish home would be built in Palestine or Argentina. To avoid anachronistic judgments, Herzl must be seen in the context of his own time. He acted within an imperial setting, in which the main players were the major empires of his day. Thus, his "Arab" protagonist in his novel *Old New Land* does not speak Arabic but Turkish, just as his Jewish protagonists do not speak Hebrew, but the languages of European empires. For him, the Arab population was a mirror image of the Jewish population: they would be culturally assimilated to the "superior" Turkish culture, just as the Yiddish-speaking Jews in Europe would assimilate to German culture. Herzl did not want to oppress the Arabs as second-class citizens in a Jewish state, but rather envisioned a multinational political entity like the Ottoman Empire, in which both Jews and Arabs would enjoy far-reaching autonomy, but not total independence.[13]

Six years after the appearance of *The Jewish State* Herzl described in detail his vision of how such a future society would look in his utopian novel, *Altneuland* (*Old New Land*). We have to keep in mind that *Old New Land* was not only written in a different genre than *The Jewish State*. During these six years, he had also become a different person. He was still a respected journalist, but now he was also the leader of a political movement that drew supporters (and critics) from all over the world.

He had met monarchs and church leaders, he was seen as a messianic figure by the Jewish masses, and he was vilified by many Jews, assimilated and Orthodox alike. He had organized five congresses and learned a great deal about the situation of Jews in every country. What is most striking in *Old New Land* is the extent to which his worldview had become more universalist. He no longer talks about a "Society of Jews" but only of a "New Society." While this new society mainly consists of Jews, other religions and nations, be they Arab Muslims or Prussian Protestants, are just as welcome. The only people excluded are fundamentalists of every creed.[14]

What is *Old New Land* about? It tells the story of a Viennese Jew and a Prussian aristocrat who decide to drop out of European society and relocate to a far-away Pacific island. On their way to the island they stop in Palestine and are shocked to find the land completely desolate. When they return to Europe for a visit twenty years later, they decide to stop in Palestine again. They do not recognize the country. The "New Society" that has been founded in the meantime has transformed the desert into a blooming landscape, peopled by a civilization enjoying the latest technology, the most exciting cultural scene, and a functioning democratic political structure. Just as in his *Jewish State*, there are few Jewish elements in Herzl's *Old New Land*. The New Society is a miniature cosmopolitan Europe lodged in the Middle East. Jews and Arabs live peacefully side by side, and there are no significant conflicts between ethnic or religious groups.

In *Old New Land* the seven-hour-day has become reality. Women enjoy far-reaching equality, including active and passive voting rights—something that did not exist in any European state at the time. Education is free of cost, as is the health system. There are pension payments and retirement homes, and electric lights hang from the palm trees. Electricity brings more than just technological progress, it fulfills an important function in helping to reduce the gap between poor and rich: "I believe that electric light was not invented for the purpose of illuminating the drawing-rooms of a few snobs, but rather for the purpose of throwing light on some of the dark problems of humanity. One of these problems, and not the least of them, is the Jewish question. In solving it we are working not only for ourselves, but also for many other over-burdened and oppressed beings."[15] Indeed, Herzl's belief in progress and especially in electricity reached far back into his childhood. Many years later he told how as a twelve-year old he had been given a book by the popular German-Jewish writer Aaron Bernstein that claimed electricity was the messiah. At first he was shocked at equating the electron with the messiah, but gradually he began to like the idea that electricity might indeed be "the Redeemer whom we are awaiting and who will liberate us from the bondage of the body and the spirit."[16]

The population of the New Society travels on a suspended railway through Haifa and receives its news from a "telephone newspaper," which sounds very much like premodern Internet.[17] During the day they sip their *Mélange* in a Viennese coffee house, at night they "go to the opera, or to one of the theaters—the German, English, French, Italian, Spanish."[18] Doctors in the Old New Land work to find a cure against malaria while engineers constructed a channel from the Dead Sea to the Red Sea to solve the water problems in the whole region.

What is the political system like in Herzl's Seven-Hour-Land? In his "aristocratic democracy" there exists a parliament, but it only convenes for two brief legislative periods a year. Important questions like the election of the president are decided by a gentlemen's agreement. There are no party conflicts. A closer look at Herzl's book reveals that the New Society is actually "not a state. . . . We are simply a large cooperative society, within which there are many small co-operatives for sundry aims. And this our Congress is, properly speaking, nothing more than the general assembly of the co-operative which goes under the name of the New Society."[19] One of the protagonists of *Old New Land* claims: "We have no state, you see, as Europe had in your time. We are an association of citizens who are trying to find their happiness in work and cultural activities."[20]

In the words of one of his biographers, Herzl "devised an original kind of polity, based on syndicalist ideals and derived in part from French anarchist thinking. There was little or no striking coercion and almost none of the forms of sovereignty associated with the European nation state."[21] All land was publicly owned, and the industries, as well as newspapers, theaters, and banks were cooperatives in the possession of workers and consumers. At a closer look, then, it would seem that his Jewish state was neither Jewish nor a state.

The ultimate cosmopolitan ingredient in Herzl's vision is the willingness of this society to be evaluated by the outside world. The international jury entrusted with this task consists of five hundred ladies and gentlemen: "the men and women whom we had invited to be our guests on this six-week spring cruise to the Levant were the finest intellects of the civilized world. A committee of writers and artists chose them from amongst the best brains in the world, of course without regard to nationality or religion. The best were invited, and they came gladly . . . ."[22] Maybe the most revealing element in this statement is the "of course." It would never have occurred to Herzl to invite only Jewish referees to judge his experiment.

These "noblest minds of humanity" arrive on the coast of Palestine on board a luxury steamer named *Futuro*, which brings them from Genoa to Haifa. Starting from Haifa they examine the whole of the land. Geologists, botanists, technicians, architects, and artists render their expert opinions on the areas of their expertise. The politicians of the New Society promise to show them the real society and not "Potemkin villages"—and they promise to respect the verdict of the international judges.

For Herzl, addressing the "Jewish question" was only a first step toward the solution of other burning questions of humankind. As his thoughts developed, so did his ambitions, until his aims extended beyond relieving the misery of merely a small group of people. The New Society would not only guarantee a safe haven for persecuted Jews, but would become a model for all nations, religions, and races: "There is an unsolved national problem, a great tragedy of human suffering that only we Jews can fully comprehend. I mean the Negro problem. . . . Now that I have lived to see the return of the Jews, I wish I could help to prepare the way for the return of the Negroes."[23]

There are of course enemies to this open and cosmopolitan society. The arch villain in Herzl's novel is an Orthodox rabbi called Dr. Geyer, an advocate for an exclusivist Jewish state. The central political divide in the New Society is the question of inclusiveness versus exclusiveness. Should the New Society be open only to Jews or also to others? Herzl's answer is unequivocal. When the Prussian nobleman Kingscourt expresses doubt over whether he would be able to become a member of the New Society, the hero of his novel, David Littwak, proclaims: "Let me tell you that neither I nor my friends make the least distinction between one man and another. We don't ask about anyone's race or religion. It is enough for us that he is human."[24] Herzl includes the Turkish-speaking Arab Reshid Bey and the German-speaking Prussian Kingscourt in the New Society and has Littwak urge: "[S]tand by the principles that have made us great: Liberalism, Tolerance, Love of mankind! Only then will Zion truly be Zion."[25] Transmitting his legacy to David Littwak (during an opera performance of *Sabbatai Zvi*), the old president Eichenstamm conveys the following message: "My last word to my people will be: See to it that the stranger in our midst feels at home."[26]

The only ones who have no place in the New Society are those who deny non-Jews equal rights. Herzl's poignant opposition to Geyer's intolerance is uttered over and over again in *Altneuland*. One character, the respected architect Steineck, becomes enraged when he speaks about Geyer: "He is a damned hypocritical minister, a bigoted pietist, a sanctimonious demagogue, a liar and an impostor. He wants to introduce intolerance into our ranks, the blasted scoundrel. I'm not easily roused, but when I see such an intolerant fanatic, I'd gladly strangle him with my bare hands!"[27]

Not only is Geyer an intolerant politician who opposes the inclusion of non-Jews, he is also an opportunist and a hypocrite. As long as it was not *en vogue* to side with the Zionists, he was their opponent. When they got the upper hand, he joined them, and Herzl let Geyer's opponents have their say: "He is the patriot, the superpatriot, the truly nationalist Jew while we others are the xenophiles, the friends of the stranger within our gates; and if we let him talk long enough he will make us believe that we are the bad Jews, if not the strangers in his Palestine!"[28] In the elections to the congress, Geyer's party loses in almost all districts against the all-inclusive liberal-minded candidates supported by Herzl's protagonists,

David Littwak and the architect Steineck (the latter based on
the Viennese Zionist Oscar Marmorek). There is no doubt in
which political camp the sympathies of the author lie.[29]

David Littwak, the newly elected president of Old New
Land, personifies the ideal of the successful immigrant who
rises from great poverty to wealth, from the ghetto to the
Jewish homeland, from slavery to freedom. His father was
a peddler in Vienna and, after much hard work, he is now a
wealthy shipping company owner and lives in an Alhambra-
like mansion near Tiberias. His fairy-tale rise through the
ranks of society had its origin at the beginning of the book
when Friedrich Loewenberg (the Herzl-like character in the
novel) decided to give all his money to this poor Viennese
family before himself leaving Europe. In gratitude to his noble
patron whom he had deemed dead, David Littwak named his
son Fritz and his home Friedrichsheim. This could hardly be
a more transparent reference to "Friedrichsruh," the home
and burial place of another of Herzl's heroes, Count Bismarck,
and to Grand Duke Friedrich of Baden, one of the few aristocratic supporters of Herzl's plans.

Modern interpreters have often gone to one of two extremes, either regarding Herzl's novel as irrelevant to his political thought or taking it at face value. While we should not
forget that this was a work of fiction, it has to be seen also as
a literary expression of the political attitudes of Herzl in the
last years of his life. He had worked for three years on this
novel, considered it as one of his masterpieces, and was soon
to realize that it was indeed his final word on what Jewish
society should look like. His biographer Ernst Pawel was right
when he observed that "in terms of political theory, *Altneuland* may have marked a significant advance over *Der Judenstaat*." He was also right when he added the observation that

"[w] ithin the Zionist movement . . . the book was for the most part greeted with consternation."[30]

This "consternation" did not disappear a century after its publication. Depending on one's political point of view, Herzl's ideals may be seen as either irrelevant or prophetic. The political right is troubled by the universalist views, which are such a prominent feature in *Altneuland*. In his *Jewish State* (2000), Yoram Hazony, the founder of Israel's Shalem Center, a right-of-center think tank, dismissed *Old New Land* as a utopian text not to be taken seriously as a political blueprint: "It is a utopia, and like all utopias, this one also invited the reader to close his eyes and believe. We know from Herzl's diaries and other sources that, far from trying actually to execute the utopian schemes presented in *Altneuland*, he never wavered from his original goal of seeking an independent and sovereign Jewish state, complete with an army and navy, borders and power politics." Thus Hazony questions all those "who have insisted on reading the novel literally, as though it were intended to be a political practical program."[31]

Even though *Old New Land* clearly belongs to a different literary genre than *The Jewish State* and is filled with the kind of kitsch so popular in fin-de-siècle Vienna, there can be no doubt that Herzl insisted it to be taken seriously. As he emphasized in the book itself, it is up to its readers if its message remains a fairy tale or becomes reality. The minute details with which he described its political system, its heroes and its villains, show where his vision of a Jewish state had arrived in 1902. When he sent a copy of the novel to Lord Rothschild, Herzl wrote in an accompanying letter: "There will, of course, be stupid people who, because I have chosen the *form* of a Utopia, which has been used by Plato and Thomas More, will declare the cause *to be* a Utopia. I fear no such misunderstanding in your case."[32] In another letter to German Chancellor von Bülow he emphasized: "In fact, I wrote the Utopia only to show that it is none."[33]

On the other side of the political spectrum, Peter Beinart cites David Littwak as one of his heroes in his book, *The Crisis of Zionism*. To be sure, he criticizes Herzl's lack of foresight when it came to Arab nationalism, but unlike Hazony who sees *Old New Land* as pure fantasy, he calls it an "impressive place." Beinart applauds the fact that Littwak can speak Arabic and that one of his close associates is an Arab engineer from Haifa. He quotes Littwak's call for tolerance and reminds his readers that the racist Dr. Geyer never gains control over the Jewish state.[34]

Old New Land was an expression of Herzl's political vision, but it was also the product of a writer who contributed countless feuilletons to the local press and wrote many plays for the Vienna stages. As such, it also has to be seen in the context of literary Vienna in the late nineteenth and early twentieth century. In fact, Herzl's novel was not the only product of Vienna's fin de siècle to draw the picture of an idealized future. Works such as Bertha von Suttner's *Lay Down Your Arms* (1889), Joseph von Neupacher's *Austria in the Year 2020* (1893), and, especially, Theodor Hertzka's *Freeland* (1890), *Journey to Freeland* (1893), and *Taken Off in the Future* (1895) all belonged to the same genre. Neither was Herzl the only author to depict a utopian Jewish state. Before *Old New Land,* other Jewish authors, among them Menahem (Edmund) Eisler, Jacques Bachar, Elchanan Leeb Lewinsky, and Sholem Aleichem had published their own visions of a future Jewish state.[35]

None of these works of fiction provided exact specifications as to the nature of the projected Jewish state, its form of government, its borders, or its degree of sovereignty. But there is one recurring principle in all of them. The future state is tolerant toward non-Jews. Jacques Bachar writes: "The Jews abolish all differences between religions, nations, and races in their state. There is only one law both for the stranger and for the citizen." There are very similar ideas in Eisler's novel, and Boris Schatz states in his vision of a Jewish state a few years later: "Not only Jews will flock to us, but also non-Jews will find their rest, because of the beauty of the land, because of the cultural achievements, and most of all because of the high moral values of our society." All authors agree that the Jews will treat minorities in their midst better than they themselves were treated as a minority over the centuries.[36]

Many of these authors also had a model state for all humanity in mind. As Rachel Alboim-Dror writes in her thorough exploration of the subject, "None of these novels intended to create just another state, but rather a unique Jewish state that would serve as a model society to all the nations of the world." She admits that many of these novels that envisioned something between a secular society and and one based on religious Jewish ideals, between a universalistic idea and particularistic Jewish values "created tensions between the longing for normalization—to be like all the other nations—and the claim to be a chosen people."[37]

Herzl's old new land was neither a religious state nor the spiritual center for the revival of a secular Hebrew culture that many of the East European Zionists envisioned. He intended to create a safe haven from persecution that would be a better version of Europe in the Middle East. His plan was also a critique of Old Lady Europa with her outdated habits and structures and widespread antisemitism. His New Society would be more dynamic, more tolerant, technically perfected, and socially just. But Europe—or at least a Western projection of Europe onto the Middle Eastern—it would nonetheless remain. It was grounded in strong feelings of European superiority and paternalism, not only toward Arabs, but also toward Oriental Jews, and more traditional Jews in general. While this appealed especially to his West European readers, part of his Eastern European audience read the lack of genuinely Jewish elements critically.

The Odessa Jewish intellectual Asher Ginsberg, better known under his pen-name Ahad Ha'am (One of the People) became the voice of this internal Zionist criticism. He had been a Zionist long before Herzl came on the stage, but his Zionism was of a different nature. He did not intend to create a miniature Europe in the Middle East, but sought instead a genuinely Jewish society, where Jewish creativity and cultural values would be central, Hebrew would be spoken, and a message of renewal would be broadcast to the remaining Jewish communities in the diaspora.[38]

HEBREW REVIVAL

Odessa reverberated with news of Herzl's First pan-Jewish Congress. All returning delegates and observers were in awe of Herzl, with one exception: Ahad Ha'am. This sober spirit was not caught by the general frenzy caused by the new messianism. Back from Basel, he announced in his journal *Ha-shiloah* that he felt at the congress like a person who "attended a wedding in mourning dress," because he sees in "Herzlism" nothing but an attempt to establish a Jewish state by diplomacy, which must end in a major disappointment.[39]

This is how Simon Dubnow described the reaction of Herzl's most important internal rival, Ahad Ha'am, to the First Zionist Congress, which was also the last that Ahad Ha'am attended. He scorned the delegates who thought they could reverse the developments of two thousand years of exile within one generation. Even if they achieved sovereignty over a certain territory—whom would it really help? In his view, more substantial, more profound transformations were needed than the creation of just another state.

Like Herzl, Ahad Ha'am too was not satisfied with creating a state like any other state. But "a light unto the nations," a model society was not enough, either. What was needed was a society different in its very substance from all others. He explained: "After two thousand years of untold misery and suffering, the Jewish people cannot possibly be content with attaining at last to the position of a small and insignificant nation, with a State tossed about like a ball between its powerful neighbours, and maintaining its existence only by diplomatic shifts and continual truckling to the favoured of fortune. An ancient people, which was once a beacon to the world, cannot possibly accept, as a satisfactory reward for all that it has endured, a thing so trifling, which many other peoples, unrenowned and uncultured, have won in a short time, without going through a hundredth time of the suffering. It was not for nothing that Israel had Prophets, whose vision saw Righteousness ruling the world at the end of the days."[40]

Ahad Ha'am accused Herzl of designing a Jewish state that would be just another, perhaps more perfected state, created by diplomats or soldiers. He, on the other hand, envisioned nothing less than modern-day prophets establishing a Jewish national home, and unlike many of his fellow East European Jews, Ahad Ha'am did not regard Herzl as such a prophet. He was simply too far removed from the Jewish people and their ways of life to understand their emotions in a profound way. Herzl wanted a small Switzerland in the Middle East; Ahad Ha'am longed for a new Judea, in which Hebrew would be spoken and Jewish culture renewed on a secular basis. Herzl wanted a state for the Jews, Ahad Ha'am a Jewish state, or to be more correct an autonomous Jewish society. Neither of them envisioned a fully independent state in the modern sense, and both agreed on a secular society.

In his long essay "The Jewish State and the Jewish Problem," written in the year 1897, Ahad Ha'am explained his position to his critics. He distinguished between Eastern and Western European Zionists and criticized those who had rejected the "old" *Hibbat Zion* movement by establishing instead a new one called *Zionismus*. These modern *Zionisten* were proud of every word of praise that was being written about the new movement written in all kinds of languages—besides Hebrew. They might be able to build a state that will provide some poor Jews with a new home—but would such a home be able to feed the spiritual hunger of the Jewish people?

In Ahad Ha'am's view, it was nothing short of ridiculous to believe that a tiny strip of land would fulfill the material hunger of all Jews—and how could it ever hold fifteen million people? The main task of Zionism in his view was to build a *spiritual* center. The leaders of the new movement in the West came to Zionism only because of antisemitism, he argued, while in the East the longing for Zion was the "natural product of a real link with a culture of thousands of years, which will retain its hold even if the troubles of the Jews all over the world come to an end, together with anti-Semitism." Thus, "in the West it is the problem of the Jews, in the East the problem of Judaism."[41] While Herzl tried to solve only the crisis of the Jews, Ahad Ha'am came to solve the crisis of Judaism as well. Instead of a "Society of Jews" or a "New Society" based mainly on economic advances he demanded a center for the Jewish spirit.

With respect to the Arab population, Ahad Ha'am was more prescient than Herzl. He feared that once their numbers grew substantially and their political aspirations became clear, they would not embrace the European newcomers. Even before Herzl entered the political arena, Ahad Ha'am had warned of a clash between Jews and Arabs, who both had claims to the same land. In the often-quoted 1891 essay in which he critically reflected on the new Jewish settlements in Palestine after his first visit there, Ahad Ha'am made his readers aware that Jewish immigrants would need to take into consideration the collective demands of the local Arab population. But we must keep in mind that even these much-quoted remarks play only a very marginal role in his essay and in his reporting from the Land of Israel in general.[42]

Herzl's *Old New Land* confirmed Ahad Ha'am's worst nightmares. He reacted to its utopianism with ridicule and shock: "In *Old New Land* nothing can surprise you. Everything is one big marvel." And he concludes, "There is only mechanical mimicry, lacking any sense of national initiative."[43] Ahad Ha'am spoke for many East European Zionists when he belittled *Old New Land* as unrealistic and in its very essence assimilatory. In his view, Herzl's state of the Jews resembled collective assimilation. There was nothing there that was Jewish, only the imitation of European culture in a Middle Eastern context. Ahad Ha'am stood in the tradition of the East European Hebrew *Haskala* (Enlightenment), which had as its primary aim not the fight against antisemitism, but the renewal of Judaism and Jewish culture.

In place of Herzl, it was Max Nordau who replied to Ahad Ha'am in the official Zionist paper *Die Welt* (The World)—even before Ahad Ha'am's essay appeared in German translation. Nordau defended the import of European ideas: "Indeed, 'Old New Land' is a piece of Europe in Asia. Herzl pointed exactly to our aspirations. We want the reunited, liberated

FIGURE 7. The Zionist journalist and activist Asher Ginsberg, known as Ahad Ha'am, around 1910.

Jewish people to remain a people of culture, as much as they are already a people of culture, and to become a people of culture where this is not yet the case. We do not imitate anyone, we use and develop what we own. We have participated in European culture, even more than in our own. It is part of us, in the same way that it is part of the Germans, French, and English. We will not allow anyone to construct a barrier between our Jewishness and our European culture. For Ahad Ha'am European culture may indeed be something foreign, and he should be grateful to us for making it accessible to him. But, for our part, we will never allow the return of the Jews to the land of their fathers to become a step back into barbarism, as our enemies calumniously claim. The Jewish people will develop its character within general Western culture, just as any other civilized people, and not outside of it, in cultureless wild Asia (*Asiatentum*), as Ahad Ha'am seems to wish." According to Nordau, Ahad Ha'am belongs to "the worst enemies of Zionism." Alluding to the "protest rabbis" who objected loudly against the First Zionist Congress in Munich, Nordau calls him a "secular protest rabbi."[44]

Herzl expressed the same thoughts in very similar words in *The Jewish State*: "We should form a portion of a rampart of Europe against Asia, an outpost of civilization as opposed to barbarism."[45] For many German-speaking Jews, Asia began just a few miles from their own places of origin. When the Galician writer Karl Emil Franzos described the Eastern region of the Habsburg Empire, where he grew up, and Romania, he called it "Half-Asia" and depicted a Jewish community that still had far to go to assimilate to modern Western civilization.[46] But no matter if Asia or Half-Asia: East European traditions, the Yiddish language, and the renewal of Hebrew were all foreign to the two leaders of the early Zionist movement,

Theodor Herzl and Max Nordau. So were the Jews of Arab countries.

Even though Herzl wanted the representatives of the Jewish communities of the Middle East to attend his congresses, his attitude toward them was highly paternalistic. He got a glimpse of their lives when he traveled to Jerusalem, and he wrote about what he saw with a sense of disgust: "When I remember thee in days to come, O Jerusalem, it will not be with pleasure. The musty deposits of two thousand years of inhumanity, intolerance, and uncleanliness lie in the foul-smelling alleys."[47] Herzl knew little about the actual problems and desires of the Jews in the Middle East. He thought it would be best to Europeanize them, just as western Jewish philanthropic organizations like the *Alliance Israélite universelle* in France, and the *Hilfsverein der deutschen Juden* in Germany intended to do by building French and German schools. The Zionism that came into existence in the early twentieth century from Morocco to Iraq, and from Yemen to Syria had its roots in traditional religious ties to the holy land. This orientation had little in common with either Herzl's West European nationalism or Ahad Ha'am's East European *Haskala*. The dreams of these communities were contained in traditional prayer books and not in theories of nationalism and enlightenment. Neither Herzl nor Ahad Ha'am spoke for the Jews of the Middle East and North Africa. But their descendants would later decisively shape the society that these and other European leaders had envisioned.[48]

Zionism was a movement that, while it left room for religious elements, was decidedly secular, though granting access to Jews from the Middle East and North Africa was unquestionably a European idea. It would remain decidedly secular for most of the twentieth century, until in the last quarter of the century religious and non-European elements became increasingly influential.

For now, however, the major divide of the movement remained within Europe and between secular Jews. Ahad Ha'am expressed this when he defined the Zionists of Western Europe by their disappointment over attempts to integrate into Western societies, while Zionism in Eastern Europe was the result of a transformation of Judaism: "The Western Jew, after leaving the Ghetto and seeking to attach himself to the people of the country in which he lives, is unhappy because his hope of an open-armed welcome is disappointed. He returns reluctantly to his own people, and tries to find within the Jewish community that life for which he yearns—but in vain. Communal life and communal problems no longer satisfy him. He has already grown accustomed to a broader social and political life; and on the intellectual side Jewish cultural work has no attraction, because Jewish culture has played no part in his education from childhood, and is a closed book to him. So in his trouble he turns to the land of his ancestors, and pictures to himself how good it would be if a Jewish State were reestablished there—a State arranged and organized exactly after the pattern of other States."[49] Western Jews, even in a Jewish state, would "remain what they always have been: Members of their non-Jewish cultures, in which they were educated since their childhood." Most East European Jews, on the other hand, are "filled with the spirit of Judaism from early on, they feel in their soul that this spirit lives on in their hearts, even if their religious convictions have undergone a basic transformation."[50]

Not all East European Jews, though, flocked to Ahad Ha'am. Herzl and Nordau also had faithful followers in Eastern Europe. Most of the congress delegates came from the East. When he toured the communities of the East, Herzl was often greeted with unrestrained enthusiasm. It was the combination of his charismatic prophet-like appearance and his Western "otherness" that created the distance necessary for true admiration. He figured prominently in Bar Mitzvah speeches, like the one held by thirteen-year old Shne'ur Zalman Hirsch in Warsaw in 1902, in which "Doctor Herzl" was a modern-day Moses leading his people out of exile. The idea of becoming like everyone else and creating "a state like any other" resonated less among the masses than the notion of a restored uniqueness. Even though Shne'ur Zalman used the formula of the Jews becoming again "a nation like all other nations," with their own territory, he or whoever wrote his Bar Mitzvah speech made clear: "We will live as strangers among the nations until we will succeed again to become a unique people in a unique country."[51] The idea of uniqueness and the desire to become a normal people blended in Bar Mitzvah speeches just as it did in congress addresses.

SOCIALIST DREAMS

For Zionists, the demand for a Jewish state meant much more than just the reestablishment of Jewish sovereignty after two millennia and the resettlement of a people from one place to another. It meant the end of what they conceived as the abnormality of diaspora life and the beginning of the creation of a new type of Jew. This major endeavor would include the revitalization of Hebrew as a spoken language, the occupational restructuring of the Jews who would be trained to work the soil, and the transformation of the Jewish body. The Zionist thinker Jakob Klatzkin formulated the tasks of Zionism as follows: "In Eretz Israel the Jewish people will regain their normality. . . . Only by being rooted in their own soil will they leave behind elitist Jewish traits and become a real people."[52]

Klatzkin thought, as did many other Zionists, that by returning to their ancient home, the Jews would become a normal people again, with an occupational structure similar to that of other people and with a stronger attachment to agricultural labor and to trade and craft professions. The relocation to Palestine was thus also a major reeducation project.

The Hebrew language would play a major role in this process. The immigrants were supposed to change not only their professions and their mentality, but also their language. The modernization of Hebrew into an everyday language, an endeavor often identified with the systematic efforts of Eliezer Ben-Yehuda, was part of transforming the "Yid" of the diaspora into the "Hebrew" in his or her homeland. Yosef Hayim Brenner, one of the most important Hebrew writers and an immigrant to Palestine before World War I, personified the radical transformation of the Jews and their language. Like with many other Zionist pioneers, religion played no role for him in this undertaking. Whoever wanted to participate in the "Hebrew revolution" could become part of the new society in Palestine. Brenner, who unlike many other Zionists, also respected the Yiddish language, longed for a Jewish state that was not different from any other state, except in the fact that the Jewish languages were spoken and their cultures valued.[53]

While Western Jews like Herzl and Nordau were generally less enthusiastic about the possibility of spoken Hebrew, they too emphasized what they regarded as a normalization of their economic situation. Addressing the Fifth Zionist Congress, Nordau said: "Only we are denied the right to live for ourselves. Only we are the natural servants of other nations, whom the master can throw out of the house if he has no need for them anymore, while they cannot terminate their service, as there is no other place for them. We Zionists want to change

FIGURE 8. The new image of the Jewish Worker in a Socialist-Zionist poster by Gabriel and Maxim Shamir.

this disgraceful situation. . . . The Jewish people can only be redeemed from its bitter misery once it leads a normal economic life on its own soil."[54]

Socialist thinkers within the Zionist movement further advanced the idea of working with their own hands on their own soil, of producing a state of workers and farmers. Aaron David Gordon, who would become an inspiration to the

Hapoel ha-tza'ir (The Young Worker—a non-Marxist socialist political stream within Zionism) and the kibbutz movements, criticized that Jews in the diaspora, as "a people that was completely divorced from nature, that during 2000 years was imprisoned within walls, that became inured to all forms of life except to a life of labor, cannot become once again a living, natural, working people without bending all its will-power toward that end. We lack the fundamental element; we lack labor, but labor by which a people becomes rooted in its soil and in its culture."[55] While Ber Borochov, one of the fathers of socialist Zionism, acknowledged that the Jewish diaspora would continue to exist, he also stressed that only in Palestine could Jews overcome their unnatural occupational structure, which had developed over the many centuries they had spent in Europe as an "extraterritorial people": "These anomalies will disappear in Eretz Israel, where the Jewish worker will penetrate into all the hitherto excluded branches of production."[56] The "territorialization" of the Jews would lead to the normalization of their situation in every respect. This meant for him the end of antisemitism, the building of a Jewish working class in their own land, and their becoming masters of their own political affairs. With respect to the Palestinian Arabs as possible competitors among the working class, the socialist Borochov was as naïve (and paternalistic) as the bourgeois Herzl. He believed that the Arab population would gradually assimilate to the Jewish newcomers; he was convinced that they, in any case, had historical roots among the ancient Hebrews and would be pleased to reconnect with them.[57] In reality, the idea of "Hebrew labor" led to an ethnically segregated labor market, which favored Jewish immigrants over the Arab Palestinian population of Palestine. The idea of the conquest of labor was also intrinsically connected to the idea of the conquest of land.[58]

Even the most secular and socialist ideas traveled with religious luggage, however. Traditional notions of messianism were translated into secular language, but their associations with the Bible and rabbinical literature were so thoroughly engrained in East European Zionists that they could not disappear. *Ge'ulat karka'ot* (the redemption of the soil) became a central slogan of the new movement, and thus provided secular meaning to a theological concept. In the words of Yehudah Mirsky, Aaron David Gordon, like many other Zionists, "abandoned traditional religious belief and practice, but held on to its reach and pathos."[59] And even though the reason why Brenner and other secular Zionists worked on the revival of Hebrew had little to do with religious connotation, the biblical text and religious tradition were still strongly evoked by their use of the language and by the deep associations their readers had. There was no denying that writing in the language of the Bible was different from writing in European languages. As Arthur Koestler would put it in his 1949 Palestine chronicle, *Promise and Fulfilment*, "Hebrew is admirably suited for producing prophetic thunder; but you cannot play a scherzo on a ram's horn."[60] Under the thin mantle of socialism and secular thought, religious concepts continued to flicker and could be reignited decades later.

The socialist Zionists were not satisfied with the mere transformation of intellectuals into peasants and merchants into craftsmen; they wanted to set an example for a new society, which would emerge out of the new Jews. Their ideal was the *Kvutza*, or as it was later called, the *kibbutz*, a collective agricultural settlement that would abolish private property and help to build the new state.[61] In terms of numbers, kibbutz members were never more than a small minority of the Jewish population in Palestine or, later, in the State of Israel. However, for many decades they were regarded as an avantgarde of the *Yishuv*. They fulfilled the demands of socialist Zionism most radically; in the idealized world of many Zionists, they had left behind both exile and the middle-class values of the old world, they had given up private property and gender discrimination.

The other type of a "new Jew" besides the *kibbutznik* was the *shomer*, the guard who protected Jewish farmers against attacks from the Arab population. Yosef Trumpeldor, who as a Russian officer had lost one arm in the Russo-Japanese War before he came to live in Palestine and who was killed in 1920 while defending the settlement of Tel Hai in the north of the country, emerged as the heroic figurehead of this new military ethos. His alleged last words, "It is good to die for our country," became a standard phrase in Zionist hagiography.[62]

Jews in their own land would not only know how to work the soil but also how to defend themselves. The ideal of the military arose in Zionist ideology as an offshoot of Max Nordau's call for the creation of "muscle Jews."[63] For two millennia, Jews had had no army of their own. If they really wanted to become a nation like all other nations, they should have not only peasants and craftsmen but also soldiers and an army, like all other states. The Jewish Legion, established by the Russian Zionist Vladimir Ze'ev Jabotinsky as a unit in the British army during World War I, was an early expression of this new military spirit. For the first time, Jews marched with the Star of David on their uniforms. The significant role that *Tzahal*, the Israeli army, today plays within Israeli society is not only a response to the continued threats to the survival of the small state, but also of an attempted normalization of centuries of Jewish history, during which Jews were not allowed to serve as soldiers.[64]

The ideal of the new Jew also challenged traditional gender roles. At least in theory, women now participated as equal members of the Zionist society. They were supposed to work the soil, take part in political decisions, and defend the new settlements with weapons in their hands. While this was translated into a partial reality, it remained in good part a myth developed in early Zionist rhetoric and historiography. In fact, women often fulfilled a double role in society: While taking on some traditionally male public functions, they continued to do the traditionally private female work: educating the children, preparing the food, and cleaning the premises.[65] If they aspired to becoming pioneers and fighters, they would have to adapt to male roles, while men were not expected to change their traditional gender roles.[66]

The "new Jewish woman" is however crucial to an understanding of the whole Zionist enterprise. Women like Manya Shohat, who helped Russians Jews defend themselves against the pogroms and later became a pioneer of one of the first collective agricultural settlements in Palestine; Sarah Aaronson, who took her life after being discovered as part of the Zionist spy ring "Nili" in the last days of the Ottoman rule in Palestine; and Hannah Szenes, as a parachutist from Palestine who was executed by the Nazis in her native Hungary after being sent there in a rescue mission, became heroines for future generation.[67]

The tension between the pull of normalization and pull of uniqueness was evident in the area of gender relations as well. Zionism tried to create a new "normality" by recruiting women to the workforce, providing (some of) them with traditionally exclusive male roles in society, and freeing those who lived in a kibbutz from the daily upbringing of their children by constructing separate children's houses. These attempts at creating gender equality should not be downplayed, but the gap between official propaganda and daily practice remained.

In summary, the "new Jews" in Palestine were to replace the eternal outsiders, the classical "other" in European societies. They were to do all the things that had been forbidden to them in exile, either by the non-Jewish authorities or by the rabbinical leadership: work their soil, defend their country, replace their "corrupted" languages with pure Hebrew, and achieve gender equality. But this intended normalization produced new kinds of otherness, for the Jewish immigrants remained strangers among the native Arab Palestinian population. They created forms of agricultural settlement unknown to the Palestinian Arabs, they used their weapons to defend themselves against attacks from the local population, they integrated women into society in a way that largely ignored the conventions in their new surroundings, and they spoke a kind of Hebrew that sounded European in the ears of both local Arabs and Jewish immigrants from Arab lands. Thus, the immigrants remained strangers in the eyes of the local inhabitants, both the traditional Jewish "Old Yishuv," and the Arab Palestinian population.

The Palestinian Arabs were beginning to form their own national movement, a process that was not caused, but certainly accelerated by the advance of Zionism. It was still a movement in creation and very much in search of itself when Zionism entered the political stage. Until the early years after World War I, as Hillel Cohen writes, "large numbers of Arabs identified themselves first and foremost by their religion, their family, their village, and the region they lived in. Even those who gave priority to their national identity as Arabs were divided on the question of what constituted the Arab nation and what its national territory was. The pan-Arab movement was sometimes stronger and sometimes weaker. Some of its adherents perceived Palestine to be part of an Arab kingdom centered on Damascus, others viewed it as a national extension of the Transjordanian emirate, while still others saw the boundaries of the British Palestine Mandate as defining a specific Palestinian Arab identity distinct from other Arab identities."[68] Similarly, Rashid Khalidi argues that Palestinian Arabs in the early twentieth century "identified with the Ottoman Empire, their religion, Arabism, their homeland Palestine, their city or region, and their family, without feeling any contradiction, or sense of conflicting loyalties."[69] The first signs of transforming these overlapping senses of identity into a national movement could be seen on the eve of World War I. In 1908 a former Ottoman official suggested expanding the existing *sanjak* (district) of Jerusalem and to include the southern parts of the vilayet (province) of Beirut in order to create Palestine as a political unit within the Ottoman Empire. In 1911, the newspaper *Filastin* (Palestine) was founded in Jaffa to give expression to a rising national movement.[70] In contrast to the hopes of Herzl and many other Zionist leaders, the majority of the Arab Palestinian population did not welcome the new immigrants from Europe, but saw in them a danger to their own emerging national aspirations.

ORTHODOX RESERVATIONS

The main protagonists of the early Zionist movement agreed on one principle when it came to the future Jewish state. Despite their differences on many other issues, they all rejected any form of theocracy and advocated a clear-cut division between state and religion. State laws should not be based on religious laws *(halakha)*. Non-Jews should enjoy equal status in every respect. But they were also concerned not to turn away Orthodox Jews from the new movement. Herzl went to great efforts to include a few rabbis and Orthodox Jews as delegates to his congresses, and Ahad Ha'am was sensitive toward the religious background of the idea of a return to Zion.

Independent of these developments, Orthodox Jews were being drawn into the politicization so characteristic of European Jews in the early twentieth century. Following the models of the Zionists, the Bundist Socialists, and other Jewish political organizations, they began to modernize their own organizational networks and to make themselves heard in the political arena. The Orthodox consisted (and consist) of extremely diversified groups. There were traditionalists who rejected any compromise with modernity, and there were the modern Orthodox who accepted integration into society while observing Jewish religious laws. In Eastern Europe there were the mystically inspired Hasidim and the *mitnagdim* (literally, opponents), a plethora of Hassidic dynasties with different religious and political outlooks: the Satmar and the Lubavitch, the Belz and the Ger, the Bratslav and the Bobov Hasidim. In Germany, there were those who preferred to secede from Reform-dominated communities, and there were others who favored the principle of unity and stayed inside the framework of communities; in Hungary there were the "status quo" moderates and the more radical Orthodox. Any thought of uniting all of these groups under one organizational umbrella was entirely illusionary. Their leaders identified their most dangerous enemies often not in the Reform movement or among the assimilationists, whom they deemed beyond any reach, but in the camp closest to them.[71]

Zionism was another major source of division within the Orthodox community. While Orthodox Jews prayed three times a day for the return to Zion, they believed that this would happen only in messianic times. The notion of a Zionist movement under entirely secular leadership and with a secular language was abhorrent to many of them. The traditionalists especially viewed the new movement as a heresy that had to be fiercely opposed. The more moderate searched for ways to combine the aims of Zionism with the principles of Orthodoxy. They founded their own group called *Mizrahi* (literally: "eastern," but also an acronym for *merkaz ruhani* or "spiritual center") in a conference in Vilna in 1902. Later, they would become known as the national religious faction within the Zionist movement, and between 1956 and 2008 they found a home in Israel's National Religious Party.

The religious Zionists (*Mizrahi*), under the leadership of Rabbi Yitzhak Ya'akov Reines, were ready to compromise. In order to help to bring Jews who were threatened by violence in Europe to the Land of Israel, they adopted a pragmatist Zionist platform. Initially, they were Zionists *despite* their messianism. Only later did they become Zionists *because* of their messianism. In this early phase, Zionism was for most of them merely a means to save Jewish lives, and not a tactic aimed at accelerating the coming of the messiah. Instead of using messianism to legitimize their support for Zionism, they neutralized messianism. It is thus no surprise that Theodor Herzl received considerable support for his Uganda plan from the *Mizrahi* faction. A Jewish homeland outside Palestine opened the possibility of rescuing East European Jews, while avoiding the theological conflict that founding a premature Jewish state in the holy land would likely bring about.[72]

The tradionalists, often called *haredim* (ultra-Orthodox), followed suit with their own political organization, when they founded *Agudat Yisrael* (Union of Israel) in 1912 in the Silesian city of Kattowitz. This organization vehemently rejected the establishment of a Jewish state in the Land of Israel and called for solidarity with the Old Yishuv, the ultra-Orthodox community living in Jerusalem and a few other places in Palestine. They tried to defend the *haredi* lifestyle of meticulous religious observance against the intrusion of secular immigrants, who built kibbutzim and coffee houses, movie theaters and nightclubs.[73] For them, any attempt to hasten the coming of the messiah was contrary to God's will, as is expressed clearly in the writings of the Lubavitcher Rebbe, Shalom Dov Baer Schneersohn. In 1899, he wrote of the newly emerging Zionist movement: "We must not heed them in their call to achieve redemption on our own, for we are not permitted to hasten the End even by reciting too many prayers, much less so by corporeal stratagems, that is, to set out from exile by force."[74]

Both the *Mizrahi* and the *Agudat Yisrael* became active in Palestine in the years after the First World War. While they did not agree with each other on most issues, they occasionally appeared united in their fight against a secular society in a future Jewish state. During the first decades of the century, religious Jews constituted so small a minority among the Zionist leadership and among the new Jewish immigrants to Palestine that their fight seemed futile. Still, in November 1918 they presented a draft "constitution" based on principles of *halakha* that would serve for a future Jewish society in Palestine.[75]

During this period, an attitude that had lain dormant within religious Zionism since its nineteenth century origins came to the fore. Some religious leaders recognized that the secular Zionists could actually be used as a vehicle to enhance the coming of the messiah. Daniel Mahla wrote: "Religious Zionism, in such a view, set out to end political quietism among Orthodox Jews, and to engage them in the activities to build up a Jewish state as an important step in the process of divine redemption. Traditionalist leaders rejected these attempts out of hand, and the two sides entered into prolonged and fierce ideological struggles."[76]

The champion of the new activist brand of messianic Zionism was Rabbi Abraham Isaac Kook, soon to become Palestine's first Chief Rabbi. In his opinion, even when they were violating Jewish religious laws, the Zionists were unintentionally performing holy deeds by propelling the Jews back to their land: "The Divine Spirit prevails in their aspirations even against their own wills." Eventually, Kook argued that the sinners would repent their sins and return to traditional Judaism. The state they will build cannot be a state like any other state, as "the State of Israel is the foundation of God's throne on earth, directed towards the unity of the Lord and His name."[77] In Jewish apocalyptic tradition, the way for the ultimate appearance of the Messiah ben David (of the House of David) will be prepared by a more violent Messiah ben Yosef (of the House of Joseph). For Kook, Zionism as a movement represented the messianic stage of this "preparatory messiah." He argued that "nothing in our faith, either in its larger principles or in its details, negates the idea that we can begin to shake off the dust of exile by our own efforts, through natural, historical processes."[78]

Even within the most traditionalist camp, there were those who now regarded the secular Zionist movement as a divine instrument. Isaac Breuer, one of the German-Jewish leaders of the *Agudat Yisrael* (and later president of their workers' party, *Poalei Agudat Yisrael*) saw the final mission of Diaspora Jewry as "national emancipation" and reassembly in the Land of Israel. Zionism was thus, in his view, a useful tool to advance the coming of the messianic age, but one that, he was convinced, Orthodoxy would eventually replace.[79]

While the Orthodox were the only Jews to demand a state based on religious principles, the early concepts of Zionism developed by its secular leaders all contained subterraneous religious elements that lent themselves to later theological reinterpretations. Herzl's obsession to create a "light unto the nations" was the secularization of a thoroughly religious concept, even though presented in a highly secular understanding. For many early leaders of Zionism, their movement constituted a secularized version of traditional messianism, and sometimes messianic allusions would work their way to the surface. Orthodox and Liberal Jews, Christians and atheists would depict Herzl as the true or a false messiah, as its harbinger, or as modern-day Moses.[80] Shortly before his death, Herzl recounted to the Russian-Jewish writer Reuven Brainin a dream he had had as a twelve-year old, in which the messiah "took me in his arms, and swept off with me on the wings of the wind. On one of the iridescent clouds we encountered the figure of Moses. . . . The Messiah called to Moses: It is for this child that I have prayed! But to me he said: Go, declare to the Jews that I shall come soon and perform great wonders and great deeds for my people and for the whole world."[81] Many years later, Israel's first president, Chaim Weizmann, recalled in messianic terminology the moment when he held the Balfour Declaration in his hands: "I felt as if a sun ray had struck me; and I thought I heard the steps of the Messiah."[82]

By designating the Hebrew language as the new vernacular to be spoken in Palestine, cultural Zionists unconsciously created a new affinity not only to the language of the Bible but also to biblical ways of thought. The socialists' talk of the redemption of the soil provided the basis for claims by some in the Labor Party after the Six-Day War that the whole of the Land of Israel was sacred.[83] Although there was no predetermined path towards a religious understanding of Zionism, the kernels of such an interpretation were contained in the movement from its outset.[84]

THE NATIONAL HOME

A STATE IN THE MAKING?

> If we were to have a Jewish majority in Eretz Israel, then first
> of all, we would create here a situation of total, absolute,
> and complete equal rights, with no exceptions: whether Jew,
> Arab, Armenian, or German, there is no difference before the
> law. . . . Complete equal rights would be granted not only to
> citizens as individuals, but also to languages and nations. . . .
>
> —VLADIMIR ZE'EV JABOTINSKY[1]

In the Sykes-Picot agreement of 1916, British and French diplomats divided the Middle Eastern regions they were about to
conquer from the Ottoman Empire into three parts: the
French would exert control over most of the northern region,
today's Syria and Lebanon, while the British would govern the
eastern and southern provinces, mainly today's Iraq and Jordan. A small strip on the eastern shore of the Mediterranean
was painted in a different color on their maps. Palestine should
receive special status and remain under international control.
This was not due to any particular resources the territory possessed nor to its specific strategic situation—but rather to the
unique religious and historical significance of the land that
encompassed the holy city of Jerusalem and other biblical
sites. Although never implemented, this plan offered a fore-
taste of the special attention this long-neglected region would
receive in the twentieth century.

Only a year later the British government, now the most important political power in the region and eager to control this strip of land by itself, gave the Zionists what they had long and fervently desired. The few lines written by the British Foreign Secretary, Lord Arthur Balfour, on November 2nd, 1917, to one of the most prominent Jewish representatives in the United Kingdom, Lord Walter Rothschild, granted legitimacy to the Zionists' goals. The Balfour Declaration was received with enthusiasm by the movement, for it made clear the British government's favorable outlook on Zionist plans: "His Majesty's Government view with favour the establishment in Palestine of a national home for the Jewish people, and will use their best endeavors to facilitate the achievement of this object, it being clearly understood that nothing shall be done which may prejudice the civil and religious rights of existing non-Jewish communities in Palestine, or the rights and political status enjoyed by Jews in any other country."[2] After Britain received the League of Nations Mandate over Palestine at the 1920 San Remo conference, the promise of a "national home" was formulated in even stronger terms. The Mandate speaks no longer of "facilitating" the achievement of this object, but of "securing" it.[3]

But what exactly did the British promise the Jews? What was a "national home"? The truth is that nobody really knew. This formula reached back to the First Zionist Congress, when "a publicly and legally assured home in Palestine" became the central demand of Herzl's new movement. Even then it was not clear if this meant an independent state or a cooperative as in Herzl's "Society of the Jews," a spiritual center as envisioned by Ahad Ha'am and his followers or an autonomous region within a multi-national empire based on the Habsburg monarchy.

There was no clear legal definition of the term "national home" and no precedent in history for the use of this term.[4] Just as the Zionist leaders believed in the unique case of a Jewish state, so the world community used terminology they would not employ in treating any other group. In this sense, the Balfour Declaration helped to further the notion of exceptionalism when it came to the Jewish state model.

Zionist leaders read the declaration in many different ways. For some, it meant that ultimately, once a Jewish majority was reached, a full-fledged Jewish state would exist. For others, it promised autonomy to the Jews in Palestine under a British protectorate as the ultimate fulfillment of their wishes. The British cabinet deliberately kept the wording vague so as not to provoke the Ottoman rulers. It was a compromise between more radical and more moderate voices, as the Report of the Peel Commission would affirm twenty years later: "We have been permitted to examine the records which bear upon the question and it is clear to us that the words 'the establishment in Palestine of a National Home' were the outcome of a compromise between those Ministers who contemplated the ultimate establishment of a Jewish State and those who did not."[5] The report also mentioned that Prime Minister Lloyd George had excluded the possibility of immediate statehood for the Jews, but thought such a possibility realistic once Jews were a majority of the population in Palestine.

THE AUTONOMY SOLUTION

After an increase of violence between Arabs and Jews, especially the 1920/21 riots in Jaffa and Jerusalem, the British government increasingly distanced itself from the interpretation that the phrase "national home" meant a full-fledged Jewish state. Thus, Winston Churchill declared in 1922 that while the

Jews possessed historic rights to the Land of Israel, that did not necessarily extend to an independent state. "When it is asked what is meant by the development of the Jewish National Home in Palestine, it may be answered that it is not the imposition of a Jewish nationality upon the inhabitants of Palestine as a whole, but the further development of the existing Jewish community, with the assistance of Jews in other parts of the world, in order that it may become a center in which the Jewish people as a whole may take, on grounds of religion and race, an interest and a pride."[6] This sounds more like Ahad Ha'am's spiritual center than an independent state with political rights.

Churchill, then Secretary of State for the Colonies, used language similar to that of the League of Nations, when it granted Britain the Mandate over Palestine and explicitly confirmed the Balfour Declaration. "The Mandatory shall be responsible for placing the country under such political, administrative and economic conditions as will secure the establishment of the Jewish national home, as laid down in the preamble, and the development of self-governing institutions, and also for safeguarding the civil and religious rights of all the inhabitants of Palestine, irrespective of race and religion."[7]

Some Zionist leaders regarded the acceptance of the Balfour Declaration by the League of Nations as the fulfillment of their dreams. Thus, Nahum Sokolow, who would later become President of the World Zionist Organization, wrote in his *History of Zionism* in 1919: "It has been said and is still being obstinately repeated by anti-Zionists again and again, that Zionism aims at the creation of an independent 'Jewish State'. But this is fallacious. The 'Jewish State' was never part of the Zionist programme."[8] Later interpreters often regard this position as a tactical deception—but one wonders why a leading

Zionist would choose the official history of the Zionist movement to spread such a view.[9]

Sokolow actually emphasized over and over at Zionist meetings that the ultimate aims of Zionism were reached with the political autonomy Jews enjoyed under the Mandate government. As President of the Executive of the World Zionist Organization, he explained this position to the Twelfth Zionist Congress in Carlsbad in 1921: "When we held our last Congress, there was no talk of the term 'Jewish people' in the international discourse; in our own eyes, we had once been a people, and we strove for recognition as a nation by others. We have finally achieved it. The national home for the Jewish people . . . . We have the title 'Jewish people.' This is a fact of world importance, this is a landmark in our history."[10] In similar terms, Austrian Zionist Adolf Böhm integrated the same claim into his own history of Zionism, which appeared in 1921: "The political goal of Zionism has been attained with the recognition of the Basel Program." In his account, he avoids the term "Jewish state" and rather speaks of a "Jewish commonwealth" (*Gemeinwesen*).[11]

The German-Jewish writer Arthur Hollitscher also came to this conclusion when he toured Palestine in the 1920s and talked with many high-ranking Zionist officials: "[T]he Jews certainly do not aspire for an independent state but for an autonomy, out of which a Jewish Palestine can grow."[12] Chaim Weizmann, the major force behind the Balfour Declaration and the new president of the World Zionist Organization, knew all too well that without a Jewish majority there would be no Jewish state in Palestine.[13] And there was a long way to go to achieve this majority. By the end of World War I, the local Jewish population was 65,000, the Arab population over half a million. Weizmann was accordingly skeptical of the

chances for establishing a Jewish state in the foreseeable future. He looked into alternative models of far-reaching Jewish
autonomy under British rule, and he defended British High
Commissioner Herbert Samuel against Zionist attacks. Samuel, although himself a Jew and sympathetic to Zionism, regarded it as his responsibility to serve first and foremost His
Majesty's Government and British interests. Weizmann explained to the Zionist leadership: "Do not forget that Eretz
Yisrael and Palestine are not identical and won't be identical
for a long time. Samuel is High Commissioner for Palestine
and we are High Commissioners for Eretz Yisrael. And perhaps one day a time will come when these two commissioners
will have a very difficult time. Let us hope that this never
happens."[14]

Even for David Ben-Gurion, the emerging leader of the
Yishuv (the Jewish population in Palestine), an independent
Jewish state was by no means his only future vision during the
1920s. He emphasized that Jewish nationalism differed from
others in that it did not want to oppress minorities. In a speech
to the Assembly of Representatives of Palestine's Jewish community in 1926, he stressed that there could not be a single
legal system in a territory with so many different national and
religious groups as Palestine. He demanded far-reaching autonomy for all groups and a decentralized government.[15] Ben-
Gurion and other Labor leaders drafted several proposals for
a future Jewish society based on autonomous rights for both
the Jewish and the Arab communities, and they developed
federalist plans for the region as well.[16]

Of course, all statements by Zionist politicians have to be
seen in the context of their specific circumstances, and they
can be interpreted as tactical considerations. But it remains a
fact that even in internal and private discussions it continued

to be unclear whether an independent state should be the ultimate Zionist aspiration. Not only did Sokolov's and Boehm's histories of Zionism explicitly abstain from references to Jewish statehood, but the deliberations at the Zionist Congresses during those years included hardly any discussions about the exact nature of a future Jewish state. This leads us to the assumption that there existed still a variety of options on future Jewish sovereignty. As historian Ben Halpern wrote: "Thus both the 'extremists' and the 'moderate' majority among the Zionists were prepared to regard 'sovereignty' as either end or means, and considered means, as either 'expendable' or as 'indispensible'—depending on the definition given to the term 'sovereignty.' "[17]

The Balfour Declaration contained another uncertainty. Palestine had not been an independent state with its own borders. Nor, during the five centuries of Ottoman rule, did the territory constitute one administrative district. The northern part of the region, the Sanjak of Acco, and the central part, the Sanjak of Nablus, were ruled from Beirut, whereas the south was governed from Jerusalem. After the British conquered the territory, they did not know exactly where to draw the borders. When British Prime Minister Lloyd George conferred with his French counterpart Clemenceau, he vaguely suggested that the borders of Palestine be defined on a biblical basis, "in accordance with its ancient boundaries from Dan to Beersheba."[18] What about the huge and sparsely populated territory east of the Jordan River? Although in 1915 the British had promised this territory to the Sharif of Mecca in the McMahon-Hussein correspondence, in the early years of British control it remained a part of Palestine. Not until 1922 did the British separate it from the rest of Palestine and name Emir Abdullah of the Hashemite dynasty as ruler of a new country called Transjordan. Even if the borders of Palestine had been clear to the British, the borders of a future Jewish national home would have been open to dispute, as Lord Balfour's letter vaguely spoke of "the establishment *in* Palestine of a national home for the Jewish people." He did not refer to the whole of Palestine or mention any specific part of it that he had in mind.

Among the Zionists, the borders of Palestine were just as blurred. The ideal borders, as mapped by the Zionist delegation at the Paris peace negotiations, included the south of Lebanon (North Galilee) and a stretch of land east of the Jordan River as far as the line of the Hedjaz railway. Weizmann also still thought that the land east of the Jordan should be part of a Jewish national home. Thus, he reiterated in his congress speech of 1921: "The question of borders will be answered when Cisjordan will be so full of Jews that we will have to expand to Transjordan."[19] Ben-Gurion, too, initially thought that a future Jewish national home could include both sides of the Jordan.[20] The right-wing Revisionists continued to claim, until the 1950s, the whole of Palestine on both sides of the Jordan for a future Jewish state.[21]

The Balfour Declaration contained the further provision "that nothing shall be done which may prejudice the civil and religious rights of existing non-Jewish communities in Palestine, or the rights and political status enjoyed by Jews in any other country." The first part of this passage referred of course to the rights of the Arab population, though they were not mentioned explicitly. There was a very brief glimmer of hope that Jewish-Arab understanding might in fact be possible when Emir Faisal (later King of Syria and Iraq) and Chaim Weizmann signed an agreement in January, 1919, mutually recognizing the right of Jews to immigrate to Palestine. But the reality on ground created a different set of facts. When Faisal's condition requiring far-reaching Arab independence in the region was not fulfilled, he declared the agreement no longer valid. In any case, it never had included representatives of the Palestinian Arabs. Post World War I, there were in fact other conflicting claims over this territory, and in March of 1920, the General National Syrian Congress declared that Palestine was nothing but the southern part of a Greater Syrian state.[22]

The resistance of the Arab population to aspirations of Jewish sovereignty grew after the Balfour Declaration and the beginning of British rule. While there were Arabs who continued to be willing to sell land to the Jews and opposed any resistance to the Jewish immigrants,[23] the majority, including the central leadership under Mufti Mohammed Amin al-Husseini (appointed in 1921), remained adamant in their rejection of mass Jewish immigration and sovereignty. Most Zionists understood by now that they would not be greeted with open arms, as Herzl had envisioned. Already at the turn of the century, Ahad Ha'am and other Zionists had pointed to the resistance massive Jewish immigration would encounter. The early immigrants, too, experienced being unwelcome. From the very first, they had to guard their new settlements against attacks from their Arab neighbors, and the postwar period saw a new quality of violence. It began with the battle over the northern Jewish outpost of Tel Hai, continued with the Nebi Musa violence in Jerusalem in April 1920, and culminated with riots in Jaffa in May of 1921, that left almost one hundred Jews and Arabs dead. Ironically, the Jaffa riots began as an intra-Jewish strife after the May Day Parade resulted in the Communist Party's demand for an independent "Soviet Palestine."[24]

For about a decade, the Zionists attempted to put in place an alternative Arab Palestinian leadership. When they realized that their attempts were futile, they tried to create friction within the Palestinian leadership by building up the Druze population and Bedouin tribes as possible allies against Palestinian nationalism.[25] There were parts of the Labor movement that romanticized the Arabs as "noble savages," but over time, even the Zionist left came to see the local Arab population as increasingly hostile, as Meir Chazan has shown.[26]

The Balfour Declaration presented yet another vague formulation when it asserted "that nothing shall be done which may prejudice . . . the rights and political status enjoyed by Jews in any other country." This obviously referred to the fact that many Jews, especially in the West, objected to the establishment of a Jewish state. They were afraid that they might be accused of double loyalties and wanted to prove that they were nothing but French or German or British citizens, who happened to be of the Jewish faith. No one wanted their national loyalties questioned, especially in times of war. In Germany, the most important Jewish philosopher of the time, Hermann Cohen, wrote several essays in which he underlined what he saw as a total symbiosis of German and Jewish traits.[27] In England, it was the one Jew among the cabinet ministers, Lord Edwin Samuel Montague, who felt least comfortable with the Balfour Declaration. He demanded the inclusion of the phrase in order to make clear that a future national Jewish home would not be interpreted as a home for every Jew around the world.

Montague was a cousin of Herbert Samuel, the first High Commissioner of Palestine, who was sympathetic towards Zionism. Although the Zionists had to realize that he represented first and foremost the interests of His Majesty's Govern-

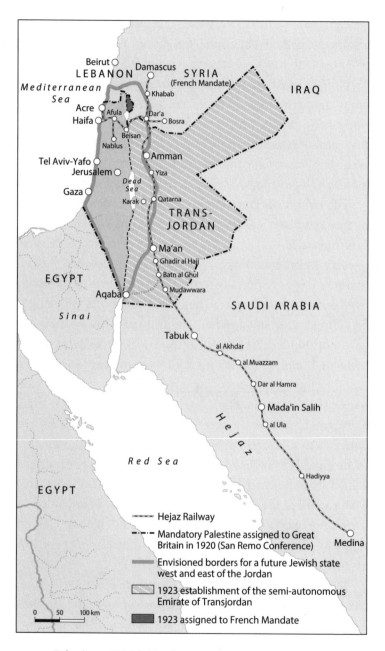

Beirut
Damascus
LEBANON
Mediterranean
Sea
SYRIA
(French Mandate)
IRAQ
Khabab
Acre
Afula
Dar'a
Haifa
Bosra
Beisan
Nablus
Tel Aviv-Yafo
Amman
Jerusalem
Yiza
Dead
Sea
Gaza
Qatarna
Karak
TRANS-
JORDAN
Ma'an
Ghadir al Hajj
Batn al Ghul
EGYPT
Mudawwara
Aqaba
SAUDI ARABIA
Sinai
Tabuk
al Akhdar
al Muazzam
Dar al Hamra
Mada'in Salih
al Ula
Red Sea
EGYPT
Hadiyya
Medina

- ·— Hejaz Railway
—— Mandatory Palestine assigned to Great
     Britain in 1920 (San Remo Conference)
—— Envisioned borders for a future Jewish state
     west and east of the Jordan
▨ 1923 establishment of the semi-autonomous
     Emirate of Transjordan
▮ 1923 assigned to French Mandate

0   50   100 km

MAP 1. Palestine as British Mandate.

ment, they were on the whole content when they took stock of the five years he had spent in office. Overall, he was sympathetic toward increasing Jewish immigration, recognized the political rights of the Yishuv, and allowed generous concession in the matter of land sales.[28]

With the achievement of the Balfour Declaration, the practical advancement of the Zionist cause became more important than ever before. Jewish immigration to Palestine and land acquisitions were the two most critical tasks. The Jewish population of Palestine increased from 65,000 in 1919 to 175,000 in 1931, and had grown to 460,000 by 1939. The purchase of lands by the Jewish National Fund and other Jewish organizations, as well as by private owners proceeded apace during this period.

The vast majority of immigrants came from Europe and were Ashkenazi Jews. Only a small fragment of the immigrants who arrived before the establishment of Israel originated in Arab countries such as Yemen and Syria. During the years after World War I, large parts of the Jewish populations in Iraq, Morocco, and Egypt felt part of their respective cultures and regarded the Zionist movement as a Western project. The Balfour Declaration was of little relevance to them. Zionism found some adherents among Jews in the Arab world, but the majority had no intention of leaving their homes. In Iraq and Egypt, leading musicians, actors and actresses, and politicians were Jewish. Sir Arnold Talbot Wilson, the Acting Civil Commissioner in Mesopotamia between 1918 and 1920, wrote in 1936 that several members of the Iraqi Jewish community had assured him that Palestine was a poor country of no practical interest for them; compared to backward Jerusalem, Baghdad, then home of 100,000 Jews (one quarter of the city's total population), was a paradise.[29] Five years later, under the increasing influence of Nazi Germany, a storm broke out in paradise, when anti-Jewish riots shattered the peace in Baghdad and other Jewish communities in the Arab world.

Internally, the structures of a "state in the making" (*medina ba-derekh*) were taking shape, although it was still far from clear what the outcome of the process would ultimately mean. In 1920, the first elections to the Yishuv's Assembly of Representatives (*asefat ha-nivharim*), a kind of pre-state parliament, took place.[30] As became clear in these elections, despite all the many differences along party lines, the most significant split was between the secular and moderately religious majority on the one hand and the *haredi* (ultra-Orthodox minority) on the other. The latter defined the Jewish community in religious rather than in national terms and refused to grant women voting rights. The *haredim* voted in separate polling stations for their own portion of the Assembly, and their votes counted twice (as women did not vote in their polls). When the Assembly convened, they proposed dissolving it immediately and holding new elections, "based on the religious spirit and the ancient Jewish tradition."[31] When this proposal was rejected, they refused to participate in subsequent elections and thus placed themselves outside *Knesset Israel*, the voluntary body consisting of the Jewish population of Palestine.

The Assembly elected a National Council (*Va'ad Le'umi*) as its executive branch, responsible for the internal affairs of the Yishuv and for the relations with the British Mandatory government. The National Council chose a smaller group, equivalent to cabinet ministers, to represent the different areas of government for the Yishuv. The Assembly also drafted a constitution for the Jewish population of Palestine. In 1927, the

British government issued regulations for the organization of the Jewish community in Palestine, a kind of constitution for the Yishuv, which differed from the internal draft constitution in a crucial point, namely with respect to the definition of the community. While the Yishuv in its majority regarded itself as an ethnic or national community, the British regulations were drafted for a religious community.[32]

The most important political body was the Jewish Agency for Palestine, which functioned as the executive of the Jewish commonwealth for all questions pertaining to immigration, settlement, education, and economic development. It was established in 1929 as the successor organization to the Palestine Office of the World Zionist Organization and was chaired from 1935 on by David Ben-Gurion. Economically, the goal for the Yishuv was to achieve a substantial extent of autarky. Initiatives like the Tel Aviv Levante Fair brought international traders to Palestine and showcased the goods the Yishuv had ready for export. Culturally, the Yishuv took pride in Tel Aviv's Habima Theater and its Philharmonic Orchestra, as well as in the Hebrew University in Jerusalem and the Technion in Haifa. Hebrew was declared an official language, alongside Arabic and English.[33] The kibbutz system of collective agricultural settlements was expanding, while Tel Aviv matured as a bustling Mediterranean city with many small and big businesses, cafés and nightlife, and Haifa became a center for the Jewish working class. Much of the new urban life was established by the Fourth Aliyah, which brought mainly Polish immigrants in the 1920s, and increased further when the Fifth Aliyah brought its many refugees from Nazi Germany and later Austria. Although the Jews did not have an official army, British officers helped to train the paramilitary organization *Hagana*, out of which the Israeli army would grow.

FIGURE 9. Lord Balfour at the inauguration ceremony of the Hebrew University in Jerusalem, 1925. Photo: akg-images/IAM

Other paramilitary organizations would emerge on the political right, most notably the *Irgun* (*Etzel*) of the Revisionist Party.[34]

Even among right-wing Revisionists, the official party line carefully avoided calling for a completely independent state. When the Union of Zionists-Revisionists was founded in 1925, the party delegates adopted a platform that avoided the terms "state" or "independent" and instead stated that "the aim of Zionism [was] the gradual transformation of Palestine (including Transjordan) into a Jewish commonwealth, that is into a self-governing commonwealth under the auspices of an established Jewish majority."[35] While many delegates took this as another circumlocution for "future state," they still conceived of it as a British dominion rather than a fully independent state, as we will see below.

The Orthodox population of Palestine received an important new institution when a chief rabbinate was introduced in 1921. It signaled an increasing integration of parts of Orthodox Jewry into the Zionist concept. Orthodox leaders now had a podium where they could voice their ideas of how a future Jewish state should look. They were eager to preserve their own autonomous school system and rejected any intrusion of secular state authorities into the realm of family law. All marriage and divorce matters should remain under the full control of the various religious communities, an arrangement the British had inherited from the Ottomans. Laws should be based on *halakha*, the corpus of Jewish religious law.[36] Non-Zionist ultra-Orthodox elements achieved a symbolic victory when the British government gave in to their demand to include, in the new regulations for the Jewish population of Palestine, the 1928 "Bylaws of *Knesset Yisrael*," which stipulated that Jews could secede from the official Jewish community (the *Knesset Yisrael*) and found their own community.[37]

Vladimir Ze'ev Jabotinsky, who would later emerge as the leader of the nationalist Revisionist party within Zionism, was well aware of the potential for a *Kulturkampf* between the ultra-Orthodox and the secular and warned against surrendering too much ground to the Orthodox. After the first struggle over women's voting rights in 1919, he wrote: "We told them that Judaism is a nation and not a religious community. We told them that among us, like in all enlightened nations, one may be a member of the nation even if one has no connection with its religion. . . . We surrendered to the militant clericalism that is fighting women's equality . . . a principle on which our organization is built. . . . We will pay dearly for this weakness."[38]

The emerging Jewish society of Palestine was in many ways autonomous by the 1930s, but it was still far from clear if autonomy would lead inexorably to an independent state. Much depended on the question of whether there would be one or two political entities in a future Palestine.[39]

THE ONE-STATE SOLUTION

While the idea of national self-determination received a significant boost after the First World War, the definitions of "nation," "nation-state," and "self-determination" remained unclear. The multi-national Romanov, Habsburg, and Ottoman empires were defeated, but the new "nation-states" that arose in their stead were often mini multi-national empires themselves. One third of Poland's population consisted of ethnic Germans, Jews, and Ukrainians; in Romania, Hungarians and other ethnic minorities made up about 30 percent of the interwar population; not to speak of the numerous nationalities under the cover of the Soviet Union. Even many of the newly created states were not nation-states in the narrow sense. Czechs and Slovaks together made up barely two thirds of the population of artificially created Czechoslovakia; and Yugoslavia was also an artificial entity, comprised of Serbs, Croats, Slovenians, Macedonians, and Bosnians. The definition of "self-determination" was also murky. There were dominions under the British Crown—Australia, New Zealand, Canada, and South Africa—that were semi-independent; in the direct vicinity of Palestine, Egypt became nominally independent in 1922, as did Iraq in 1920, but both remained under British control, while the newly formed Lebanese Republic and Syria remained under French control. In the transition from an Imperial era to an era of national self-determination, there were mandates and dominions, commonwealths and trusteeships. And there was a national home. The definitions of these terms were anything but unequivocal; they depended on the context of their time and space. To see the path from Herzl to Balfour to the

Declaration of Independence as predetermined, leading necessarily to statehood in the modern sense means reading history backwards. Even the Hebrew term *atzma'ut*, created by Ittamar Ben-Avi, the son of Eliezer Ben-Yehuda and the "first Hebrew speaker," underwent a metamorphosis during the 1930s and 40s, along the way from autonomy to independence.[40]

Thus, both one-state and two-state solutions varied according to what was meant by "statehood," and there were numerous variations on the two concepts. The main divide, though, was clear: the first model tried to integrate the Jewish and the Arab population while allowing far-reaching autonomy for both groups, while the latter version aimed at a separation of the two population groups, possibly reached after population transfers, as was practiced most prominently between Greece and Turkey after the First World War.

Both the left and right had blueprints for a one-state solution for Palestine.[41] A small group of intellectuals, mainly of German-speaking background, who called themselves *Brit Shalom* (Covenant of Peace), favored the immediate declaration of a Jewish-Arab commonwealth. Among them were scholars like Gershom Scholem and Hans Kohn, journalists like Robert Weltsch, and high-ranking Zionist officials like Arthur Ruppin. While they differed in the details of the implementation, they all rejected the traditional nation-state model and preferred a cultural center along the lines of Ahad Ha'am's ideas. Some of them, like historian Hans Kohn, rejected the state as such, deeming it an "artificial construct."[42] According to Ernst Simon, who later became professor of education at the Hebrew University, Zionism offered an opportunity to topple "the idol of the state, that means the misbelief that there is no form of peoplehood and community without the forced institution of the state."[43]

To be sure—not all Brit Shalom members objected to the idea of the state in general. But a nation-state in which one group would be dominant ran against their convictions. Their ideal was a bi-national state in which Arabs and Jews would enjoy equal rights. Jewish nationalism for them was about spirit and culture, and not about power and territory. Brit Shalom suggested that an equal or a proportional portion of Jewish and Arab representatives should staff every significant institution of the state.[44] They feared that once there was a traditional majority-minority relation between the two groups, real dialogue would no longer be possible. Instead of *rov* (majority) they rather talked about *rabim* (the multitude) when referring to the future of the Yishuv. For them, moreover, military action contradicted the spirit of Judaism. Hans Kohn championed a British protectorate in which Jews and Arabs would enjoy individual autonomy without the need for any armed forces, while Ernst Simon favored a model based on the Swiss cantons, in which the various Jewish and Arab majority regions within Palestine would have autonomy in most political matters. For Brit Shalom members the vague term "national home" had great appeal. Hugo Bergman, who was a close friend of Franz Kafka in his Prague years and later became rector (provost) of the Hebrew University, declared: "We do not strive for a state but for a national home."[45]

Overall, Brit Shalom members believed that Israel was obliged to fulfill a special mission among the nations. A Jewish state that was like any other state would do little besides providing "a home to a few million Jews, like Lithuania or Montenegro." A future Jewish state, they argued, must be different from all other states and must serve as a light unto the nations. For these intellectuals, the idea of the nation-state had lost all legitimacy in the wake of World War I. Indeed, the

Jewish state could become a model "anti-state." In the end, Brit Shalom failed because it drew its members almost exclusively from the intelligentsia, and because there was no Arab counterpart willing to listen to its plans.

The political right also promoted a one-state solution, though it arrived at it from a very different direction. Its ideal state consisted in a strong state or dominion, on both sides of the Jordan River. In order to achieve its sovereignty, it might be necessary to use weapons. Its leader, Vladimir Ze'ev Jabotinsky, grew up in Odessa in a family that had absorbed the Russian culture of its surroundings, but—unlike Herzl—he had also been immersed early on in the study of Hebrew and imbued with a love for the Land of Israel.

As Michael Stanislawski described him, Jabotinsky was "an East European Jew, born and bred, but the most Gentile-like East European Jew one could possibly imagine, far more cultivated, gentlemanly, sophisticated than his followers could ever hope to be, but still undyingly committed to his people, sacrificing his life to them and for them."[46] Jabotinsky and Herzl were both writers and journalists who had strong emotional ties to their native languages (Russian and German) and to their childhood homes. In 1937, at the peak of his political career as a Zionist, Jabotinsky published, in Russian, a novel titled *The Five*—a moving confession of his emotional bonds to his native city of Odessa.

Jabotinsky was just as much a European and a cosmopolitan as Herzl. He was at home in Odessa, Rome, and London, but like Herzl kept an emotional distance between himself and the Middle East: "The Middle East and all that is implied by that concept are foreign to me. I don't appreciate its beauty. I don't understand its traditions. Its music makes me wince and its thought fails to interest me. I would feel more at home with a tribe of Eskimos at the far end of Labrador. People tell me the fault is mine, not the Middle East's—and in fact, I do appear to suffer from a congenital defect that prevents me from fathoming the region's subtleties, just as I suffer from one that makes Stravinsky's music leave me cold."[47] And like Herzl, he too had a condescending view of Arab civilization (it was "primitive and polygamous") and of Orthodox Jewish religious practice.[48]

But in contrast to Herzl, Jabotinsky knew, besides his many European languages (among them several Italian dialects), two Jewish languages as well.[49] He translated Edgar Allan Poe into Hebrew, and he learned Yiddish well enough to become the orator most sought after by the Jewish masses of Eastern Europe. He was convinced that the Jews were connected to their ancient homeland more than any other people, because they had remained faithful to it in their thoughts and prayers despite over two millennia of dispersion.[50]

One theme Jabotinsky rarely discussed was Jewish culture. To be sure, in contrast to Herzl, he believed that Jewish society in Palestine should be Hebrew-speaking, but with a rather unorthodox twist. Thus, he promoted the use of Latin letters for Hebrew, just as Atatürk had replaced the Arabic letters of the Turkish language with Latin ones. Jabotinsky's modern Hebrew would be free of "Arab sounds," and would become a Europeanized Mediterranean language.[51] His main reason for becoming a Zionist, like Herzl's, was not the fear of assimilation but antisemitism. Even if they wanted, Jabotinsky argued, the Jews of Europe could never fully integrate into European societies and therefore they needed their own state. In this sense, both are quite distinctive from Ahad Ha'am, of whom Jabotinsky deridingly remarked that he aimed to set up "an amusement park for Hebrew culture."[52]

The demand for a Jewish state, Jabotinsky argued, was a historical necessity if Jews were to return to a path of normality: "Every nation on earth, every normal nation, beginning with the smallest and the humblest who do not claim any merit, any role in humanity's development, they all have States of their own. That is the normal condition for a people."[53] He regarded the Jewish claim for statehood as on a different level from the demand for an Arab state in Palestine. When the Arab demand is compared to "our Jewish demand, to be saved, it is like the claim of appetite versus the claim of starvation."[54] Jabotinsky tirelessly insisted on political goals. The majority population of the country would have to be Jewish, both sides of the Jordan River should become part of the Jewish state, and the British should keep the promise they made in the Balfour Declaration. As early as 1923 he made clear what a Jewish state meant for him: "Its meaning is a Jewish majority. That's how Zionism began and that's the basis on which it will continue to work until its realization—otherwise it is condemned to fail."[55] A state with a majority Jewish population: that was Jabotinsky's vision for a Jewish state, nothing less— but also nothing more than that—was required.

Only a small faction within the Revisionist party demanded the immediate establishment of a Jewish state. Jabotinsky left open the question of when such a state should come into being. Neither in 1938 after the German annexation of Austria and *Kristallnacht*, nor in the wake of the British White Paper of 1939 that constituted a retreat from the Balfour Declaration did he call for immediate formation of a Jewish state. Speaking out against radicals in his party, such as Avraham Stern and Uriel Halperin (aka Yonatan Ratosh), he made it plain that for him a sovereign Jewish state was still a long-term and not a short-term goal.[56]

There is no doubt that Jabotinsky shared some views with the nationalistic right movements of his time. When he founded Betar, the militaristic youth wing of the Revisionists, he composed a hymn for the group using the martial language that would come to typify the movement. Again and again he expressed his conviction that the fight for a Jewish state would not be decided through prayer or negotiation, but only through a bloody struggle, at the end of which a race of new Jews would emerge with a state of their own:

> From the pit of decay and dust
> With blood and sweat
> Shall arise a race
> Proud generous and cruel.

Jabotinsky and the Betar movement borrowed some elements from the nationalistic movements of Europe, including Fascist Italy, though Jabotinsky was highly critical of blind trust in the Duce: "Buffaloes follow a leader, Civilized men have no 'leaders,'" he wrote in 1926. But there were Maximalists within the Revisionist Party who promoted authoritarian ideals, and as the historian Colin Shindler has written, "While the Duce cult was disparaged by Jabotinsky, he also realized that he could utilize its attributes to further his aim of building a mass movement in Poland."[57]

Jabotinsky accused Weizmann and Ben-Gurion of being too lenient toward the British and the Arabs, and insisted on a more confrontational policy towards the British government, which refused to allow him entry to Palestine after he published his radical views in the Revisionist paper *do'ar ha'yom*. His demands included a speedy acceleration of immigration, and the building of a Jewish army. When he failed to gain support for these demands in the Zionist Organization, he and his fellow Revisionists left it and founded their own New Zionist Organization in 1935.

For Jabotinsky, the confrontation between Jews and Arabs was rooted in the fact that both sides shared historical rights to the same land. This was not a struggle between right and wrong, but between right and right. Jabotinsky understood the statehood claims of the Palestinian Arabs better than most other Zionists, but he did not accept their denial of Jewish claims. He considered the beliefs of left-wing Zionists in the possibility of compromise naïve. In his best-known essay, "The Iron Wall," he reiterated the right of the Jews to immigrate to Palestine even against Arab resistance. In national conflicts, there is not always an abstract truth, Jabotinsky maintained: historical truth lies in the eyes of the beholder. If necessary, the Jews have to fight for their homeland by force.[58]

At the same time Jabotinsky never doubted the necessity of granting Arabs equal rights in a future Jewish state and, throughout almost his entire life, he opposed plans to expel them from their native lands.[59] His agenda called for both individual and collective rights for the Arab population. The Jewish state on both sides of the Jordan River was a vast territory, but he did not conceive of it as a nation-state.[60] He was well aware of the autonomy theories governing national minorities in the Habsburg Empire, which had after all been the topic of his dissertation in the law faculty at the University of Yaroslav.[61] He was also the author of the introduction to a Russian translation of a treatise by the Austrian Social Democrat Karl Renner, the leading proponent of national autonomy in the Habsburg Empire. These theories were embedded in his visions for the future Jewish state. In 1918 he wrote an unpublished treatise, over 100 pages in length, suggesting a bi-national administration of Palestine, and in 1922 presented a federalist proposal for a Middle Eastern federation consisting of Muslim (Syrian and Mesopotamian), Muslim-Christian (Lebanese), and Jewish (Palestinian) cantons, each with a high degree of autonomy. A year later he presented another federation plan together with Chaim Weizmann.[62]

Czechs and Slovaks had built a state together, and so had Serbians and Croats. In Belgium, French and Flemish speaking population groups lived peacefully side by side, as did German-, French-, and Italian-speakers in Switzerland. Why then was it inconceivable that Jews and Palestinian Arabs, two peoples with related historic roots, might live together?

Jabotinsky's objections to a two-state solution, which would entail a transfer of the Arab population and to the degradation of their status to second-class citizens, have to be seen in the context of his life-long fight for the minority rights of East European Jews. Jabotinsky feared that granting Palestinian Arabs anything less than full national minority rights in a Palestine with a Jewish majority might have negative repercussions for the Jews who remained in Europe. More than that, it was also a matter of understanding nationalism and defining normality within the theory of nations. To "become a state like any other state" meant one thing to Western Europeans who had grown up in a nation-state, and another to Central and Eastern Europeans, for whom multi-national empires with many national minorities were the norm. Jabotinsky, like most Zionists from Eastern Europe, clearly distinguished between the categories of citizenship and nationality. One state could make room for several nations and grant them all collective rights.[63]

Jabotinsky changed some details in his future visions of Palestine, but he remained consistent in his support of equal rights for all citizens and full autonomy for the Arab popula-

FIGURE 10. Vladimir Jabotinsky in London, 1925.

tion in a Jewish state, provisions that he hoped to see in the future constitution of this state.[64] If we want to know how he envisioned a future Jewish state, we have to look at his last book, which appeared posthumously, first in England under the title *The Jewish War Front*, and then two years later in the United States as *The War and the Jew*. This book, which has been too often overlooked by scholars, includes a model constitution for a future independent Palestine.[65] Jabotinsky wrote it in January and February of 1940, when the fate of European Jews seemed sealed after the conquest of large areas of Jewish population by the Germans. He set out, he explains to warn "my fellow-Jews (if they still need the warning, which I doubt) that equal rights are, at best, a very perishable kind of good, infinitely prickly, to be handled and used with caution, moderation and tact." In concrete terms, he formulates as "the purpose of this book . . . to press a claim for the inclusion of the Jewish problem in the war-aims of the Allied nations."[66]

Although Jabotinsky advocated the restoration of individual rights for the Jews after the war and demanded their autonomous collective rights wherever they chose to live, he regarded—as he already had before World War II—mass evacuation as the only possible solution. This distinguished him from most other Zionist leaders, who encouraged the emigration of smaller numbers of organized Zionists. Jabotinsky ruled out Territorialist solutions as unrealistic for the vast majority of the Jewish masses. They would not come to a mirage, a Fata Morgana Land. Only the historic homeland of the Jews would be able to take them in. Jabotinsky referred to what he called the "Max Nordau plan." In 1919, the old associate of Herzl had suggested the immediate immigration of half a million Jews to Palestine, followed by several more millions in the years to come.

Jabotinsky's state looked like a Jewish-Arab federation rather than a Jewish nation-state. He started out by saying that it might reassure the world "to learn how not the moderate but precisely the so-called 'extremist' wing of Zionism visualizes the constitution of the Palestine of the future."[67] The state he envisioned was a parliamentary democracy and a pluralistic society. He left no doubt that when he spoke of the Jews (or the Arabs) he was referring to an ethnic and not a religious community. Jabotinsky drew on the draft constitution that he worked out in the early 1920s and which was adopted by the Revisionist Executive in 1934.[68]

In this draft constitution, all inhabitants would not only enjoy equal individual rights, but both Jews and Arabs would share equal collective autonomous rights: "In every Cabinet where the Prime Minister is a Jew, the vice-premiership shall be offered to an Arab, and vice-versa. Proportional sharing by Jews and Arabs both in the charges and in the benefits of the State shall be the rule with regard to Parliamentary elections, civil and military service, and budgetary grants. . . . Both Hebrew and Arabic shall be used with equal legal effect in Parliament, in the schools, and in general before any office or organ of the State. . . . The Jewish and the Arab ethno-communities shall be recognized as autonomous public bodies of equal status before the law. . . . Each ethno-community shall elect its National Diet with the rights to issue ordinances and levy taxes within the limits of its autonomy, and to appoint a national executive responsible before the Diet."[69] Jabotinsky rejected any kind of ethnic cleansing, believing on the contrary that it would be advantageous for the state that the Arab population remain within Palestine. He left no doubt as to the necessity of granting them all the rights of a national minority: "After all, it is from Jewish sources that the world has learned how 'the stranger within thy gates' should be treated."[70]

What his paradigm proposed was a loose federal state rather than a full-fledged nation-state.[71] Jabotinsky made clear that even in 1940 full independence was not necessarily the ultimate Revisionist understanding of a Jewish state: "The Revisionists' idea of an independent Palestine was then (1934) a Dominion within the British Empire, as it is still to many of them."[72] The idea of a Jewish state as a "seventh dominion" of the British Empire (comparable to Canada, Australia, and New Zealand) originated with veteran Labor politician Josiah Wedgwood in the mid-1920s and was indeed revived on occasion throughout the 1930s and 40s. It was often seen as a near fit to the Revisionist vision.[73]

Did Jabotinsky favor a model state or rather a state like any other? On first glance, his biographer Hillel Halkin is right when he argues that Jabotinsky did not envision a model state like Herzl: "The Jews, in his opinion, had no moral uniqueness or mission in the world—no mission of any kind except to take their rightful place among the nations."[74] But a closer look reveals that Jabotinsky, like so many others, would not be satisfied with establishing just another state, another "Albania." As realistic as Jabotinsky always seemed to be, his plans for a future Jewish state nevertheless had utopian elements. He did not talk about a seven-hour workday or women's rights, but he was Herzl's equal when it came to his aspirations for a better society. Grounding himself on the theories of the Austrian social philosopher Josef Popper-Lynkeus (who had called for a Jewish state even before Herzl), Jabotinsky demanded that the basic needs of every citizen should be satisfied: food, clothing, housing, health services, and education. Referring to the biblical jubilee year, he also demanded the return of private property to the state after fifty years.[75] There was no existing state in the world that Jabotinsky could have taken as an example for this idea. His goal is especially remarkable, as it came from an outspoken proponent of private property and opponent of socialism.

Jabotinsky voiced a conviction that the children of the next generation would experience the disappearance of hunger, wars, and homelessness, just as his own generation was witnessing the disappearance of illiteracy. In all of this, the Jewish state should be a trailblazer. The person, who was perhaps best known for his support of a Jewish army and who once had written, "I would like to see military training become as common among Jews as lighting Sabbath candles once was,"[76] suggested the demilitarization of the future Jewish state: why waste millions of dollars on guns and warships?[77]

THE TWO-STATE SOLUTION

The two-state solution was not discussed as a serious alternative for Palestine until the mid-1930s. Partition of the land west of the Jordan River became a viable option only as a result of the continuously worsening situation for Jews in Europe, coupled with the escalation of Arab resistance to increasing Jewish immigration. In 1936, the Arabs of Palestine staged a general strike and launched what would later be known as the Great Revolt against the British to protest the increase in Jewish immigrants. Between 1936 and 1939, Arab Palestinian nationalism received an enormous boost, while violence against the Yishuv increased. Even in the more liberal circles of the Zionist movement, this uprising, which was brutally crushed by the British, was considered also a declaration of war against Palestine's Jews.[78]

These tensions led the Mandatory authority to look for alternatives to the present status of Palestine. In the summer of 1936, the British government appointed Lord William Peel, former secretary of state for India to head a commission seeking a solution for the Palestine conflict. After an extensive tour to Palestine and the questioning of numerous political players on both sides, the commission presented its results in the form of a long and detailed report that began with a historical overview and gave credence to both Jewish and Arab claims to the territory under question. It also summarized the British responsibility for the Jews of Palestine: "There are 400,000 Jews in Palestine. They have come there not only with our permission but with our encouragement. We are answerable, within reason, for their welfare. We cannot, in the present state of affairs, abandon them to the good intentions of an Arab government."[79] At the same time, the Arabs in Palestine should not be compelled to live in a Jewish state, especially given the fact that in 1936 Jews constituted a minority. Peel considered a "cantonization" of the territory, in which each canton or district—Jewish or Arab—would govern its own affairs completely autonomously, while the Mandatory government would remain in control of foreign affairs, defense, customs, and a few other areas.[80] He concluded that such an arrangement was bound to fail, as it demanded cooperation between Jewish and Arab cantons, which he could not foresee. Thus, the only solution possible was the partition of Palestine.

The Peel Plan suggested creating a small Jewish state consisting of a coastal strip, stretching roughly from south of Tel Aviv to the north of Haifa and the Galilee, a British enclave that would include Jerusalem, Bethlehem, and a coastal access point around Jaffa, and an Arab state occupying the rest of Palestine. Mixed Arab-Jewish cities would be ruled by the Brit-

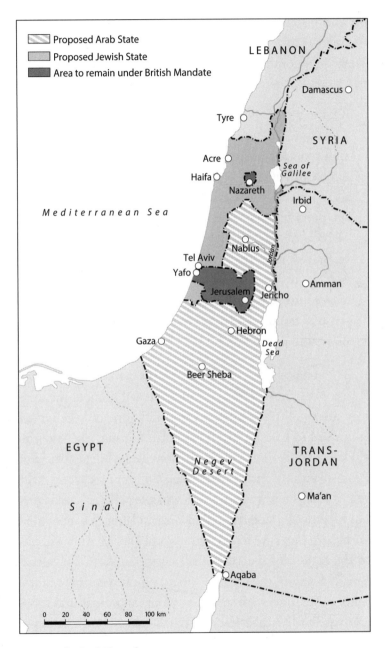

Proposed Arab State
Proposed Jewish State
Area to remain under British Mandate

LEBANON

Damascus ○

Tyre ○

SYRIA

Acre ○
Haifa ○

Sea of Galilee

Nazareth ○

Irbid ○

Mediterranean Sea

Nablus ○

Jordan

Tel Aviv ○
Yafo ○

Jerusalem ○
Jericho ○

Amman ○

Gaza ○

Hebron ○

Dead Sea

Beer Sheba ○

EGYPT

Negev Desert

TRANS-JORDAN

Sinai

Ma'an ○

Aqaba ○

0   20   40   60   80   100 km

MAP 2. The Peel Plan of 1937.

ish administration. The reactions of the Zionists were divided. Clearly, the tiny Jewish state did not live up to Zionist dreams. Their disappointment was expressed in a declaration signed by Hebrew writers:

> [Our heart] . . . lies with the heart of the Jewish people in Eretz Israel and the Diaspora in fearing the royal commission's conclusion regarding partition of the Land of Israel, which amputates our land, cuts off entire limbs and robs us of Jerusalem, the cradle of our civilization in the past, our glory in the present, and our hope for the future. The Hebrew writers will fight together with the entire House of Israel for the reestablishment of Israel in its complete homeland. The association calls . . . on all ranks of the Yishuv to unite as one body with national discipline and a sense of responsibility and to avoid any action counter to our cultural position.[81]

The religious Zionists missed Jerusalem, the right-wing Revisionists Transjordan, the moderate left thought the territory too small for substantial immigration, and the far-left continued to hold on to a bi-national solution. The latter included not only the small Brit Shalom camp, but also socialist Zionists around the *Shomer ha-tza'ir* group, for whom "the role of Zionism was not to attain separate political sovereignty but to settle the land through dedicated labor in cooperation with the progressive forces in the world and the Arab workers in the region for the sake of the common battle for Socialism."[82] Many in the socialist kibbutz movement opted for a unified Palestine, with sufficient room for agricultural cooperatives, but like their leader Yitzhak Tabenkin, they did not insist on full political sovereignty. Tabenkin stood for those

in the Labor movement for whom the land was more important than statehood. They were willing to wait for independence, so long as they did not have to give up any portion of
the territory between the Mediterranean and the Jordan River.

On the political right, claims for land went even further
and took in both sides of the Jordan River. Jabotinsky summed
up Revisionist opposition to partition in his speech before the
Royal Commission in the House of Lords on February 11th,
1937. It constitutes also the core of a book he published in 1938
under the same title as Herzl's foundational book, *The Jewish
State*, published four decades earlier.[83]

The ultra-Orthodox Jews were ambivalent in their attitude
toward partition. A 1937 congress of the non-Zionist *Agudat
Yisrael* maintained, officially, the position that "the Land of
Israel is indivisible, because God determined its borders."[84]
But some of their leaders, Rabbi Ozer Grodzinski among
them, distinguished between the borders of a Jewish state before the coming of the messiah and afterward. On that basis,
a temporary solution with Jewish control over smaller parts
of *Eretz Yisrael* was within the realm of the possible.[85] The
Aguda's central committee seemed to be more concerned with
the prospect of a secular Jewish state, no matter its borders,
than with the partition of the land. It made clear that it rejected "outright any attempt at despoiling the Land of Israel
of its sanctity and [considered] the proposal to establish a secular Jewish state in Palestine as a hazard to the lofty role of the
Jewish People as a holy nation." A Jewish state would be imag-
inable for them only "if it were possible for the basic constitution of this state to guarantee Torah rule in the overall public
and national life."[86]

The religious-Zionist *Mizrahi* movement categorically rejected the partition plans with the argument that it is not up

to humans to divide a country given to the Jews by God. But when it came to *halakhic* arguments that would support such a ruling, they remained conspicuously silent. Ashkenazi Chief Rabbi Yitzhak Halevi Herzog, who had succeeded Rabbi Kook, vacillated. Publicly he shared the general Orthodox refusal to accept partition and—together with the Sephardic Chief Rabbi—called for public resistance to such measures. But during the meeting of the Woodhead Commission, which was appointed in 1938 to follow up the recommendations of the Peel Commission, and before the *Mizrahi* central committee, he signaled his consent for a partition plan.[87]

Despite considerable opposition from all political camps within the Zionist movement, the majority, led by Chaim Weizmann and David Ben-Gurion, opted to accept the Peel Plan as a basis for negotiations. As Ben-Gurion summed it up, this was their only hope to offer a refuge to the many Jews who were desperately waiting to get out of Europe, and it was a unique historical opportunity: "I see this plan in its entirety not as the lesser evil, but rather as a political triumph and historic chance that we have not had since the day our land was destroyed. . . . I prefer this plan in its entirety over the existing regime."[88] When the Twentieth Zionist Congress convened in Zurich in 1937 it still seemed that full political sovereignty was not the only possible interpretation of the Balfour Declaration, but rather one option among others, as underlined in a resolution stressing "that inherent in the Balfour Declaration was the possibility of the evolution of Palestine into a Jewish State."[89]

Despite all misgivings as to the size of the proposed territory, the World Zionist Organization immediately began to take action. The Jewish Agency, founded in 1929 as the prestate governing authority for Palestine, began plotting the exact borders and considering possible population transfers.[90] The cautious support of the Zionists remained, however, inconsequential, as not only did the Arabs reject any partition plans, but the British government too rejected the plans its own commission had drawn up as impractical.

In the interwar period, Zionists saw their goal of normalizing Jewish history as within reach. Finally, so they thought, the Jews would have a state like every nation. But they also sensed that it could not just be a state like any other state. They were well aware of the fact that a Jewish state centered on the holy sites of the world religions would be viewed with special eyes by the world. And the Zionists themselves had the ambition to build what would be a model state for the whole of humanity. They were promised a "national home," though it was unclear what exactly this would mean. It was at just this juncture, when the realization of the promise felt tangible, that the Jews were once more thrust into the center of world history. They became the main target of the Nazi terror in Germany and the object of the most systematically executed genocide in modern human history. The Holocaust, as it would later be known, became the paradigm of modern genocide, and the Jews were identified as the eternal victim in human history.

It was under these tragic circumstances that Zionist leaders began to change their plans and concentrate their efforts on a Jewish nation-state. As Gil Rubin has shown, toward the end of his life and under the impact of the outbreak of the war, Jabotinsky considered a "transfer" of Palestinian Arabs, which would entail enticing or forcing them to move to other Arab countries, such as Iraq or Saudi-Arabia.[91] His ideas were based on Greek/Turkish and Baltic models, and even more so on the 1939 South Tyrol Option Agreement, in which Hitler and Mussolini had given the German-speaking population of South Tyrol the option to move from Italy into the German *Reich*. In the context of Palestine, a plan along these lines was first formulated by the Peel Commission, which favored population exchange between Jews and Arabs in the event of the establishment of two states.

We will never know if Jabotinsky, the former opponent of expulsions and proponent of equal rights for an Arab minority in a Jewish state, would have abandoned his traditional positions after the war. It could well be that the extinction of Jewish life in Eastern Europe would not only have made his concerns for the Jews' political fate obsolete, but might also have destroyed his life-long faith in the viability of minority rights. Other leading Revisionists—among them Eliyahu Ben-Horin and Joseph Schechtman (who extensively researched population transfers in other parts of the world)—further developed these transfer plans, as did Ben-Zion Netanyahu, who served as Jabotinsky's last private secretary and was the father of later Prime Minister Benjamin Netanyahu.[92]

In the meantime, David Ben-Gurion decided that it was time to remove any remaining doubt as to what was now the one goal of the Zionist movement: the establishment of a fully sovereign Jewish commonwealth. The term "state" was still not mentioned, for Ben-Gurion's thinking was that it could become a part of the British Commonwealth. When Ben-Gurion gathered six hundred leading Zionists in the New York Biltmore Hotel in May of 1942, the first news of the genocide had just reached them. The necessity for a Jewish state rose to a new level of urgency—and yet that goal seemed further from realization now than ever before during the last two decades. In its White Paper of 1939, the British government had limited Jewish immigration to Palestine over the next five years to 75,000—this at a time when Jews constituted less than one third of its population. The implementation of the White Paper would, of course, have ruined the chances for an eventual Jewish majority, as it made any further immigration dependent on the consent of the Arab majority. The Biltmore Program demanded a revocation of the White Paper and the opening of the gates of Palestine to Jewish immigrants.[93]

The dramatic departure of the British government from the spirit of the Balfour Declaration left the Zionist movement face to face with a major dilemma. Once war broke out, the British knew all too well that the Zionists had little choice but to fight on their side against Nazi Germany. At the same time, the Zionists fiercely opposed British policies with regard to Palestine. While the mainstream center and center-left factions laid aside their disappointment over British policies until the greater enemy, Nazi Germany, had been defeated, the position of the right-wing Revisionists was less clear, especially after Jabotinsky's death in 1940. During the war, the seeds of the militant postwar battles against the British were sown. Some radical factions started the fight while the war was still on-going.[94]

At that point, only a small minority within the Zionist camp objected to the two-state solution. Intellectuals, mainly German-speakers and Americans, founded a small successor-group to the extinct *Brit Shalom* under the name of *Ihud* to promote the notion of a bi-national state. They were led by American Reform Rabbi and Chancellor of the Hebrew University, Judah Leib Magnes. Among the movement's leading spirits were Henrietta Szold, the long-time leader of the women's Zionist organization Hadassah, and the philosopher Martin Buber. In Buber's words, it was "impossible to for any length of time build with one hand while holding a weapon with the other." Thus, Buber considered the Biltmore policy a *fata morgana*—a mirage. In his response, Magnes borrowed the term when he blamed Buber for the failure of the one-state solution: "You thought and believed that Zion could be built not with blood and fire but through tireless creative work and mutual understanding with our neighbors. You know very well that in the history of mankind states have almost invariably been built only with blood and injustice . . . we have fallen prey to the Fata Morgana of the state."[95]

THE ELSEWHERE SOLUTION

While Jabotinsky was dreaming of a Jewish state on both sides of the River Jordan, and Weizmann was lauding the Peel Plan as a first step towards Jewish statehood, and Ben-Gurion was demanding full sovereignty for the Jews in the Biltmore Program, other Jewish visionaries were on expeditions in East Africa, Northwest Australia, and Suriname. They belonged to a movement that had split from Zionism and called itself Territorialism. Against the background of increasing antisemitism and persecution in Europe, the Territorialists aimed at obtaining sovereignty for the Jewish people immediately, and in an area less disputed than Palestine.

The Zionists rejected their plans unequivocally. For them, a Jewish state could only be established in the ancient Jewish homeland.[96] Jabotinsky in fact had once applied his favorite epithet, the "Fata Morgana Land" to any other place that might be chosen for the Jewish state."[97] But the Territorialists had prominent activists among them, such as Isaac Nachman Steinberg, the People's Commissar of Justice in Lenin's first Soviet government (1917), the acclaimed British-Jewish writer Israel Zangwill, and the famous German writer Alfred Döblin, author of one of the most celebrated novels of the Weimar

Republic, *Berlin Alexanderplatz*. These Territorialists did not regard themselves as the renegades of the Zionist movement, but as the true legatees of Herzl's original plans.

After all, Herzl himself had proposed Argentina as a viable solution in his *Jewish State*, and wrote in his diary in June 1895: "I am assuming that we shall go to Argentina."[98] He had realized at the First Zionist Congress that many Jews, especially the Jews of Eastern Europe, wanted to see a future Jewish state in the traditional Jewish homeland, but he remained open to at least temporary solutions in other parts of the world. He negotiated with the Portuguese ambassador over a possible settlement in Mozambique, and he was interested also in the Belgian Congo. He seriously considered Cyprus, and for a short while the small Egyptian coastal strip in Egypt around El-Arish. In 1903, in the wake of the Kishinev pogrom, he presented the Zionist Congress with a proposal of the British government and urged the delegates to seriously consider the "Uganda Plan," according to which Jews would settle in East Africa (today's Kenya). For many delegates, especially those from Eastern Europe, this proposal was a sacrilege. In the end Herzl's proposal that they initiate negotiations achieved a thin majority of 295 votes, while almost as many voted against it or abstained.[99]

It is remarkable, especially when compared to later developments, that even among the national-religious camp there was quite a lot of applause for Herzl's Uganda attempts. The leader of the religious Zionists, Rabbi Yitzhak Ya'akov Reines, wrote Herzl in December of 1903 that he welcomed the Africa initiative, because his party was looking for remedies against the suffering of the people, and the people were closer to his heart than the land.[100] Religious Zionists realized that the Uganda plan offered them a unique opportunity to solve their basic dilemma by establishing the Jewish state outside the land of their religious longings. If it were implemented, they would be able to promise European Jews immediate relief—and leave it up to the messiah to bring them back to their true home at some later date in the future.

Most surprising perhaps was the fact that the Uganda scheme was also championed by some of the earliest and most prominent pioneers of modern Jewish settlement in Palestine. Just like Reines, Eliezer Ben-Yehuda, who had settled in Jerusalem as early as 1881 and is usually considered the father of the modern Hebrew language, gave priority to the needs of the people over the needs of the land. He supported the group he called "the Africans": "You call yourself Zionists of Zion or Palestinian Zionists, and we call ourselves Africans, Ugandans. Gentlemen, we are not ashamed of these expressions. But we are no Africans or Ugandans, we are with the people. That's what we are! You are with the land, and we are with the people [*atem artzi'im ve-anu ami'im*]. For us the people is the most important thing. We say: If the people can be in the land [of Israel], even better. But if this is not possible, then we will build up another country for the people, as long as this helps to avert the dangers threatening our people!"[101]

The atmosphere within the Zionist leadership was rife with tension. The explosion came on December 19, 1903, during a Hanukkah Ball in Paris, when a young student named Chaim Zelig Luban aimed two shots at Herzl's closest associate, Max Nordau, screaming, "Death to Nordau the African." Nordau survived the shots and was able to help another delegate who was injured. Ironically, Nordau himself was among the critics of the Uganda Plan.[102]

Nordau lived many more years, but only a few months later, the founder and leader of the Zionist movement died in a clinic near Vienna. The idea of a temporary or permanent Jewish home outside of Palestine did not come to an end with Herzl's death on July 3, 1904, or with the rejection of the Uganda Plan by the Seventh Zionist Congress in 1905. A small group of Zionists reorganized as Territorialists who propagated a Jewish homeland in any place they could obtain. This movement was led by the British writer Israel Zangwill, who had once introduced Herzl to London society. In his 1901 essay, "The Return to Palestine," Zangwill had emphasized the uniqueness of Zionism when compared to European colonialist movements: "Mother-lands have always created colonies. Here colonies are to create a mother-land, or rather re-create her."[103] Zangwill also paraphrased a familiar statement used by British Christians, such as Lord Shaftesbury, when talking about a possible Jewish settlement in this region: "Palestine is a country without a people; the Jews are a people without a country."[104] In 1905, Zangwill came to a different conclusion. Palestine, he now realized, already had its Arab population, and it was opposed to the new immigrants. The Jews, therefore, would have to look for another piece of land, one that was less densely populated and whose inhabitants would welcome them.[105]

Zangwill was convinced that if the Jews in the wake of the Kishinev pogroms were to receive a territory that offered them "British Home Rule, Jewish national customs, and a Jewish Governor," then even its most fervent opponents would have to concede that the Zionist movement was successful.[106] Weizmann called Zangwill "the true ideologist of East Africa," when this region was discussed by the Zionist leadership.[107] After the failure of this plan, Zangwill founded his own Jewish Territorialist Organization (ITO), and over twenty years he sought indefatigably for a "New Judea" in Africa, in Australia, and in the Americas. He negotiated over territories in Angola and North Africa, and with the American-Jewish philanthropist Jacob Schiff he discussed plans to settle Russian Jews in Galveston, Texas.

Zangwill experienced one disappointment after the other. Again and again he would hear of some allegedly unpopulated territory somewhere, only to determine later that it was unsuitable for a Jewish homeland, either for geographical reasons or because it actually was *not* uninhabited. When somebody told him that he might perhaps find empty space on the moon, he replied sarcastically: "Not even there, I fear. For there is a man in the moon, and he is probably an Anti-Semite."[108]

Zangwill died in 1926, having never come close to the realization of his goals. In fact toward the end of his life he had rejoined the Zionist movement. But before he died he was able to witness the beginnings of another Jewish homeland project, one that originated in a different part of the world and from very different motives. The Soviet Union was home to one of the world's largest Jewish populations and it was trying to redefine the relationship that had existed between the Czarist Empire and its Jewish subjects. Under Lenin and Stalin, Jews were listed as a "nationality" in their official documents, but unlike Ukrainians, Georgians, and other minorities, they were not granted full status as a national minority, as they lacked a territory. Here again was the idea that the Jews were not a "normal nation," because they lived dispersed, in this case throughout the western parts of the Soviet Union. Jewish Socialists, organized in the *Bund*, and Jewish autonomists argued that they did not need a territory in order to be considered a nation, but both groups were outlawed in the Soviet Union. Instead, the Soviet leadership established a special Jewish section of the Communist party, called *Yevsektsia*. The

Yevsektsia had no better luck, however, when it came to solving the riddle of how Jews could function as a separate nationality minus a territory of their own. If they were to be treated like all other national minorities, then they would have to have their own territory. And if they didn't have one, then they should be granted one.

Leading Communists seized on this idea, seeing it as an opportunity to transform the Jews from a mainly merchant population into peasants. An early proponent of granting the Jews an autonomous region in the Crimea, where they would undergo this rapid occupational transformation, was Michail Kalinin, since 1919 the titular head of state of the Soviet Union. The first Jewish settlements in the Crimea, founded around 1930, had names like Kalinindorf and Stalindorf (Kalinin Village and Stalin Village). Yuri Larin, Stalin's advisor on Jewish affairs, had himself grown up in the Crimea. He was convinced that the big cities would be breeding grounds for antisemitism and that turning Jews into peasants would eliminate the old abnormalities.[109] Soviet party functionaries worked together with the American Jewish Joint Distribution Committee, from capitalist America and under the leadership of the Moscow-born Joseph Rosen, to resettle the Jewish masses from the Pale of Settlement to the Crimea.[110]

The plans floundered for a number of reasons, among them the resistance of the local Ukrainian and Tatar populations. Russian and Ukrainian peasants were themselves interested in settling the fertile land in the Crimea. Stalin gave up the region but not the idea. His next proposal for a projected Jewish mass settlement named a rather unlikely place: a Far Eastern province of his vast empire called Birobidzhan. The creation in 1934 of an autonomous Jewish region in this thinly populated remoteness near the Chinese border served several purposes at once: first, it was supposed to be an alternative to Palestine and thus would eliminate the remnants of Zionism in the Soviet Union; second, it would pioneer settlement in an underdeveloped region near the Trans-Siberian Railway; and third, the plan would, it was hoped, raise enthusiasm for the Soviet cause in the major Jewish communities of Eastern Europe and thus advance the world revolution.

In May 1934, President Kalinin declared: "We consider Birobidzhan a Jewish national state." Enthusiasm among Russian Jews was tepid, to say the least. Only a few thousand agreed to make the move to this new Yiddish-speaking "red Palestine" in Siberia, and most of them returned after a short time. By the outbreak of the war, the number of Jews in all districts of the Soviet Union that allowed some degree of Jewish autonomy was only 136,000, 4.5 percent of the total Jewish population.[111] But Stalin could nonetheless claim that he had founded a Jewish state and that another one in Palestine was no longer needed.

For the Territorialists, meanwhile, the need for a Jewish state became ever more urgent. The clouds of war and terror were darkening over the Jews in Europe, but Birobidzhan remained a place where they did not want to go, and Palestine was a place they were not allowed to go. The Conference of Evian, convened by President Roosevelt to discuss the plight of Jewish refugees, only underlined the truth: no state was ready to open its doors—with the conspicuous exception of the Dominican Republic, whose dictator Trujillo thought he could "whiten up" his country with European immigrants.

Hitler had no intention of giving the Jews their own territory, although some Nazi officials had for a while considered a "Madagascar option," previously suggested also by Polish nationalists.[112] After 1933, some prominent voices among Ger-

FIGURE 11. A street sign welcoming visitors to Birobidzan in Russian and Yiddish.

man Jews renewed the call for a territorial solution for the Jewish people. Among them was one of the most popular novelists of Weimar Germany, Alfred Döblin, whose *Berlin Alexanderplatz* was a bestseller when it appeared in 1929. After Hitler came to power in Germany, Döblin published a collection of essays titled *The Flight and Exile of the Jewish People.* In it he included an essay entitled "The New Judea."

"The New Judea" presented Döblin's idea for a new home for the Jewish people. Palestine could hold a maximum of only one million people, he argued. He was interested in a permanent home for many millions. Australia, Peru, and Angola were places he considered.[113] The rise of Hitler to power was for him what the Kishinev pogrom had been for many Zionists thirty years earlier. Döblin, a highly assimilated Jew like Herzl, proposed a global Jewish government that would assuage the misery of the Jews of his time. He was in close contact with the Austrian Jewish journalist Nathan Birnbaum, who was the first to use the term "Zionism" and who later became an ultra-Orthodox Jew and supported the Territorialist *Freiland* movement. He wrote to the writer Thomas Mann that he had begun to learn Yiddish.[114] The territorial solution alone, however, would not solve the Jewish question for Döblin. He urged finding a spiritual solution as well, for in his eyes Western Jewry had lost the struggle for emancipation. Just as Judaism received a new religious foundation after the destruction of the second temple, it now stood in need for a new secular foundation. Döblin's ideas were translated into Hebrew and printed in one of Palestine's most important cultural journals, *Turim*. Döblin, who was deeply convinced that Territorialism was Herzl's true legacy,[115] then moved on to a different refuge. In 1941, while in exile in France, he converted to Catholicism. After the war he returned to Germany, where he spent his last years without ever visiting the Jewish state.

With the spread of the Nazi power over Europe and its increasing threat to Jewish existence, some Zionists too reverted to territorial solutions. In Argentina, for example, Eugenio Villa called for the establishment of a "Judea" in South Rhodesia, a stopgap until Israel could be founded in Palestine.[116] He received no backing from the Zionist movement.

Even after the war, the systematic search for a Jewish homeland outside of Palestine continued. The most important representative of Jewish territorialism during the 1930s and 40s was Isaac Nachman Steinberg, who as we saw earlier had served in 1917/18 as Lenin's first People's Commissar of Justice. He later left the Soviet Union and became one of the founders of the YIVO Institute for Jewish Research, before founding the *Frayland-lige far Yidisher Teritoryalistisher Kolonisatzye* (Freeland League for Jewish Territorial Colonization). The league's purpose was to locate a territory suited to serve as a home for the Jewish people in Australia, South America, or South Africa. Adam Rovner, the historian of the Territorialist movement, characterized Steinberg as follows: "[He] is one of the most important Jewish figures in the twentieth century you've probably never heard of."[117]

During the 1930s, Steinberg lived for four years in Australia, where he tried to turn the remote Kimberley region in the little populated northwest into an autonomous homeland for the Jews. To his own astonishment, his revolutionary past actually helped in his negotiations with the Australian government.[118] Steinberg did not intend to establish an independent state in Australia, but only to offer the Jews a safe haven free of persecution: "Is there any benefit to mankind in creating a new, a Jewish State? Would it contribute to the world's peace or to the greater development of the Jewish people itself?" he asked—and replied: "I myself doubt the value of a Jewish state, even in Palestine."[119]

When the Kimberley project failed, Steinberg began negotiating for a Jewish homeland in Tasmania, and when this too failed, he entered into talks with the Dutch government about Suriname (Dutch Guyana), which lasted until 1948, by which time the Jewish state was already a reality.[120] In fact in June of 1947, the parliament of Suriname, as well as the government of the Netherlands, had approved the Freeland League's scheme for large-scale Jewish colonization in the unoccupied sections of the country."[121] It was only after the establishment of the State of Israel in May 1948 that the Dutch government broke off the negotiations.[122]

In the end, Territorialism was an utter failure. But its various attempts to solve the plight of the Jews in the first half of the twentieth century show clearly how multifaceted Jewish nationalism was before the establishment of the State of Israel. What many observers have read as a straight-lined development beginning in 1897 and coming to fruition in 1948, was in reality a good deal more circuitous. It was a combination of circumstances, culminating in the Holocaust and the world's determination to create nation-states that rendered alternate solutions, such as a bi-national state or a territory outside the historical Jewish homeland, obsolete. The UN General Assembly's decision on November 29, 1947, to partition Palestine came at a moment when other similar resolutions were being passed, most notably, the resolution to divide former British India into two states, one Hindu and the other Muslim.

The UN decision paved the way for a future Jewish (and Palestinian) state. But for six million of Herzl's spiritual children and grandchildren, who were killed in Auschwitz and other places of horror, it came too late. Neither did Herzl's biological heirs live to see the establishment of the state their father and grandfather had envisioned. Herzl's oldest daughter Pauline died in 1930 in Bordeaux, probably of an overdose of morphine. When her brother Hans, who had converted several times to different Christian denominations, heard that his sister was ill, he rushed from England to Bordeaux. He came too late and took his own life in the same hotel room in which his sister had died. His last wish was to be buried in the same coffin with her. Herzl's younger daughter, Trude, had a few more years to live. After the birth of her son Stephan Theodor in 1918 she was confined to a mental hospital, where she spent most of her remaining years. In 1942, the Nazis de-ported her to Theresienstadt, where she died the following year. Stephan Theodor Neumann was now the only heir remaining. He survived the war in England, studied at Oxford, changed his name to Stephen Norman, and became a soldier in the British army. When he traveled through Palestine in 1946, he was enthusiastically received as the last living Herzl, but only a few months later, in November of 1946, still deeply depressed by the dark news from Europe, Herzl's only grandson jumped to his death from the Massachusetts Avenue Bridge in Washington, DC.[123]

Thus, the history of the Herzl family ended just at the moment when the State of Israel was born. It is a story still little known in Israel—and for that matter around the world, as it does not accord with the heroic image of the founder of Zionism. Only in recent years, due to the insistence of an Israeli historian, has it been discussed in Israeli media, and as a result, Herzl's last request has finally been granted. Herzl and his parents had been reburied on Jerusalem's Mount Herzl in a solemn ceremony on August 17, 1949 (the newly introduced "Herzl Day"), but a committee had decided not to accede to the terms of his will by bringing the bodies of his two children buried in Bordeaux to Israel. In 2006, their remains were reinterred on Mount Herzl in Jerusalem.[124]

ORIGINAL ISRAEL

A STATE DEFINING ITSELF

> The normality that a Jewish state exists
> is in itself an abnormality.
>
> **—CLAUDE LANZMANN**[1]

When the UN General Assembly decided on November 29, 1947, to divide Palestine into a Jewish state alongside an Arab state, it was not yet clear what that state's name was going to be. In the Hebrew Bible, the territory had several names. *Eretz Yisrael*, the Land of Israel, was a popular term in Jewish tradition throughout the centuries. But there was also "Judah" (or Judea), the southern kingdom that continued to exist after the destruction of northern Israel in 722 BCE, and which lent its name to the Jewish people. "Zion" too was much-used. After all, Jews uttered their desire to return to Zion in their daily prayers, and the Zionist movement was named after Mt. Zion in Jerusalem. A small group favored the name "Canaan," the ancient designation of the land before its conquest by the ancient Hebrews.[2]

Although the founders of the new state were secular, the religious connotation of the name Israel can hardly be disputed. "Israel" (the name means "the one who wrestles with God") was the name given to Jacob after he fought with a mysterious being (Genesis 32:24–28), usually interpreted as an angel sent by God. For most Zionists, the biblical account was irrelevant, as they associated the country's name with the label later given to the Jewish people (*am yisrael*) and to the land (*eretz yisrael*). But for religious Jews, the biblical connotation remained. For them, Israel was not just any "seven-hour-land," as promised by Theodor Herzl, but precisely that piece of land promised to the Jews by God. The future tension between secular and religious Israelis thus began just here: with the different readings of the name given to the state.

Even after the name "State of Israel" (*medinat yisrael*) was chosen, it remained unclear how the state would define itself with respect to the Jewish people, which in its majority still lived dispersed around the globe. The term "Jewish state" was mentioned five times in the Declaration of Independence. There was no doubt that the UN partition plan of Palestine in 1947 envisioned a Jewish and an Arab state. But what was the meaning of a Jewish state? Did "Jewish" refer to the Jewish people or to Jewish religion? Who would be a Jew in a Jewish state? And would the existence of a Jewish state finally lead to the normalization of Jewish history or would it constitute yet one more peculiarity in this long history?

WHAT IS A JEWISH STATE?

David Ben-Gurion was the founding father of the young state, and his notions of what a Jewish state meant were pivotal during Israel's first two decades. His ideas on the normalization of Jewish history were, however, full of contradictions, just as Herzl's had been. Israel's Declaration of Independence, read aloud and partially drafted by Ben-Gurion, mentioned explicitly that the Jews, as a result of finally having their own state, have become "a nation like any other nation"—but Ben-Gurion adamantly resisted the notion that the State of Israel

FIGURE 12. On May 14, 1948, David Ben-Gurion declares the independence of the State of Israel under a portrait of Theodor Herzl.

would just be "a state like any other state." It should rather be a light unto other states, a model society just as Herzl had envisioned it in his novel *Old-New-Land*.

"There is a festive atmosphere and profound joy in the country. And again I feel like a mourner among the party guests, just as on November 29th," wrote David Ben-Gurion in his diary on May 14th, 1948, referring to the UN decision to partition Palestine. Then he started a new volume of his diary with the words: "The State of Israel was founded at four o'clock in the afternoon. Its fate lies in the hands of the army."[3]

A few hours earlier the British had lowered their flag and Ben-Gurion had proclaimed the State of Israel. This decision had been taken only two days earlier by a provisional government, the People's Administration (*minhelet ha'am*), with a vote of six versus four votes. Some members thought it wise to delay the proclamation in the face of an impending war. The Arab states were unambiguous in their decision not to recognize a Jewish state, and it was not clear until the last minute that the new state would have the backing of the United States. Nobody knew if it would be able to defend itself against attacks from Egypt, Syria, Jordan, Lebanon, and Iraq. When the provisional government asked the *Haganah* (the pre-state army) leadership to predict the state's chances of survival, the response was: fifty-fifty.[4]

At the end of Israel's War of Independence, the young state had not only defended the area allocated by the United Nations, but had actually made territorial gains. Jerusalem became a divided city, and until 1967 Jews had no access to their holiest sites. The composition of the new state was decidedly different from its pre-war configuration. Most of the Arab population had fled or been driven out of Palestine. When the war was over in early 1949, the 700,000 Jews constituted over 80 percent of Israel's population.[5] Within the next two decades, the Jewish segment of the Israeli population rose to almost 90 percent. Many of the new Jewish immigrants came from Arab countries, where their lives were threatened or where they feared repercussions arising from the ongoing conflict. The State of Israel had achieved what had always been considered necessary for its existence: a clear Jewish majority.

On this basis, the old Zionist goal of normalizing Jewish history seemed within reach. Israel's Declaration of Independence stressed that it was "the natural right of the Jewish people to be masters of their own fate, like all other nations, in their own sovereign State."[6] Finally, the Zionist dream seemed to have come true. But the reality fell short. Nothing went the way the movement's leaders had envisioned. After all, most of the people for whom the state had been built were

Legend:
- State of Israel as outlined by UN Partition Plan
- Territory outside UN-borders, conquered by Israel between 1948 and 1949
- West Bank, occupied by Jordan
- Gaza Strip, occupied by Egypt

LEBANON

Sidon

Damascus

Tyre (Sur)

SYRIA

Acre

Haifa

Nazareth

Sea of Galilee

Irbid

Mediterranean Sea

Jenin

Tel Aviv

Nablus

Jordan

Yafo

Ramallah

Jericho

Amman

Jerusalem

Bethlehem

Gaza

Hebron

Dead Sea

Beer Sheba

ISRAEL

EGYPT

JORDAN

Negev Desert

Ma'an

Sinai

Eilat

Aqaba

0 20 40 60 80 100 km

MAP 3. Israel's borders, 1948–1967.

no longer alive. In the words of David Ben-Gurion, "For hundreds of years the Jewish people offered up a question-prayer: can a state be found for the people? No one considered the horrifying question: will there still be a people for the state once it is established?"[7]

The question what independence actually meant was still being discussed in the days and weeks before and after the official founding of the state. Count Bernadotte, the UN mediator for Palestine, suggested that an Arab-Israeli union be put in place on both sides of the Jordan River, which would be presided over by King Abdullah of Jordan. Some Israeli cabinet members were willing to consider this option, while Ben-Gurion suggested that Israel "join a federation, but only as a completely independent state"—whatever such a construction might entail. In the days before the proclamation of independence, Golda Myerson (Meir) went on her famous mission to speak personally with the king, who promised to grant Jews "full autonomy" within his monarchy.[8]

After the outbreak of war, the discussion of possible federal models became more theoretical, but it did not totally disappear. The far left remained committed to a bi-national state west of the Jordan River, while the Revisionist right still argued for a state on both sides of the Jordan. None of these concepts carried any significant political weight after the end of the war, but theoretical models were still floating around. In Joseph Heller's 1949 edition of *The Zionist Idea*, the author, a committed Zionist, wrote: "Whether or not the State of Israel will in the future have to become an autonomous member of a wider, more comprehensive political union depends on the circumstances which cannot yet be determined. If yes, Israel may be faced with a choice of supreme importance: either to join a Near East federation, consisting mainly of

Moslem states, or to join the British—or possibly, an Anglo-Saxon—commonwealth of nations."[9]

In the eyes of much of the world, this new state was not just a state like all other states. Which other nation had had to wait almost two thousand years to reestablish its sovereignty? And which other nation had experienced its most devastating destruction just a few years before its greatest triumph? The decade when the Jewish state was born was also the decade when a third of the Jewish people were murdered. The proximity of trauma and triumph only added to the old Jewish sense that theirs was a singular fate, a historical path different from that of other nations, the very feeling that the state's founders had been so eager to eradicate.

Leading Jewish personalities used a language of the miraculous when speaking of the new state. One of the leaders of Liberal Judaism in Great Britain, Rabbi John Rayner, who had escaped from Nazi Germany in his youth, wrote: "A miracle is an event that astonishes by its unexpectedness, that defies what are generally taken to be the laws of nature or of history, that is considered by most people as impossible before it happens, and shames their incredulity before it does. The establishment of the State of Israel was a miracle in that sense."[10] David Ben-Gurion, who was greeted like a secular messiah by the Jewish survivors when he visited the Displaced Persons' camps in Germany, is often quoted as having said, "In Israel, in order to be a realist, you must believe in miracles."[11] Shimon Peres once wrote: "The founding of Israel . . . had its roots in the miraculous. The fact is, Israel abounds in miracles."[12] Nahum Goldmann, the long-time leader of the World Jewish Congress and the World Zionist Organization, regarded the Zionist political idea "as absolutely unique and fantastic. You may claim that it is senseless or that it is magnificent, but in either case it remains unique."[13] And even today many people explain Israel's existence in a way supernatural. In a modern collection of texts on Zionism written by American Jews, the word "miracle" appears again and again. For Bradley Shavit Artson, Vice-President of the American Jewish University in Los Angeles for example, "Israel's existence is a miracle," and for Rosanne Miller Selfon, President of Women of Reform Judaism, "Israel mirrors a modern miracle."[14] The concept was adopted by secular liberal Israel as well. One of its most celebrated heroes, the writer David Grossman, admitted in a moving speech delivered at a memorial of the assassination of former prime minister Yitzhak Rabin in 2006: "I am totally secular, and yet in my eyes the establishment and the very existence of the State of Israel is a miracle of sorts that happened to us as a nation—a political, national, human miracle."[15]

The fact that it was (and remains) so common for liberal politicians, secular writers, and Reform leaders to characterize the very being of the Jewish state in supra-natural terms, adds to the likelihood that interpretations of Israel's existence will take on religious coloring. If Israel is a miracle, it cannot be judged by the standards of a "normal state" but stands outside the course of ordinary history, just as Christian and Jewish theologians had over centuries judged the course of Jewish history to be a divine mystery.

Against the backdrop of such strong convictions as to Israel's miraculous birth, clinging to the idea that the new nation would accomplish a normalization of Jewish history, that it would be a "nation like any other nation" was not easy. The popular Israeli writer A. B. Yehoshua admitted as much: "The Holocaust . . . provided indisputable proof to all those who hold to notions of a unique Jewish destiny. How much our destiny and place in the world differ from those of other peoples became most horribly apparent in World War II. The yellow badge affixed to the Jew's garment was but a physical representation of what had always been known: that we are different. To seek to escape this singular destiny is futile—this the Holocaust proved. The different historical path of the Jewish people was only emphatically made more apparent by the horrible experience of the Holocaust."

Yehoshua held fast to the belief that the establishment of Israel was an attempt to escape from the special role Jews played in history. He argued "that the Holocaust proved once and for all the urgency of normalization for the Jewish people, the need to be a nation in the family of nations with equal rights and obligations."[16] He found evidence in Israel's Declaration of Independence to support his interpretation: "The catastrophe which recently befell the Jewish people—the massacre of millions of Jews in Europe—was another clear demonstration of the urgency of solving the problem of its homelessness by reestablishing in Eretz-Israel the Jewish State, which would open the gates of the homeland wide to every Jew and confer upon the Jewish people the status of a fully privileged member of the community of nations."[17]

The Holocaust was of course not the only legitimization for the establishment of a Jewish state. Israel's Declaration of Independence reads like a history book, and it is history that serves as the basis of all Jewish claims to the land. As historians have noted, in contrast to the American Declaration of Independence which stresses the rights of individuals, the Israeli Declaration stresses the rights of a collective, the Jewish people.[18] The text speaks of the importance of the Land of Israel as the birthplace of the Jewish people: "Here they first attained to statehood, created cultural values of national and universal

significance and gave to the world the eternal Book of Books."[19]
The document also emphasizes that the connection between
the Jews in exile and their homeland was never broken. Although they lived far from their ancestral home for many
centuries, they prayed unceasingly for their return and supported the Jewish community still living in Palestine. The
historical part of the declaration concludes with the important
events of the twentieth century: the Balfour Declaration, the
Peel Plan, and the UN partition plan. The authors of the text,
mainly secular and Socialist Jews, were very careful not to
include the name of God. Only the term "Rock of Israel" appears in the text as a compromise nod to the Orthodox. While
secular Jews can pretend that it has other meanings as well,
for religious Jews it was always clear that this is just another
term for God.

Thus, just as with the name of Israel, a religious subtext
was inscribed into Israel's founding document. Originally
meant to reach out to a small Orthodox minority, it had the
potential to cast the state's very being in a divine light. This is
especially relevant, as in absence of a constitution, Israel's Declaration of Independence is the document that comes nearest
to defining the nature of the state. There were several reasons
why a constitution was never drafted. The Orthodox objected
to any constitution that would not be in line with *halakha*,
Jewish religious law. Such a constitution would have been
unacceptable to the secular majority. David Ben-Gurion himself gave up on the idea of drafting a constitution in 1950,
mainly for the reason that it might restrict the power of the
government and the parliament, both dominated by his own
Mapai (Social Democratic) party. In lieu of a formal constitution, basic laws were drafted over the course of many decades.
While some legal scholars regard them as the equivalent of a

constitution, there can be no doubt that Israel lacks a single powerful foundational document that defines its essence with the kind of thoroughness that a declaration of independence cannot achieve.[20]

One other foundational document has influenced Israel over the course of its existence and that is the "status quo agreement," written in the form of a letter that Ben-Gurion sent to representatives of the ultra-Orthodox Agudat Israel Party in June 1947. While Ben-Gurion or, for that matter, his opponents from the right-wing parties, had no doubts about the secular nature of the state, he found it crucial to appease the communities of Orthodox Jews, especially in light of their severe decimation during the Holocaust. Ben-Gurion believed that this tiny portion of the Israeli population would diminish even further over time. Thus, any concessions made to them would be of rather symbolic nature in a society that would, in his view and that of most of his contemporaries, become increasingly secular.

Ben-Gurion's letter granted far-reaching rights to the Orthodox minority in a number of areas. The Sabbath would be the weekly day of rest, dietary laws (*kashrut*) would be observed in all state institutions and the army, all matters of personal law (especially marriage and divorce) would be delegated to religious courts alone, and religious schools would be granted educational autonomy. A year later, Ben-Gurion allowed ultra-Orthodox youth to be exempted from the otherwise compulsory military conscription if they were enrolled in an institution of religious study (a *yeshiva*). In 1948, only four hundred young men fell under this exemption, and Ben-Gurion could not have foreseen that seventy years later, tens of thousands would be exempted each year. In reality, Ben-Gurion was instrumental in implementing next to the secular

Western system of law that remained dominant, a second competing system, based on traditional Jewish religious laws, *halakha*.

Ben-Gurion later himself regretted instituting the exemption for Orthodox yeshiva students and other concessions to the ultra-Orthodox. In a letter to his successor Levi Eshkol, he wrote, "I am not of the opinion that you need my advice on matters of government, and of course I would not consider giving it, but the unruliness of fanatics crosses all bounds," (he was referring to the violent demonstrations by the ultra-Orthodox on Saturdays in Jerusalem). "I am of the opinion that I am responsible for this to some extent: I released yeshiva students from army service. I did so when their number was small, but now they are increasing. When they run amok, they represent a danger to the honor of the state. We cannot appear to the world like Alabama or South Africa."[21] As a solution to the problem, he explicitly recommended drafting ultra-Orthodox men.

The status quo and the military exemption pointed to the still-unanswered question of what a *Jewish* state actually meant. For Ben-Gurion, as for most of the other secular founders of the state from both the left and the right, "Jewish" referred first to the Jewish nation and not to the Jewish religion. The Orthodox minorities—both the *haredi* (ultra-Orthodox) and the national-religious—on the other hand, always foregrounded the religious element of Jewishness. The status quo agreement was too vague to settle the issue: it allowed for different interpretations.

Take for example the Sabbath. It was never stipulated what exactly was meant by "a day of rest." Could the airport operate and the national airline fly? Could busses run? Shops and restaurants be open? These questions have received different answers at different times and in different locales. Or take the marriage and divorce laws. Israel has retained the pre-state laws that go back to the Ottoman Empire. There is no official civil marriage, and only religious courts can rule over personal matters. This means in practice that a Jew can only marry a Jew, a Muslim only a Muslim, and a Christian only a Christian. By implication it also enforced gender inequality, as a Jewish woman has fewer rights in a rabbinical court than a Jewish man, for example in matters concerning divorce.

Just as Ben-Gurion and the secular majority had to give up some of their core principles, so did the religious Zionists whose origins were in the Mizrahi movement. They realized that their state would not be what Rabbi Avraham Isaac Kook had once termed "the foundation of the throne of God on earth." Instead of a sign of complete redemption, they now considered the state as either a "first sign of redemption" or the "beginning of the flowering of redemption." For non-Zionist ultra-Orthodox, the theological dilemma posed by this Jewish state was much larger. Even though they had lost most of their adherents, their European leadership, and their structures as a result of the Holocaust, Agudat Israel remained adamant in their rejection of a Jewish state, even after the end of the war. Its president, Jacob Rosenheim, reassured his base in 1946 that a sovereign Jewish state that would be "a nation like all other nations," with secular leaders who violated the Sabbath, "would strike a severe blow at the concept of a return unto the Lord" and should be rejected. Another leader of the movement, Rabbi Itzhak Levin, declared that "a Jewish state in Palestine which does not conform with the Torah is a profanation of God in Israel and among the nations and a danger to the Jewish religion."[22] They also observed, however, that while it was impossible to support such a state, it should not be publicly opposed either, as the name of God might thus be profaned. This did not deter the leader of the more extreme Satmar Hasidic group, Rabbi Joel Teitelbaum, to call the State of Israel Satanic and blame Zionism for the Holocaust.[23] It is important to understand these internal Orthodox discussions as the background of Ben-Gurion's status quo letter, which was after all also an effort at political compromise and an (ultimately successful) attempt to put large parts of the Orthodox at peace with the idea of a predominantly secular Jewish state.

Thus, the seeds for a future *Kulturkampf* between the secular and the religious were planted at the very hour of Israel's birth: the name of the state alluded to mythical biblical origins, the vague reference to the divine name in its Declaration of Independence gave room for messianic interpretations, constant reference to its miraculous birth placed the state outside any secular interpretation of history, the lack of a constitution enabled the future undermining of the founders' values, and the appeasement policy of the "status quo" gave Orthodox elements considerable power over everyday life in the new state. Religious symbols were held in high esteem. Even the national flag with its blue and white stripes was designed to resemble a *tallit*, a prayer shawl. Like Herzl fifty years earlier, Ben-Gurion also thought it important that a secular concept receive a religious blessing. The Mizrahi leader Rabbi Yehuda Leib Fishman-Maimon delivered the *shehecheyanu* prayer, which marks a special occasion in life, similar to the message by Rabbi Samuel Mohilever that had been recited at the First Zionist Congress.

As long as Israel was a society with an overwhelmingly secular Jewish population and a silent religious minority, the status quo worked relatively well and religious symbols remained nothing but symbols. When, beginning in the 1970s, the religious contingents grew more powerful and assertive, Ben-Gurion's compromise began to fall apart. By refusing to draft a constitution and by letting the pre-state status quo become a permanent state of affair (though with some minor changes over time), Ben-Gurion and his affiliates invited a future redefinition of the nature of a Jewish state. With the unexpected growth of the Orthodox population, a religious definition of Israeli society became more prevalent over time. Without intention and without being able to predict the future course of history, the founders of the state had laid the groundwork for the demise of their own values, which were rooted in a secular liberal society.

There is one other element that contributed to Ben-Gurion's seemingly contradictory policies. Like many other early Zionists, he deeply believed in the uniqueness of the Jewish national movement, while at the same time arguing for the normalization of the Jewish people. Ben-Gurion was certainly aware of the ambiguous associations religiously literate readers had with the sentence in the Declaration of Independence stating that the Jews "like any other nation" (*ke-khol am ve'am*) had a natural right to determine their own affairs as a sovereign state. He knew that in the book of Samuel the leaders of the people asked God to "make us a king to judge us like all the nations" (*ke-khol ha-goyim*; Samuel 8:5). Samuel had tried to convince them that a king would exploit them as all kings do and that only God should be king of the Jewish people. But they remained adamant and insisted "that we also may be like all the nations" (Samuel 8:20).

Ben-Gurion was knowledgeable in biblical and rabbinical traditions. And it seems also that despite his secular lifestyle he believed in the redemptive nature of the establishment of a Jewish state. In 1950 he gave a lecture called "Uniqueness and Mission" to a group of military leaders, in which he pointed out that Jewish history, by integrating immigrants from so many different countries, had proved itself a unifying force. He made clear that there was no difference between his national goals and a universalist mission. The Jewish state was, according to him, the beginning of both Jewish and general human redemption.[24] In another speech before young officers during the War of Independence, he emphasized that they should not only take care of their bodies' performance and their physical stability, but that during the war they must also remain true to the unique traditions within Jewish history.[25]

In 1949, while the war was still on-going, Ben-Gurion met twice with a group of Jewish intellectuals, among them the philosopher Martin Buber, the historian Benzion Dinur (Dünaburg), and the writers Leah Goldberg and Moshe Shamir to discuss questions pertaining to the essence of a Jewish state, including its cultural setup and immigration matters. Buber told him that the Jewish state could not be just another state, it had to be a state with a higher purpose. These immigrants don't just move, they ascend (from the Hebrew *ole*) to this country "to achieve something they would not achieve in any other country."[26] During the 1950s Ben-Gurion would regularly open his house to a group of intellectuals with whom he would read the Bible. He was also interested in archaeological enterprises that traced the Jewish heritage back to biblical times.

While he neither lived according to Jewish religious laws nor believed in God in any traditional way, it is thus quite clear that Ben-Gurion was deeply inspired by the Hebrew Bible and shaped by his study of Jewish history. According to Nir Kedar, his "Judaism was based on a set of humanistic-political values which were articulated by the biblical prophets and were present throughout history in Jewish thought and praxis."[27]

Ben-Gurion was born in 1886 in the Polish shtetl of Plonsk, where the majority of the population was Jewish and experienced antisemitism on a daily basis. He always stressed, however, that his Zionism did not grow out of negative experiences of exclusion, but rather from positive longings for a national Jewish renaissance. This kind of Zionism, mixed with a good dose of socialism, produced in him a yearning for a better society not only for Jews, but for all humankind. In this sense, Ben-Gurion was Herzl's heir. If Herzl was a modern Moses who led the Jews out of exile, Ben-Gurion was a modern Joshua, who led them into the Land of Israel. Just as Herzl held the seven-hour-day holy, and Jabotinsky believed in the obligation of the state to feed all its citizens, so Ben-Gurion was convinced that the young State of Israel had the power to perform good deeds beyond its borders.

Development aid to poor African and Asian countries was for him more than just a political measure; it served also to deliver a deeply ethical message. Israel regarded itself as a mediator between the first and the third worlds. Exporting its agricultural and technological knowledge would befit its role as a model nation. In 1972, Israel had diplomatic relationships with thirty-two African countries that were ignoring anti-Israel protests from the Arab world; many of them even had embassies in Jerusalem. To be sure, economic and strategic ties also played a crucial role here, as in all other diplomatic relationships. But for Israel there was more at stake. In 1960, Ben-Gurion characterized these relationships, in a paternalistic tone reminiscent of Herzl: "Israel has been granted the great historic privilege . . . of assisting backward and primitive peoples to improve themselves, develop, and advance."[28] At the same time, many African politicians stressed during their visits to Israel that their own nations had suffered under colonialism and endured oppression for many centuries, just as had the Jews.

Ben-Gurion's long-time foreign minister Golda Meir stated that she was "prouder of Israel's International Cooperation Program and of the technical aid we gave to the people of Africa than I am of any other single project we have undertaken." The Tanzanian president Julius Nyerere called her "the mother of Africa." The first foreign prime minister to visit the young state of Israel was Burma's U Nu in 1955, and six years later Ben-Gurion visited Burma for two weeks, where he took the opportunity to study Buddhism.[29]

Ben-Gurion's attitude towards African and Asian states was, however, only one small symptom of his profound belief in the special mission of the Jewish state. In many speeches and articles he reiterated the conviction: "From the beginning we were a people set apart. We became a people of the book, of the Prophets, of the End of Days, the Eternal People."[30] In 1957, still entrenched in the consequences of the Sinai Crisis, Ben-Gurion found time for an extensive exchange of thoughts with the philosopher Nathan Rotenstreich. In his notes, Ben-Gurion emphasized the connection of Israel's existence with biblical history, while he downplayed the relevance of two millennia of exile. He regarded the modern State of Israel as a continuation of the ancient kingdoms of Israel and Judah. Young Israelis, he argued, would find the consciousness for their new state not in the Zionist writings of Herzl, but rather in the Bible. The prophets "are closer, more instructive and had more vital sap for the generation born, growing up, and living in Israel," he told them "than all the speeches and discussions at the Basel Congresses." For him the State of Israel was a messianic fulfillment in a "social-cultural-moral sense."[31]

Israel's founder held fast to a Palestinocentric and secularized messianic vision of Zionist history that appalled Rotenstreich, who saw Ben-Gurion's view as the mark of a "termination of history, the termination of life in real time, whereas we, setting up the Jewish state, are entering history."[32] Ben-Gurion reiterated his vision a year later at the "ideological assembly" convened by the Jewish Agency to discuss the state of Zionism and Israel among leading intellectuals. He was opposed not only by Israeli intellectuals, but also by the American Jewish thinker Mordecai Kaplan, who proposed a "Greater Zionism" that would include an affirmative position toward the continued existence of a Jewish diaspora, and by the president of the World Jewish Congress, Nahum Goldmann, who argued for a more inclusive historical view of the Jewish experience: "A nation cannot choose the parts of history it likes and discard what it does not like."[33]

As prime minister, Ben-Gurion had a special forum in which to summarize his thoughts on topics he considered to be of intellectual relevance: the Government Year Book, which regularly carried an essay of the Prime Minister. His longtime bureau chief Yitzhak Navon, who would later become Israel's president, noted that Ben-Gurion took a lot of time and effort writing and discussing these essays, and waited impatiently for their appearance in print: "From the moment the article went to press he would pester us with annoying questions: When will the article appear? When will the Yearbook appear? Finally, when the book was presented to him he would rejoice with the composition, the work of creation, as if it were his first article to be published."[34] As Navon notes, if there was a common thread to all of Ben-Gurion's articles, it was his deep belief that the fate of Israel was different from that of all other nations and that the Jewish state had to serve as a light unto the nations.

Ben-Gurion underlined that there was nothing to be learned from recent history, but much from the biblical past. Modern Israel had to reconnect with ancient Israel and disregard the last two millennia of diaspora history: "Only the people of Israel, uprooted bodily though they had been from the land of their origin for almost two thousand years, were the one nation to continue their ancient tradition in their own language and culture as though there had been no interruption or severance in the thread of their history."[35]

Ben-Gurion's language is full of biblical and messianic allusions, which led him to the universal mission of the Jewish people and ultimately to the Jewish state: "The renascence of Israel has not been, and will not be, restricted narrowly to the making of sovereign instruments of local scope for the Jewish nation only. It will find its full and supreme expression in the revelation of its eternal spirit and the fulfillment of its historic mission for the salvation of mankind. . . . We are building the State with prophetic vision and messianic longings, to be an example and a guide to all men. The words of the Prophet remain true for us: 'I will give thee for a light to the Gentiles, that thou mayest be my salvation unto the end of the earth.'"[36] He used this language year after year: "The Messianic vision that has lighted up our path for thousands of years has prepared and fitted us to a light unto the nations. Moreover, it has imposed upon us the duty of becoming a model people and building a model state."[37]

Herzl had envisioned a model state. Ben-Gurion, its first prime minister, tried to implement it. He repeatedly recalled the constant tension between particularism (the uniqueness of the Jewish people) and universalism (the model state role): "Two basic aspirations underlie all our work in this country: to be like all other nations, and to be different from all the nations. These two aspirations are apparently contradictory, but in fact they are complementary and interdependent. We want to be a free people, independent and equal in rights in the family of nations, and we aspire to be different from all other nations in our spiritual elevation and in the character of our model society, founded on freedom, cooperation, and fraternity with all Jews and the whole human race. This aspiration is not the outcome of a feeling that we are a chosen people, but an imperative necessity for our survival, because we are few and our position is different from that of all other nations: the great majority of our people is still scattered abroad . . . ."[38]

Ben-Gurion reiterated his belief in the uniqueness of the Jewish state: "Our country occupies also a unique place in the intellectual and cultural history of mankind." As a result, "everything that happens in this country is watched closely by the whole world, more than similar occurrences in countries much larger in their area and their population. . . . The establishment of Israel in our time is different from the establishment of any other country in the modern period."[39] More than that, "the struggle of the Jewish people is unique in the history of mankind" and therefore, "[i]n contrast to all laws of logic and reality, without any example in the history of mankind."[40]

Nahum Goldmann, chairman of the World Zionist Organization in the post–World War II era, who otherwise agreed with little that Ben-Gurion said, supported the idea of Israel's global mission. On the occasion of Herzl's centenary, he asked,

"Do you think that what other nations admired about Zionism was the fact that the Jews, too, wanted a state with ministers, ambassadors, cabinet crises and a flag? As if the world had not enough states. . . . In the historical perspective, what inspired the finest of the Jews with enthusiasm for Zionism was precisely its Utopian aspect." Jews, he continued, have still to cling to the great humanitarian ideals, "not the short-sighted, provincial realism of some groups in Israel."[41] A few years later Goldmann accused Ben-Gurion of elevating the state, forgetting that a state is nothing but a means to materialize the identity of a nation. "It would be the greatest danger for Israel to lose its special character and be satisfied to be a state like all other states. To me it is clear that a Jewish state can only survive if it constitutes a unique phenomenon in our world; if it becomes a state like any other state, its triumph will be only the collective assimilation of the Jews."[42] In contrast to Ben-Gurion, Goldmann followed the lead of Ahad Ha'am, regarding Israel as a spiritual center while the Jewish diaspora would continue to exist.[43]

The notion of the future coexistence of the Jewish diaspora and a Jewish state did not disappear with the establishment of the State of Israel. The most important voice in its support was the philosopher Simon Rawidowicz, who vehemently fought for the preservation of two equal centers, which he called, alluding to the ancient two centers, Jerusalem and Babylon.[44] Ben-Gurion disagreed: "There can be no such thing in the Diaspora as Jewish culture, as Simon Rawidowicz believed. At the most there can be a cultural ghetto, even if in the favorable sense of the word."[45]

In a letter to Rawidowicz, Ben-Gurion claimed: "The Jew in the *golah*, even a Jew like yourself who lives an entirely Jewish life, is not able to be a complete Jew, and no Jewish community in the *golah* is able to live a complete Jewish life. Only in the State of Israel is a full Jewish life possible. Only here will a Jewish culture worthy of that name flourish."[46]

Rawidowicz insisted that the name of the new state, Israel, was irritating and misleading. How could anyone distinguish in the future between the people of Israel and the state of Israel, he asked, if both were called by the same name? And he criticized the notion of a Christian or Muslim Israeli as a contradiction in itself, for "Israel" in its true meaning signifies the Jewish people. The new state should always be called *Eretz Yisrael* (the Land of Israel) or *Medinat Yisrael* (the State of Israel), and not just "Israel."[47] But Ben-Gurion remained adamant in his definition of the Jewish state. It reconnected the Jewish people with its land and its history. For him that was "what connects and identifies the Israel of the year 1948 with the Israel in the Bible."[48]

Ben-Gurion was convinced that Jews could have a fully satisfying existence only in their own state, where they would be able to defend themselves and live according to Jewish values. In contrast, he referred to the Jews in the diaspora as "human dust": "We have turned human dust, gathered from all over the world, into an independent, sovereign nation, occupying a respectable place in the family of nations."[49] He held fast to this opinion until the end of his life. In a 1966 interview, he insisted that for him, the purpose of the State of Israel was a twofold one: "These two interdependent purposes, to be a covenant of the people and a light to the Gentiles, are the purposes that determine the future of the renewed State of Israel."[50] For Ben-Gurion, only if Israel increased its "moral and intellectual superiority, will we become a Chosen People, a faithful bulwark for the Diaspora, an educational example for the peoples and a desirable partner for our neighbors on a basis of cooperation for the development of the entire Middle East and for increasing peace in the region and in the world."[51]

The vision of the state's founding father was secular, but his language was loaded with biblical references, religious terminology, and messianic allusions. Notions of the chosen-ness and uniqueness of Israel were woven into many of his programmatic articles and speeches and, in a later generation, they would be easy prey to be taken out of context by leaders from different political camps or religious outlooks.

WHO IS A JEW IN THE JEWISH STATE?

Ben-Gurion's idea of the uniqueness of the Jewish state was based on his notion of the uniqueness of the Jewish people. But who exactly was the Jewish people? Israel's Declaration of Independence guarantees all Jews the right to "return" to Israel, assuming that all their ancestors had fled ancient Palestine. The Law of Return of 1950 formalized this promise, which was not without parallel in other countries. Thus, for example, Germany allows the "return" of ethnic Germans, whose ancestors left German lands centuries ago, and similar laws exist in Greece, Spain, and many East European states. The difference with respect to the Jews was that in their case ethnic and religious identities overlapped, and it was not always clear if they regarded themselves or were regarded by others as members of an ethnic or of a religious group.

Over the years Ben-Gurion and other Israeli lawmakers realized that it was growing increasingly complicated to define just who is a Jew—and thus entitled to become an Israeli citizen. When Ben-Gurion presented the Law of Return to the Knesset, he based it on the uniqueness of the Jewish people and spoke once again of the State of Israel as a beginning step toward redemption: "The Law of Return and the Nationality Law which are before you are closely connected and have a common ideological basis that derives from the historical uniqueness of the State of Israel, a uniqueness that relates to the past and the future. . . . These two laws determine the special character and purpose of the State of Israel which carries the message of the redemption of Israel."[52]

The law underlined that Israel's gates were open to all Jews.[53] But it did not clarify who was considered a Jew for the purpose of this law. During the coming years and decades, lawyers, scholars, and politicians would fight over the proper definition of who was a Jew. It was a question not only relevant for purposes of immigration, but also for one's identity card (which contained the category "nationality"), and for getting married in Israel. Without at least a tentative answer to the question of who was a Jew, there could be no answer to the question of what was a Jewish state.

When Ben-Gurion realized this, he took an unusual decision. On October 27th, 1958, Israel's prime minister sent out a query to fifty religious leaders and public intellectuals in the Jewish world, asking that they help to finally resolve this question of who is a Jew, and also suggest how to handle the status of children born to Jewish fathers and non-Jewish mothers. The letter was triggered by a coalition crisis. The majority of cabinet ministers had decided that it was an individual decision. It was up to everyone to decide themselves whether they or their children were Jewish and should be characterized as such on their official identity cards. The National Religious Party protested, insisting that only the rabbinate could decide who was Jewish, and as a consequence left the coalition.[54]

What were the answers to Ben-Gurion's questionnaire? Among the Orthodox there was broad agreement that the query was, to begin with, illegitimate, and thus their replies were rather brief. In their opinion, the question of who was a Jew had been answered two thousand years ago, and if doubts should arise (against all odds), then only Orthodox rabbis should decide this issue. After all, they argued, didn't Israel have two Chief Rabbis? It was their prerogative to decide who was a Jew.

Typical of those who held this view was Rabbi Yehuda Leib Maimon, one of the founders of the religious Zionist *Mizrahi* movement, a signer of the Israeli Declaration of Independence, and Israel's first Minister of Religion: "The question 'Who is a Jew?' has been answered for thousands of years, ever since we became a distinct nation. According to our eternal Torah and tradition, a Jew is a person who was born, at the very least, to a Jewish mother. No power in the world can or is entitled to revoke this ruling, which is the primary foundation of the whole of Judaism. . . . If, for some reason, there should ever arise any doubt as to this traditional ruling, one must request the opinion of the Chief Rabbinate, which alone has the authority to rule on matters of *halakha*."[55]

The writer Shmuel Y. Agnon, himself an observant Jew and a few years later a recipient of the Nobel Prize for Literature, agreed with the position of the religious establishment and gave Ben-Gurion some well-meant advice: "As a person on whom the safety and welfare of the state rest, you would do well to refrain from concerning yourself with matters of religion, whether for good or ill, in order to leave yourself free for matters of state."[56] Agnon missed a point here. Ben-Gurion was well aware that what he was inquiring about was not a matter of religion. He was interested in the definition of who was a Jew primarily as it concerned nationality status. Since the Knesset had passed the Law of Return and state authorities were to implement it, and since state authorities and not the rabbinate had to decide how to define nationality for the purpose of identity cards, his concern was not about the religious definition of a Jew.

Nor did other intellectuals hold back on advising Ben-Gurion. The educator Ernst Simon quoted from the Prime Minister's letter in which he stated that in Israel "there is no fear that the Jews will become assimilated among the non-Jews." Simon went on to warn him: "There is, however, good reason to fear the collective assimilation of the entire nation if it should, Heaven forbid, be gutted of its minimal Jewish substance."[57] Simon's colleague at the Hebrew University, the philosopher Shmuel Hugo Bergmann, suggested eliminating the notation of religion in official use altogether: "I believe in the special sanctity of the Jewish people as a 'holy nation' in which nationality and religion are one and the same."[58]

There were also Jews outside Israel, whose opinion Ben-Gurion valued. The philosopher Alexander Altmann, who had fled Nazi Germany and lived as a scholar in Manchester before moving on to the United States where he taught at Brandeis University, went further than his Israeli peers: "I must state that there is no place for the question of religion and nationality on the identity card of a modern democratic state." Like Simon, he too thought that religion and nationality could not be separated in the case of the Jews: "The ancient Israelite tribes merged into a nation solely under the influence of religious experiences, and the history of the nation and the religion are identical. . . . The whole of the national effort of the Jewish people stems from unity between religious faith and the desire to ensure the survival of the nation. Anyone who jeopardizes this unity is presumably jeopardizing the very heart of the nation."[59]

Isaiah Berlin, the famous Oxford philosopher, stated that Israel as a liberal state could not "define the status of its citizens or even of its residents in purely religious terms." Contrary to Simon and Altmann, Berlin believed that "there must exist a category of persons who will be entitled to register themselves as Jews by nationality, but not by religion."[60] All this was further complicated by the demand of Harvard philosophy professor Harry A. Wolfson, who suggested creating the new and distinct category of the "Hebrew."[61]

The divergent views of Jewish intellectuals were of little help to Ben-Gurion in solving the riddle of Jewish identity. What was perhaps the most pragmatic answer came from Israel's Attorney General and later Supreme Court justice, Haim Cohn. He evaded the religious and philosophical dimensions of the debate by concentrating solely on its legal dimension: "The meaning of 'Jew' in Knesset legislation is not identical to its meaning in religious law."[62]

Cohn's argument became indeed the basis for most Israeli legislation related to this question. The courts did not pretend to clarify the question of who was a Jew in religious terms, but tried instead to create a basis only for their legal decisions as to who was a Jew in terms of nationality. The determination of who was a Jew in religious terms fell to the rabbinate, the determination of who is a Jew in terms of nationality had to be decided by the state.

For many years, the state avoided an exact definition of "Jewishness" as it pertained to the Law of Return. Finally, in 1970, an amendment was drafted stating that "for the purposes of this Law, 'Jew' means a person who was born of a Jewish mother or has become converted to Judaism and who is not a member of another religion." The amendment was very careful to state that this definition was not intended as a revision of any rabbinic statement, but was valid only "for the purposes of this law." Another clarification in the same amendment stated: "The rights of a Jew under this Law and the rights of an *oleh* (immigrant) under the Nationality Law, 5712–1952, as well as the rights of an oleh under any other enactment, are also vested in a child and a grandchild of a Jew, the spouse of a Jew, the spouse of a child of a Jew and the spouse of a grandchild of a Jew, except for a person who has been a Jew and has voluntarily changed his religion."[63] When read carefully it becomes clear that Israeli legislation did not try to declare non-Jewish spouses or grandchildren of Jews as Jews in any religious sense. It rather aimed to extend the rights granted to Jews as possible immigrants in the sense of the "Law of Return" to their spouses, children, and grandchildren. The lawmakers were well aware that while the amendment granted them legal residence in Israel, it did not tell the rabbis who should be a Jew in terms of religious law.

These clarifications had become necessary after two prominent cases were settled by the Israeli Supreme Court, in 1962 and 1970, respectively. The first concerned Oswald Rufeisen, or as he called himself then, Brother Daniel. Rufeisen was a Polish Jew who—posing as an ethnic German—had helped to save the lives of hundreds of Jews in the Mir Ghetto during the war. After his true identity was revealed, his own life was saved by Catholic nuns, and he subsequently converted to Catholicism, joined the Carmelite order, and was ordained as a priest. In the 1950s he moved from Poland to Israel, where his brother, his only surviving relative, had settled. He applied for Israeli citizenship claiming that while he was a Catholic by religion, he remained a Jew by nationality. The Israeli government denied his claim, maintaining that whoever converted to another religion ceased being Jewish both in terms of religion and in terms of nationality. He was granted Israeli citizenship by naturalization, but he insisted that he should be granted citizenship on the terms of the Law of Return.[64] In a well-known decision of 1962, rendered around the same time as the court was considering Adolf Eichmann's appeal, the Israeli Supreme Court supported the government decision. This issue was of such importance that for the first time five justices, instead of the usual three, were summoned to preside.

In their deliberations, the justices appealed to Jewish history. So long as Judge Silberg, an Orthodox Jew, was paying his respect to Oswald Rufeisen as a person of tremendous courage during the Holocaust, he reflected the opinion of the court. But not everyone agreed when Silberg went on to say that Rufeisen was asking for too much: "... what Brother Daniel asks us to do is to erase the historical and sanctified significance of the term 'Jew' and deny all the spiritual values for which our people gave their lives in different periods of our long dispersion . . . ." Silberg emphasized that it was not the courts' task to determine who was a Jew in a religious sense. In that sense, he argued, Brother Daniel might well be considered Jewish, as according to rabbinical views one cannot leave the Jewish religion. But the task of the court was to identify who is a Jew in a secular sense, "as it is usually understood in common parlance—and this I emphasize—by the ordinary simple Jew."[65]

But surely this was an impossible task for a judge. What judge could objectively and accurately divine the opinion of "the ordinary simple Jew"? It was a most unusual basis on which to determine a verdict. But Judge Silberg was confident in his answer and continued to elaborate: "The answer to this question, is, in my opinion, sharp and clear—a Jew who has become a Christian is not deemed a 'Jew.'" This, Silberg declared, was the opinion "shared by *all* [emphasis in original] Jews who live in Israel (save a mere handful) . . . we do not cut ourselves off from our historic past nor deny our ancestral heritage. We continue to drink from the original fountains." Only a naïve person, he argued, could believe "that we are creating here a new culture." Israel, in his view, was a further chapter of the Jewish culture that had persisted over the centuries: "The Jew living in Israel is bound, willingly or unwillingly, by an umbilical cord to historical Judaism." Justice Silberg continued to give history lessons in court, speaking about the historical heroes and martyrs of the Jewish past, biblical Jewish festivals and the revived Hebrew language, all of which were the basis of the Jewish society in Israel.

But the court proceedings proved better than any argument that the matter was not as simple as presented by Silberg. While he claimed that there was general agreement among all Jews as to who was a Jew, there was not even general agreement among the justices of the court. A dissenting voice was that of Justice Haim Cohn, who argued that it was not up to a court to decide who was Jewish in the sense of nationality. Rather, that should be left entirely to the subjective understanding of the person who declared himself a Jew.

In the course of the court discussions, it became clear that one and the same person might be a Jew in a certain situation and a non-Jew in another. As Avishai Margalit correctly stated, a person might be considered a Jew by a rabbi even though he had converted to another religion, but the same rabbi would not consider him a Jew when he was called to the Torah in synagogue. The definition of who is a Jew was, thus, a situational definition. One might add, it was also a time-bound definition. A court in 1962 did not consider Brother Daniel a

Jew, but a court one generation later might well have come to a very different decision. What was an "ordinary simple Jew" to most Israelis was one thing in the 1960s and another thing fifty years later.[66]

Despite the theoretical changes over time and the possibility of a situational definition of one's Jewishness, the court decision of 1962 has remained valid to this day. In concrete terms, it means that there is no clear distinction between ethnicity and religion when it comes to Jewishness in Israel. A person who converts to the religion of Judaism becomes a Jew also in an ethnic sense, while a Jew who becomes a Christian automatically loses his ethnic identity as a Jew.

Only seven years after the decision on Brother Daniel, another case came to the attention of the Supreme Court, which dealt also with the question of who is a Jew. This time the issue was not about a convert but about the children of a Jewish father and a non-Jewish mother living in Israel. Benjamin Shalit had met his wife in Scotland, returned with her to live in Israel, and became an officer in the Israeli navy. After his children were born, the registrar denied them the entry "Jewish" under "nationality" on their IDs because their mother was not Jewish. The father protested and the matter was referred to the Supreme Court.

In their deliberations, the justices once again discussed the general understanding of who is a Jew. One justice emphasized that being Jewish should neither be understood as a virtue nor a flaw. A son of a Jewish mother who fights as a terrorist against Israel remains a Jew, albeit a wicked Jew. A non-Jew who sacrifices his life for Israel is not turned into a Jew by his deeds: "'Jewishness' is not a prize awarded to people as an honorary degree for their virtues and their efforts on its behalf. 'Jewishness' is a religious-legal qualification applied or conferred under certain conditions alone, and the petitioner's children do not meet these conditions . . . ." The court ruled in favor of Shalit's petition by a slim 5 to 4 majority, but a later amendment to the Law of Return made clear that a converted Jew cannot be considered a Jew.

At the same time, the amendment enlarged the number of potential new immigrants greatly by including the children and grandchildren of Jewish mothers *and* fathers, Jewish grandmothers *and* grandfathers, and all of their spouses. The Knesset accepted this amendment but rejected the court's recommendation that the category of nationality on Israeli identity cards be abolished.[67] Ben-Gurion himself might have had a special interest in these questions, as his son Amos had married a non-Jewish woman. Their first daughter, Ben-Gurion's granddaughter Galia, was considered non-Jewish by the Orthodox rabbis because her mother had originally converted in a non-Orthodox ceremony.[68] For the first time in modern history, Jews in Israel were not a minority seeking protection. They were now themselves the majority that had to deal with an Arab minority in their midst—a minority that did not want a Jewish state and that regarded Israel's birth not as an occasion for celebration but as *nakbah*, a catastrophe. Thus, to define who was a Jew in a Jewish state also meant deciding how non-Jews should be treated in a Jewish state. There were voices, such as the labor union leader and later government minister Pinchas Lavon, who in classical Zionist fashion sought to create not just a model state but a model policy on minorities: "For the first time we will be a majority living with a minority and we shall be called upon to provide an example and prove how Jews live with a minority."[69] But in the face of reality, this proved unrealistic—and for two reasons: The first was the understandable resistance of Palestinians to living and being treated as a minority in a country where, until 1948, they had constituted a large majority; the second was the equally understandable desire of the Jews to exercise their right to a state of their own, in which they might enjoy the privileges that had so long been denied them. It was just as Jabotinsky had observed long before the state was founded: this was not an issue of right against wrong but of right against right.

The Law of Return, its amendment, and its various inter-pretations, like the later Citizenship Law, were important elements in the larger dynamic. The project was nothing less than the creation of a society, one in which all were supposed to be equal, but where some, as it turned out, were more equal than others. While Palestinian Arabs had to provide evidence that they lived in Palestine without interruption from the time when the State of Israel was established in order to gain Israeli citizenship, the Russian-born Christian wife of a person with a Jewish grandfather did not (and does not to this day) need any such proof. These laws naturally cemented relations between diaspora Jews and Israeli Jews, as between secular and religious Jews, while at the same time widening the gap between Israel's Jewish and Palestinian citizens. It is not the (Israeli) citizenship in their passport that drives a wedge between them, but rather the (Jewish or Arab) nationality in their internal identity papers. With all its difficulties in defining who was a Jew, the Law of Return thus fulfilled the double task of creating a safe haven for Jews from around the world and of guaranteeing a Jewish majority population in the state in the foreseeable future. While it was not able to solve the dilemma of internal Jewish definitions, it established a demarcation line against those who were not part of the core nation, namely the Palestinian Arabs.

There were other legal grounds underpinning distinctions between the Jewish majority and the Arab minority population, among them two laws that retroactively sanctioned the seizure of Palestinian property: the 1950 Absentee Property Law, which "rendered permanent the ostensibly temporary expropriation," and the 1953 Land Acquisition Law that legalized the seizure of any land not cultivated since 1948 by the "non-absentee" Palestinian population. By 1954 one third of Jewish Israelis were living or working on land appropriated through the absentee law.[70] Most of Israel's Palestinian citizens were under martial law, which lasted until 1966 (in "mixed cities" like Haifa, Jaffa, Ramle, and Lod it was lifted as early as 1951). Moreover, not all citizens of Israel had identical obligations. Palestinian citizens were not (and are not) conscripted to army service, and with few exceptions, especially among the Druze and Bedouin populations, do not serve in the army. They live in their own villages, towns, or neighborhoods, and send their children to separate schools. They are not part of the collective Israeli narrative and the Jewish ethos of the state. They are elected members of the Knesset, but excluded from the nation's political elite and from decision-making processes. Those who had fled or were expelled from Israel after its independence did not receive permission to return to the state. And, finally, there is the symbolic value of the Star of David in Israel's flag, the phrase of "a Jewish soul" in its national anthem, and the dominance of the Hebrew language, which made and makes it difficult for non-Jews to emotionally identify with the Jewish state.

Those critics who condemn the Zionist project as a "colonial settler state"[71] have maintained that Israel "was established by forcibly removing most of the indigenous majority from within its borders and then extending to those who remained a discrete set of rights and duties that only the settler community could determine."[72] On the other hand, those defending Israeli measures that keep the Arab population at a distance, argue that they are safeguards against a potential Trojan Horse within Israeli society: "The Israeli Arabs are a time bomb. Their slide into complete Palestinization has made them an emissary of the enemy that is among us. They are a potential fifth column. In both demographic and security terms they are liable to undermine the state. So that if Israel again finds itself in a situation of existential threat, as in 1948, it may be forced to act as it did then."[73]

There are also more nuanced ways to explain the status of Palestinians citizens in the Jewish state than by pointing the finger at the "colonial settler mentality" of the Jews or the "fifth column threat" of the Arabs. Explanations that condemn Zionism as a form of Western imperialism and colonialism, or even as the product of an alleged Jewish sense of superiority (as French President Charles de Gaulle did in an infamous phrase in the wake of the Six-Day War),[74] overlook the immediate historical context and its enormous emotional impact.[75] For most Jews (and many non-Jews), it was not just the eternal question of historical rights and who preceded whom as the "original" population of the land, but the very recent shadow of the Holocaust that informed their right of national sovereignty. If the pogroms of Russia, racist antisemitism in Germany and Austria, and the Dreyfus Affair in France were the immediate backdrop to the rise of political Zionism, the tragic consequences of the Holocaust quite plainly laid the foundations for the State of Israel.

Images of the piles of dead bodies in the camps at Bergen-Belsen and Buchenwald and of survivors on board of the

Exodus 1947, who were sent back by British authorities from the coast of Palestine to the "blood-stained soil" of Germany, were still fresh in the world's memory when Israel was born. In that hour, those who established this Jewish state were driven by one dominant thought: that in order to never again be victims, they would need their own state complete with all its symbols, myths, and privileges—even if these benefits came at the expense of others. The Marxist historian Isaac Deutscher, certainly no apologist for Israel, is credited with first telling the oft-to-be-retold parable about the Jew jumping from a burning building, who lands on a Palestinian, injuring him inadvertently by saving his own life.[76]

One could not very well expect the Palestinians to embrace the Zionist project and to live peacefully as a minority in a country they considered their own. After the first decades of Israel's existence, they had made certain material and cultural advances, and they enjoyed more rights of free speech and political diversity than the citizens of most Arab states. They also realized, however, that they paid a high price for these gains: they had no political sovereignty. Thus, it was hardly surprising that on the eve of the Six-Day War and Israel's territorial expansion, two thirds of Israel's Palestinian Arab citizens did not recognize the right of existence of the very state in which they lived.[77] Humiliation at being second-class citizens in their own land nourished their feelings of resentment, as expressed perhaps most painfully and angrily in Mahmoud Darwish's poem "Identity Card." It concludes with the following verses:

> Write down!
> I am an Arab
> You have stolen the orchards of my ancestors

And the land which I cultivated
Along with my children
And you left nothing for us
Except for these rocks.
So will the State take them
As it has been said?!

Therefore!
Write down on the top of the first page:
I do not hate people
Nor do I encroach
But if I become hungry
The usurper's flesh will be my food
Beware ! Beware ! Beware !
Of my hunger
And my anger![78]

Despite their growing anger, during the first two decades of the state's existence, "Palestinian national consciousness went through a latent period and remained submerged within the rise of the larger Arab national movement, driven by pan-Arabism, which ignited the imagination of many Arabs in Israel."[79] There are many reasons for this relative calm. In large part, it was the outcome of an internal struggle between the Palestinians during the last years of the British Mandate. While "the mainstream national movement maintained that the Zionist movement had to be fought to the bitter end . . . [t]he other camp . . . believed that the Zionists could not be defeated and that the common good of Palestinian Arabs demanded coexistence with Jews."[80] The 150,000 or so Palestinian Arabs left in Israel after 1949 lacked a strong middle class, a political elite, and structures that would enable organized resistance. For many years, the only political party that took account of their collective interests was the Communist Party—but most of them were far from identifying as Communists. Another factor behind the political quiescence of Israel's Palestinian population was the sophisticated system of state control, and a degree of fear of the Israeli army and police.[81] Finally, the relative success of attempts to integrate the Arab population into the new state's economic and cultural life should not be entirely overlooked. Their material situation slowly improved, as did their educational opportunities, their healthcare, and their housing. Many did not want to endanger these advantages.

WHERE IS THE NEW CANAAN?

In the early years of statehood there was also more radical opposition to the assumed connection between the Jewish state and the Jewish people. Already before the establishment of the State of Israel, a group of intellectuals had formed for the purpose of severing ties altogether between the Jewish diaspora and the Jews in their homeland. They called themselves "Canaanites," referring to the population that had lived in the land before the biblical Hebrews. For them, normalization of Jewish history meant only one thing: the end of Jewish history. There would be Jews who continued to live in the diaspora, and there would be Hebrews who lived in the Land of Israel.

For the Canaanite movement, which originated in the 1940s, Zionist ideology had achieved nothing but a relocation of diaspora Jews to the Middle East, a ghetto territory sunk in hostile surrounding, a "solution" that only landed the Jews in yet another state of exile. The Canaanites' understanding of normalization was that the Jews, once in their own state, would again become an Oriental people, closely connected to their Semitic relatives and would relinquish the condition of a universal people scattered in all the corners of the earth. Ties between the "Canaanites" in Israel and the "Jews" in the diaspora must be severed entirely, just as North Americans or Australians had detached themselves at one point from the British. Once the Jews had their own state, so they believed, they would cease being Jews and become Hebrews, an Oriental people with close ties to the Arab peoples around them, with whom they also shared historical ties. The Canaanites remained small in numbers, but they counted among them some influential intellectuals of the early State of Israel.

The term Canaanism is usually credited to Avraham Shlonsky, then literary editor of *Ha'aretz* and one of the most important Hebrew poets. He used it to describe a group of young poets (*Ivri'im ha-tze'irim*). The spiritual head of this group was Yonatan Ratosh who had grown up as Uriel Halperin in Warsaw and came to Palestine with his family at the age of 12 in 1920. He soon became an activist in Jabotinsky's Revisionist Movement. While in Paris he met Revisionist activist and Semitic language scholar A. G. Horon, who claimed that Hebrew was the language spoken in the region at large in antiquity. Ratosh and Horon saw as their mission there the uniting of the Jewish population in Palestine with those Muslims and Christians who lived in the region and who—in their view—were once part of a large Semitic family of nations, Hebrew in its origin. The outcome would be a modern Hebrew empire, reaching from the Mediterranean to the Euphrates.[82]

The most radical declaration of the Canaanite movement was Yonatan Ratosh's 1944 "Opening Speech at the Meeting of the Committee with Representatives of the Cell." While the murder of European Jewry was at its worst point, the Canaanites underscored their total separation from Diaspora Jewry and the Zionist movement: "As long as the land of the Hebrews is not be cleansed of Zionism and the hearts of the Hebrews made pure of Judaism, all efforts will be in vain and every sacrifice a wasted one. . . . [A]s long as the Hebrews will not fully recognize that Jewish history is a foreign history to us . . . Hebrew splendor will remain locked away, and the road to the Hebrew future will remain a desolate one."[83]

Not blood but soil became the main element of the Canaanite ideology. They wanted to unite all peoples of Semitic heritage into one state under Hebrew dominance. Ties with Jews who continued to live outside this state would be cut. The modern Canaanites in Israel had, they believed, nothing in common with people who were of Jewish religion and lived in Europe or America. This idea of a Hebrew nation separate from Diaspora Jewry attracted intellectuals from the left and the right. Uri Avnery, a German immigrant, who would later become one of Israel's leading left-wing intellectuals, a member of Knesset, and the publisher of the influential magazine *Ha-olam ha-ze* (This World), would sympathize with this idea, as did the right-wing Revisionist Hillel Kook (aka as "Peter Bergson," and the nephew of Palestine's first chief rabbi), who wrote in 1946: "We must state it clearly: the Jews in the United States do not belong to the Hebrew nation. These Jews are Americans of Hebrew descent."[84]

For the Canaanites, Hebrew-speaking Jews and their Arab-speaking neighbors would form one empire based on common heritage and territory. Once its ties with the Jewish diaspora were cut, the Canaanite empire would be what some Zionists had always proclaimed: a state just like all other states.

Of course, for most outside observers, the Canaanite way was anything but a normalization of Jewish history. Zionists objected to the suggestion that the doors of Palestine be closed for future generation of Jewish immigrants, and Arabs felt that the Canaanite plan was an imperialist and paternalistic concept that would put them under the thumb of a small Jewish minority.

Ratosh, though, held on to his view. Even after the Six-Day-War, he declared: "[There] emerged in this country at the turn of the last century a new nationality, namely that of the Hebrew nation. This new nationality emerged from within the geographic and linguistic framework of the classic Hebrew nation, which antedates Judaism."[85] Ratosh wanted to abolish the Law of Return and demanded schooling, army service, and immigration "without difference of extraction, faith or denomination." If Israel succeeded at integrating Kurdish and German and Yemenite Jews, the new Canaan might also integrate the Arab *fellahin*.[86]

The Canaanites' intention to integrate just like all other nations within the Middle East also went against the Zionist goal of becoming a "light unto the nations." Boaz Evron, a leading intellectual within the movement, expressed this rejection, in an interview after the Six-Day War: "I do not think that Israel, in order to justify its existence, must be a 'light unto the Gentiles.' No state needs or is required to justify its existence. Why must we?"[87] Baruch Kurzweil, an opponent of Canaanism and Israel's most important literary critic, regarded the movement as an ever-growing threat to the rule of secular Zionist thought. Some critics even saw in Ben-Gurion himself a secret supporter of Canaanism, as he distanced himself increasingly from the Jewish diaspora and from the history of the Zionist movement. According to Israel's most influential scholar of Jewish Studies, Gershom Scholem, "Ben-Gurion encouraged the Canaanites because he skipped directly to the Bible and rejected all exile. But he leapt into the moral Bible, while they turned to the pagan Bible."[88] For Scholem, the Canaanites were a modern faction that was paving a path out of Judaism: "Their victory would lead not to the creation of a new Hebrew nation but to the evolution of a small sect which in the tempest of historical dialectics would come to ruin. . . . The State of Israel is of value only because of the consciousness of Jewish continuity."[89]

The episode of the Canaanites may have pointed the way to an alternative history of Israel, but their plan had no chance of realization. The great majority of both Jews and Arabs rejected it. Jewish immigrants from Arab countries, whom the Canaanites were hopeful might accept their ideas, showed the least sympathy for this brainchild of a few Ashkenazi intellectuals. The Jews who immigrated from Yemen in 1949, from Iraq in 1951/2, and later from North Africa, and who substantially changed the nature of Israel's population, were not shaped by a European national movement but had internalized traditional and often religious feelings for the holy land, and arrived in Israel as a result of anti-Jewish and anti-Israeli sentiments in their countries of origin. Those who had other options usually did not go to Israel, as for example the Algerian Jews who were French citizens and almost in their entirety chose to live in France. Those who came to the Jewish state shared neither the utopian views of Theodor Herzl nor the socialist ideals of collectivism. The plans of the Canaanites were not attractive to them. Their relations to their Muslim neighbors were often strained, with memories of persecution and expulsion still fresh. Those who had experienced Jewish life under Arab rule were least likely to favor a joint Jewish-Arab enterprise.

Although Jews who came to Israel from Iraq and Syria, Egypt and Libya were migrating to a country in their geographic proximity, they were also taking a cultural journey from the Middle East to Europe. Israel was then a state with a clear Ashkenazi majority, with European values, and with basically all leadership positions in politics, economics, and culture occupied by European immigrants. The immigrants from Arab countries were considered by the European-Jewish establishment as in need of a reeducation if they were to fit into the dominant and allegedly higher Ashkenazi culture. In some extreme cases, state authorities took babies away from Yemenite Jewish mothers, whom they regarded as unable to raise their children, and passed them on to Ashkenazi parents.

While Canaanism in its radical form proved a failure, the implementation of the classical Zionist ideal of a "new Jew" who would be completely detached from the image of the diaspora Jew, was more successful. This ideal Jew became to be known as the "sabra," the Israeli-born Jew. Named after the cactus fruit (*tzabar*), which is prickly outside but sweet inside. It was a new character type that was intended to be tougher than the supposedly weak diaspora Jew. Sabras rejected Jewish history as an integral part of their identity, but regarded themselves instead as born anew in the Land of Israel. It is telling that the person credited with the birth of this image, the journalist and writer Dan Ben-Amotz, in his autobiography concealed the fact that he was actually born in Poland as Moshe Tehillimzeiger and only immigrated to Palestine as a teenager.

FIGURE 13. Moshe Dayan (right) with Jordanian officers, 1949.

A "typical" sabra, actually born in a kibbutz (although he grew up in a moshav, a similar agricultural cooperative, with more emphasis on the individual's achievements and lifestyle), was Moshe Dayan, who would become the embodiment of military heroism in Israel. On the occasion of the funeral of Roi Rotberg, who was shot in 1956 by Arab infiltrees while defending Kibbutz Nahal Oz near the Gaza Strip, Dayan coined the words that would become the classical description of the sabra: "We are a generation that settles the land and without the steel helmet and the cannon's maw, we will not be able to plant a tree and build a home. This is the fate of our generation. This is our life's choice—to be prepared and armed, strong and determined, lest the sword be stricken from our fist and our lives cut down."[90]

The sabra ideal was yet another attempt at fulfilling the dream of normalizing Jewish history by constructing a counter-ideal to the stereotype of the diaspora Jew. For other Israelis, though, normalizing their lives did not mean correcting Jewish history but rather integrating into the lifestyles of the Western world. Thus, during the 1960s, a new individualism arose in reaction to Ben-Gurion's "statism," to the kibbutz ideal of collectivism, and to the military spirit of *Tzahal* (the Israeli army), as embodied in the *Palmach* generation (the elite unit of the pre-state militia). The writer S. Yzhar used the term "Espresso generation" to brand young intellectuals who spent their time in coffee houses.[91] The women's journal *Ha-isha* announced a Miss Israel competition, which championed a female ideal quite different from the pioneer ideal promoted by the nation's leaders. Some young people joined the communist-inspired *matzpen* group, founded in 1962, which endorsed extra-parliamentary opposition and borrowed many positions from student protest movements around the world. Social unrest, from the Wadi Salib protests in Haifa to the Black Panther movement, shook the inner stability of the country and increased the dissatisfaction of Jews from Arab countries who increasingly felt like outsiders.[92]

The state tried to marginalize all of these movements that were directed against the collectivist ideal best embodied in Ben-Gurion's idea of statism (*mamlakhtiut*), the ideal that had dominated Israel's society during its first two decades. Official state institutions not only left their imprint on the country's economy, its legal system, and its education, but also on its cultural values.[93] The latter was composed of an eclectic mix of patriotism, socialism, and collectivism. A refusal to grant permission to the Beatles to perform in Israel in 1965 is representative for this attitude, as was the long-time resistance of

David Ben-Gurion and the Mapai party's leadership to the introduction of television. When finally, in 1968, the first Israeli TV channel launched, it was state-controlled and remained the country's only station for twenty years.[94]

By 1968, Ben-Gurion's successor, Levi Eshkol, had already been in office for five years. The transition from Ben-Gurion to Eshkol was a step, though only a small step, toward a new generation of politicians. Only nine years younger than his predecessor and like Ben-Gurion born in Eastern Europe, Eshkol belonged to the old guard of the Labor Party and represented its values. He lacked Ben-Gurion's charisma and is often characterized as a pragmatist who had no clear vision. He did, however, gradually introduce more openness and flexibility to political discourse, and the mere fact that the towering founding father of the state had handed over the scepter of leadership (and failed to grab it back a year later) marked a change not to be underestimated.[95]

Eshkol tried to bridge the gap between the dominant left and the oppositional right with a significant gesture. In contrast to Ben-Gurion, he allowed in 1964 the reinterment of Vladimir Jabotinsky's body in Israel's national cemetery at Mount Herzl, in near proximity to the graves of Israel's political leaders. The former Revisionists, transformed into the Herut (Freedom) party after the establishment of the state, gathered around the leadership of Menachem Begin, who played the role of perpetual opposition leader during the first two decades of Israel's statehood.

Much more than Jabotinsky, Begin put to use the idea of a special mission of the Jewish people in history and embraced religious values that were foreign to the secular founders of the movement. A Holocaust survivor himself, who had lost many family members in his native Poland, Begin was adamantly opposed to Ben-Gurion's rapprochement with West Germany and was unforgiving towards persons whom he regarded as Nazi collaborators. Most prominent among them was the Hungarian Zionist Rudolf Kastner, who was assassinated by a far-right extremist before he was cleared by a verdict of Israel's Supreme Court in 1958.[96]

The bitter rhetoric between Ben-Gurion and Begin, between the left and the right that had characterized the first two decades of Israeli politics would be laid aside when Israel faced an existential crisis. The political parties would join forces to form a national unity coalition that would for the first time include a cabinet post (without portfolio) for Menachem Begin. This moment of national unity arrived in June of 1967, when a new chapter of Israeli history began.

GREATER ISRAEL

A STATE EXPANDING

Well, the neighborhood bully, he's just one man
His enemies say he's on their land
They got him outnumbered about a million to one
He got no place to escape to, no place to run
He's the neighborhood bully

The neighborhood bully just lives to survive
He's criticized and condemned for being alive
He's not supposed to fight back, he's supposed to have thick skin
He's supposed to lay down and die when his door is kicked in
He's the neighborhood bully

—BOB DYLAN, "NEIGHBORHOOD BULLY," 1983

On November 10th, 1975, the 37th anniversary of *Kristallnacht*, the UN Plenary Assembly passed a resolution with 72 votes against 35 with 32 abstentions claiming that Zionism was "a form of racism and racist discrimination." This was the historic low in a rocky relationship between the United Nations and its member state Israel.[1] The UN had helped to create the State of Israel but there was not much love for the Jewish state in this and other international bodies. The story of Israel's alienation from international organizations reaches back to the 1950s. Thus, already in 1954, the World Health Organization's Eastern Mediterranean Region (EMRO) had split into two sub-committees: Sub-committee A consisted of all the Arab states, sub-committee B of Israel alone.[2] But it was only after 1967 that Israel was ostracized from the UN and many of its affiliated organizations. In 1974, UNESCO decided by a majority decision of its member states to withhold assistance from Israel in the fields of education, science, and culture because of Israel's alleged "persistent alteration of the historic features . . . of Jerusalem."[3] In 1982, the UN General Assembly branded Israel "not a peace-loving member state," thereby questioning its right to remain a UN member under article 4 of the UN charter, which states that the UN is open to all "peace-loving states."[4] During the late 1970s and early 1980s, almost half of all UN plenary resolutions directed against any specific state or states condemned Israel alone. Israel was excluded over these decades from all regional groups and thus suffered considerable restrictions as a UN member state.[5] After two thousand years, there was once again a Jewish state, but it was a state in isolation. Most countries did not have diplomatic relations with Israel during the 1970s and 80s, while its neighbors were officially still at war with the Jewish state. Until the late 1970s Israelis could not cross any border of their country legally.

Herzl's idea that the Jewish state would serve as the model society for all humankind seemed to have done an about-face a quarter century after its founding. For a large part of the world, Israel was not a model state but a pariah state.[6] No other was viewed with so much distrust and no other had its very right of existence questioned as frequently as did Israel. When Saul Bellow, the Canadian-born Nobel-prize winning novelist toured Israel in 1975, he came to the following conclusion: "The Jews did not become nationalistic because they drew strength from their worship of anything resembling German *Blut und Eisen* but because they alone amongst the peoples of the earth, had not established a natural right to exist unquestioned in the lands of their birth. This right is still not granted them, not even in the liberal West."[7] Israel was now regarded by many in the West, as well as closer to home as an imperialist, colonial, and anachronistic state. Within only a few years, in the view of large parts of the world, the Jews had been transformed from victims to persecutors, David had become Goliath. What had happened?

SEVENTH DAY REALITIES

Six days in June 1967 changed the very essence of the Jewish state. As a reaction to increasing threats from Egypt to eliminate "the Zionist entity" and triggered by President Nasser's closure of the Strait of Tiran at the southern tip of the Gulf of Aqaba, the Israeli army initiated a preventive strike on June 5th, 1967. After a few hours almost the entire Egyptian air force had been destroyed, after two days East Jerusalem was under Israeli control, and after six days the war, which by now also involved Jordan, Syria, Lebanon, and Iraq was over. Israel ruled the Sinai Peninsula, the Gaza Strip, the West Bank of the Jordan River, East Jerusalem, and the Golan Heights—a territory more than three times larger than just a week earlier. Most significantly, the Jewish state now administered a substantial Palestinian population.[8]

The relationship between Israel and the Jewish world also began to shift considerably in 1967. While before the Six-Day War solidarity between Jewish communities and Israel was mainly passive and largely restricted to financial support, a wave of enthusiasm such as never had been known before swept over Jews around the globe. The memory of the Holocaust was still very much alive, and with it came the realization that now, unlike in Europe a quarter century earlier, American Jews actually could help Jews in their hour of exis-

MAP 4. Israel after the Six-Day War, 1967.

Within the map:

Israeli territory from 1949 until 1967

Territory conquered by Israel during the Six-Day War (June 5 – June 10, 1967)

Tripoli

LEBANON

Beirut

Damascus

SYRIA

Golan

Mediterranean Sea

Acre

Haifa

Nazareth

Jenin

Nablus

Tel Aviv

Allenby Bridge

Ramallah

Amman

Jerusalem

Jericho

Bethlehem

Gaza

Hebron

Dead Sea

Beer Sheba

ISRAEL

Negev Desert

JORDAN

Ma'an

Port Said

Suez Canal

Cairo

Suez

Sinai

Eilat

Aqaba

EGYPT

Golf of Suez

Golf of Aqaba

SAUDI ARABIA

0 20 40 60 80 100 km

Sharm el Sheikh

tential danger. During the war, many took to the streets to express solidarity with the Jewish state, others traveled to Israel to fill positions in civil life that had been vacated by soldiers on reserve duty. After the war, Israel's image had changed from that of a tiny nation in a far remote part of the world to a major military power. Israel was no longer the poor little brother who needed support but a strong state that would defend the lives of Jews in all corners of the world. In the eyes of many observers, this new identification with Israel became the new secular religion for most American Jews.[9] Some joined in the actual religious enthusiasm that was spreading in Israel over the reunification of Jerusalem and the conquest of the holy sites in Hebron and interpreted these events as the beginnings of the messianic age.[10] American Jewish organizations, such as the American Jewish Committee, which had traditionally been cautious in their position towards Israel, became unequivocal in their support after 1967.[11]

In Europe, too, many Jews were astonished at the triumph of the Israeli military and Israel's sudden control over Jewish holy sites. The French Jewish scholar André Néher, who held a chair in Jewish Studies at the University of Strasbourg and was a close collaborator of the philosopher Emmanuel Levinas, experienced a genuine awakening with the Six-Day War. In the wake of the war, he called on all French Jews to immigrate to Israel, and regarded the unification of Jerusalem as not only a military triumph, but "an event of mystical and messianic significance."[12] In Munich, as in other German cities, large street demonstrations were held in support of the Jewish state, featuring leading political speakers.[13]

In Israel, this transformation among diaspora and especially American Jewry was duly registered. In the words of one of Israel's leading intellectuals, Gershom Scholem, who served as president of the Israeli Academy of Sciences and Humanities from 1968 to 1974, "Till the Six Day War they were saying that the real State of Israel is in New York, since the largest and most creative concentration of Jews was located there. Today they have stopped speaking in this style. Something happened to them. They have had the feeling, prior to the Six Day War, that here in Israel there was going to be a second Auschwitz, while their hands were tied and they were unable to do anything. They would not even be able to say afterwards that they didn't know, as they did after the Holocaust, for it was published in the press, in the Arab propaganda, on television. And that was a severe trauma: the sense of recurring Holocaust that arose among the Jewish intellectuals abroad."[14]

The Six-Day War, a military triumph of a dimension almost unprecedented in history, had of course an even more profound impact on Israeli society itself. The self-confidence of Israelis rose. Through its enlarged territory the small country's security seemed safer than before. The distance between Tel Aviv and the Jordanian border had been barely fifteen miles before the war, now a larger security buffer was added. The new euphoria was nourished by religious sentiments as well: the *kotel*, the Western Wall of Jerusalem, was now under Israeli control, as was the Cave of the Patriarchs and Matriarchs in Hebron.

The year 1967 was in many respects a second founding of the State of Israel. Just as in 1948, there was talk of a "miracle," but this time it was dressed in explicitly religious language. The messianic reading of the events of June 1967 resulted in a reinterpretation of the very existence of the state. The dawn of a messianic era seemed to have broken. Moshe Unna, one of the few Orthodox rabbis who was actually critical of such language, wrote: "The events were not only sensed but also explained as an 'obvious miracle.' The belief in immediate redemption, in which religious Zionism is grounded, was transformed into active fervor during those days. Many saw in these events signs of the coming of the messiah. . . . The obligation was now to keep the Promised Land and not to return it to strangers."[15]

Israeli intellectuals differed widely in their understanding of the events. On the eve of the war, Ehud Ben Ezer had conducted numerous interviews centered on the spiritual condition in Israel. Back then, most of his interviewees stressed the special moral obligation of Israel to be a model state, "a light unto the nations." Martin Buber, the first president of Israel's Academy of Sciences and Humanities, had warned against an attitude that identified "revival" with "normalization." Like his old acquaintance, Ahad Ha'am, Buber saw the risk of a "national assimilation, one more dangerous than any individual assimilation for the latter affects only the individuals and families concerned, while the former eats at the kernel of Israel's selfhood."[16] Yeshayahu Leibowitz, an Orthodox Jewish scientist, philosopher, and (for many) Israel's moral conscience, had stressed "the unique historic destiny" of the Jewish people. Israel could not be a state like any other state. He even suggested relinquishing its membership in the United Nations, as its historic role must be "in accordance with this historic and national uniqueness."[17]

When Ehud Ben Ezer to some of his interviewees after the 1967 war, many liberal intellectuals feared that stressing the role of Israel's uniqueness would now have a very different meaning: it would no longer express the prophets' ideal of a "light unto the nations" but lend support to the rising hubris over its triumphant victory and to the new form of messianic euphoria. They saw their role now as advocating for a sense of normality. No one took up this role more passionately than the writer A. B. Yehoshua. He believed that without the conflict, Israel actually would have reached the Zionist goal of normalization: "I believe that the basic aim of Zionism has been fulfilled. I do not consider Zionism an all-embracing ideology, neither a way of life nor some kind of social philosophy, but first and foremost a historical act, the aim of which was to bring about a certain normalization of the Jewish problem by concentrating part of the Jewish people, territorially, in a state of their own. Had we not become involved as we did with the Arabs, Zionism would indeed have brought this normalization to the Jewish people, and its main task would be almost completely fulfilled."[18]

After 1967, Yehoshua saw many of Israel's most important achievements endangered. He expressed serious worries over the fact that many Israelis viewed their victory as the beginning of the messianic age and retroactively interpreted the establishment of the state as yet another part of a divine plan. For him this religious interpretation of Zionism constituted a "betrayal of Zionism which sees settlement in all the territories of Greater Israel as a value that is messianic and sacrosanct, which sees not the Jewish people's survival and normalization as the main thing, but a situation of expansion and territorial settlement, and a life in continuous conflict with the Arabs, and hence with the entire world."[19] Fifteen years after the war, Yehoshua's colleague Amos Oz confessed: "Perhaps there was, on all sides, a latent messianism. A messiah complex. Perhaps we should have aimed for less. Perhaps there was a wild pretension here, beyond our capabilities—beyond human capabilities. Perhaps we must limit ourselves and forgo the rainbow of messianic dreams."[20]

During the decade after the Six-Day War, intellectuals world-wide repositioned themselves on the question of Israel's special role among the nations. In Paris, Jean-Paul Sartre's journal, *Les Temps Modernes*, issued a special issue on *Le conflit israélo-arabe* in June 1967. Israel's new role as an occupying power that would shape its image, especially with the European left, began to take shape. In Chicago, Saul Bellow took up a position against Sartre, who claimed that one had to expect more from Israel than from other states. Bellow replied: "But since Israel's sovereignty is questioned and world opinion is not ready to agree that it is indeed a country like other countries, to demand more is cruelly absurd."[21] In Cambridge, the philosopher and literary critic George Steiner scorned Israel as a provincial "Jewish Albania," which caused Gershom Scholem to remind him of the historical task of Zionism to return the Jews to the normal course of history: "He is trying to live outside of history, while we in Israel are living responsibly, inside of history."[22] Scholem admitted that Zionism did not yet achieve this task. The world-renowned scholar of Jewish mysticism and messianism recognized, perhaps more than anyone else, the immediate danger that justifying the recent events through messianic and teleological arguments posed.

There were also intellectuals in Israel who were swept away with the religious and nationalistic trends in the post-67 era and saw, finally, an opportunity for Israel to achieve what it had failed to do in 1948: to restore the completeness of the land and to create a Jewish state in the Greater Land of Israel. Some of them, among them the writers Shmuel Yosef Agnon, Nathan Alterman, Uri Zvi Greenberg, und Moshe Shamir, signed a petition demanding that the territories occupied in 1967 never be returned.[23]

FIGURE 14. Shlomo Goren, Chief Rabbi of Israel's army, blows the shofar at the Western Wall after Israeli troops take control of Jerusalem's Old City on June 8th, 1967.

For Alterman the events of 1967 had eliminated the temporary distinction between the State of Israel and the Land of Israel, between the biblical territory and the modern secular state: "The land and the state are henceforth one essence," he wrote.[24] His colleague Moshe Shamir, who like Alterman had once been part of secular socialist Zionism, saw in the reunification of Jerusalem a sign of the approaching Messianic era. Zionism's task was finally fulfilled, he argued.[25] Shamir, who later became a member of the right-wing Likud party in the Knesset and cofounded the nationalistic Tehiya Party, was convinced that Israel would never be accepted by its neighbors. For him, the Six-Day War was just one more in the long chain of events aimed at the destruction of the Jewish people. The Jews, he claimed, were unlike any other people. They had been the target of unjustified attacks over millennia. The

Jewish state would not be able to change this basic feature of humanity, but it could lend the Jews new self-confidence. Only in their own state would they be strong enough to take on the fight against the rest of the world.[26]

As historian Noam Zadoff demonstrated, Moshe Shamir's identification with the idea of a Greater Israel represents continuity rather than a break with the ideals of the old Israeli left. A kibbutz member for a few years, and deeply immersed in the socialist ideals of the left-wing *Hashomer ha-tza'ir* movement and the Mapam party, Shamir's thinking had always combined socialism and nationalism, and Marxist ideals with the goals of a Greater Israel. When the latter seemed within reach after 1967, his nationalist sentiments overpowered the socialist ones. Shamir was joined by some former leaders of the left-wing establishment, most notably former Mapam and kibbutz movement leader Yitzchak Tabenkin, in his conviction that the land conquered in the Six-Day War should not be returned. He also became a proponent of the idea that the kibbutz movement had become complacent and was replaced by the settler movement whose pioneering spirit sought the achievement of the Greater Israel idea.[27]

Soon after the war, some warning voices raised concern about the ensuing euphoria. Among the most articulate was philosopher Yeshayahu Leibowitz, who claimed that Israel had transformed the military triumph of the Six-Day War into a historical disaster on the seventh day: "On the seventh day we had to decide—and we were free to decide—whether that war was one of defense or of conquest. Our decision turned into a war of conquest, with all that it implied. Not only was the character of the state altered; the very foundation of its existence assumed a new aspect. The change was not simply of quantity but of substance."[28] Leibowitz belonged to the declining faction in the national-religious camp that clung adamantly to the original Mizrahi position. For him, the State of Israel solved practical problems for the Jewish people, but should not be regarded as a tool advancing the redemption of the Jewish people and the advent of the messianic age. He argued that the Jewish religious laws, *halakha*, were shaped in a time when Jews had no state. They were appropriate for a diaspora people but could not be applied as state law without major adaptations. Thus, for him, Israel was a "state of the Jews" rather than a "Jewish state."[29]

The consequences of the Six-Day War, Leibowitz argued, altered the character of the state and replaced older values with new ones. He pointed to the *kotel*, the Wailing Wall, as an example. The secular Zionist pioneers did not quite know what to do with the remnant of Herod's outer temple walls, which had served as a symbol of the old religious Jewish community in the Land of Israel. When this part of the city was under Jordanian occupation after 1948, the leadership of the state created a new sanctified space in the western part of the city on Mt. Herzl, where the remnants of Theodor Herzl and his family were reinterred, and where the leaders of the new state and its fallen soldiers were to find a permanent home. When Herzl's tomb was built, it was deliberately placed on an axis with the Western Wall so as to juxtapose the symbol of national destruction with the symbol of national revival.[30]

In an essay published twenty years after these events under the title, *ha-kir o ha-har* (The Wall or the Mountain), A. B. Yehoshua juxtaposed the Western Wall and Mount Herzl. For Yehoshua, these two places symbolized two opposing modes of memory in the State of Israel. The *kotel*—as the Western Wall is known in Hebrew—was for him a purely religious symbol that called to mind the destructions of the Jewish past. It had neither redeeming value nor aesthetic quality. Mount Herzl, on the other hand, was a place that projected pride for

FIGURE 15. Jews pray at the Western Wall before 1948, when it was accessible only through a narrow alley.

the whole nation. As opposed to the Western Wall, which is dominated by the commanding sight of the two Muslim holy places above it, Mount Herzl was, "a complete place, an autonomous unit, which is not hit or threatened by any foreign element." In his vision of a future Jewish-Palestinian com-

FIGURE 16. Jewish men and women (separated by a barrier) pray at the Western Wall in July 1967, just after the creation of a large plaza.

monwealth, Yehoshua saw the Western Wall reduced to minor status as part of the religious landscape of East Jerusalem, while Mount Herzl would become the undisputed symbol of memory for secular Israel.[31]

Contrary to Yehoshua's hopes, the *kotel* was reclaimed right after the events of 1967 as the symbol not only of Jewish but also of Israeli Jerusalem and of the state in its new shape. Before the war, there was only a small alley in front of the wall, bordered by the so-called Moroccan quarter. Within days the quarter was razed and a huge new plaza rose in its stead. This site became the symbolic center of the new state, including its secular population. It became the site of public swearing-in ceremonies for Israeli soldiers and for Bar Mitzvah celebrations by Jews from around the world. On Shabbat and the Jewish holidays, thousands gathered there in prayer. Leibowitz, the religious Jew and philosopher, sarcastically suggested putting up a discotheque at the site and calling it the "Divine Discotheque." The newspaper *Ha'aretz* published Leibowitz's letter under the headline "Diskotel."[32]

The recapture of the wall was indeed *the* iconic moment of the 1967 military triumph. In an address to the Knesset in 1995, then Prime Minister Yitzhak Rabin, who in 1967 had been Chief of Staff of the Israeli Defense Forces, recalled his impressions: "There was one moment in the Six-Day War which symbolized the great victory: that was the moment in which the first paratroopers . . . reached the stones of the Western Wall, feeling the emotion of the place; there never was, and never will be, another moment like it. Nobody staged that moment. Nobody planned it in advance. Nobody prepared it and nobody was prepared for it; it was as if Providence had directed the whole thing: the paratroopers weeping—loudly and in pain—over their comrades who had fallen along the way, the words of the Kaddish prayer heard by Western Wall's stones after 19 years of silence, tears of mourning, shouts of joy, and the singing of 'Hatikvah'" [the Israeli national anthem].[33]

Religious and national elements were intertwined from the very moment the wall was captured by Israeli troops. When the staff of the Israeli army loaded the command-car in which they were to follow the paratroopers to the Western Wall, they took along a Torah scroll, a shofar, and a bench—to perform exactly the acts the British authorities had once prohibited. Performing them showed Israel and the world that the Jews had returned to the wall and were in full control of it.[34]

The centrality of the capture or "liberation" of the wall was reinforced by visual images of the Israeli military appearing at this site in the middle of the Six-Day War. David Rubinger's iconic photographs of Israeli paratroopers being moved by the two-thousand-year-old stones and of Military Chief Rabbi Shlomo Goren blowing the shofar show a blending of military and religious messages. They helped to turn the wall from a symbol of national destruction into a symbol of military triumph.

The new symbolism of the wall for secular Jews was captured well in the lines that Eliezer (aka Elie) Wiesel wrote on June 16, 1967: "It is me standing and looking at [the wall], as if struck by a dream. Looking at it, holding my breath, as looking at a living body, omnipotent and almighty. A human essence that transcended itself—and those observing it—beyond and above time. An essence that transferred me into a far away and uncanny place, in which stones too, have their own will, their own fate and memory."[35]

The swearing-in ceremonies for Israeli soldiers held at the wall contributed further to this merging of its religious and military meanings. The site became again a place of international pilgrimage, with the pilgrims paying homage now also to Israel's military triumph, as the *Jerusalem Post* stated in 1971:

> [. . .] Tisha B'Av [the fast day in memory of the destruction of both temples] at the Western Wall is becoming ever more an international Jewish Holiday and ever less a day of mourning. To the tens of thousands of Israelis and tour-

ists who swarmed to the Old City last night when the fast commenced, the Wall was obviously more of a reminder of the Israeli victory four years ago, than of the Jewish defeat and destruction of the Temple 1901 years ago.[36]

Clearly, the erstwhile religious connotation of the wall was now supplemented or replaced by its national meaning. In a poll taken in the early 1980s, only 7.4 percent of secular Israelis viewed the wall as a primarily religious symbol, while every second nonreligious Israeli regarded it as primarily a national symbol, with the rest viewing it as of equal religious and national significance.[37]

The main political question now was not about Jerusalem, but about the future of the rest of the newly conquered territories. The Hebrew University's best-known historian, Jacob Talmon, a prominent opponent of the concept of a Greater Israel, remembered how Prime Minister Levi Eshkol had assured him personally that he had no interest in keeping these territories: "He was happy that 'at last we have something we can bargain with.'"[38] Talmon prophesied in 1970: "Should this state of war between Jews and Arabs, which has lasted already 50 years continue for another 50 years . . . there will be no victors and no vanquished, but mutual general destruction." And he continued: "The preoccupation with security, however natural and justifiable, so often becomes a self-defeating obsession. Which state in the world has ever enjoyed security, and particularly now in the age of nuclear, chemical and biological warfare? The axiom of the eternity of Arab hatred and active hostility is suicidal."[39]

Among the young, there were also voices of warning. One of them was the twenty-eight-year old writer Amos Oz, who together with Avraham Shapira and other kibbutz dwellers, interviewed Israeli soldiers about their experiences in the war. This collection, which became a bestseller and was translated into English under the title *The Seventh Day* was not a story of heroism and martyrdom but rather a tale about the burden of triumph. Oz warned early on of the consequences of occupation: "For a month, for a year, or for a whole generation we will have to sit as occupiers in places that touch our hearts with their history. And we must remember: as occupiers, because there is no alternative. And as a pressure tactic to hasten peace. Not as saviors or liberators. Only in the twilight of myths can one speak of the liberation of a land struggling under a foreign yoke. Land is not enslaved and there is no such thing as a liberation of lands. There are enslaved people, and the word 'liberation' applies only to human beings. We have not liberated Hebron and Ramallah and El-Arish, nor have we redeemed their inhabitants. We have conquered them and we are going to rule over them only until our peace is secured."[40]

The public debate over the future of the newly acquired territories would emerge as the major rift in Israeli society over the next fifty years. Immediately after the war, Prime Minister Levi Eshkol entrusted a small committee consisting of four military intelligence officials with the question of what to do with the newly acquired lands. On June 14, 1967, the committee came to the conclusion that there should be two main guiding principles: "the security of the State of Israel" and "achieving peace." The ideal solution that they recommended required achieving "both security and peace . . . the establishment of an independent Palestinian state, under the Israeli Defense Forces, and in agreement with the Palestinian leadership." The committee endorsed withdrawal to the 1949 armistice lines with the exception of East Jerusalem. The document summarized its proposals as follows: "We repeatedly emphasize that if we wish to arrive at a peace agreement, and an agreement that [will] last for long, we must be generous and daring as we approach the Palestinians. Any other way—even if it leads to achievements in the present—would only sow the seeds of destruction for the future."[41] Shortly after the war, Oz published an article in which he questioned whether Israel in fact had any historical borders, maintaining that its historical borders had always changed over time.[42]

Should Israel hold on to the territories or give them back? If only some territories would remain part of Israel—then which ones? Should the legitimation for keeping control rest in security interests or rather ideological and theological considerations? The Israeli public was divided. One month after the war, 60 percent thought that at least a part of the conquered territories should be returned in exchange for a peace agreement with the Arabs. But 90 percent were in favor of keeping East Jerusalem under any circumstances, and 85 percent thought the same about the Golan Heights. One third wanted to keep all of the territories.[43] Many Israelis waited for the phone call from the Arab leaders that never came, to use Moshe Dayan's famous phrase. Instead of an offer to exchange land for peace, the Arab world decided to make no concessions toward Israel. At the Arab leaders' summit that began on August 29th, 1967, in Khartoum, they issued their "three no's": no to peace with Israel, no to negotiations with Israel, and no to the recognition of Israel. The adamant position of the Arab leaders played into the hands of those in Israel who regarded the territories as more than just a bargaining chip.

To this day Israel continues to be without clearly defined and universally recognized borders. There are the borders of the UN partition plan of 1947, the borders of the 1949 armistice, and the borders of the land controlled by Israel since

1967. There are the traditional borders of the Revisionists—the party of Jabotinsky and Begin—who held fast to the idea of a Jewish state on both sides of the River Jordan until the 1950s. And there are the borders created by Menachem Begin's government after the return of the Sinai Peninsula to Egypt and the annexation of East Jerusalem and the Golan Heights in the 1980s. Later came the border of the "Separation Barrier" next to the "Green Line," land swaps, and plans of complete annexation. But there is no border universally recognized by the world community or agreed internally by Israel's public.

MESSIANIC VISIONS

The age of euphoria came to an end at the latest only six years after it had begun. When Egypt and Syria attacked Israel in a surprise action on the Jewish holiday of Yom Kippur in October of 1973, the Jewish state struggled for its survival. It took only a few days but significant human losses before the Israeli army had restored its earlier predominance. Israel was more isolated in the international community than six years before. Most Western European countries, under pressure from an Arab oil embargo, refused to aid Israel. Internally, the government of Golda Meir was made responsible for being unprepared by the Arab attack.

Golda Meir (Myerson) had become prime minister after the death of Levi Eshkol in 1969. Like her predecessor, she belonged to the old guard of the Labor Party, but she became the symbol of a new development in world politics as well. She was the first democratically elected woman prime minister in the world who did not follow a family member as the country's political leader.[44] Meir was no feminist, but for many observers her political career in the young state of Israel—which included the posts of ambassador to Moscow, labor minister, and foreign minister—served as proof that Israel was not only a light unto the nations, but also a model state as regards gender equality. A closer look reveals, however, that in fact less than 10 percent of Knesset members were at that time women. By 1988, their percentage had dropped to under 6% (7 out of 120 Knesset members), and no other women has so far been elected prime minister or president, although two women served as chief justices. The traditional public/private gender dichotomy continued to exist in Israel, just as in many other Western states, despite a much different and progressive rhetoric.[45]

Less than one year later, after the Yom Kippur War, Golda Meir resigned as prime minister. She was followed by Yitzhak Rabin, who stepped down in April of 1977, after a small private bank account that his wife had opened in Washington during his tenure as Israeli ambassador was discovered. Shimon Peres was acting prime minister until new elections were called in May 1977. The political scandals, the economic crisis, and unrest among the Palestinian population, combined with the feeling of many Jewish immigrants from Arab states that they were second-class citizens led to a political earthquake. When news anchor Chaim Yavin announced the election results, he began with the historic words: "Ladies and gentlemen, a revolution [*mahapakh*]."[46]

After decades in opposition, the leader of the nationalist right, Menachem Begin, had come to power. Begin's Zionism was carved of different stuff from that of his opponents. He had grown up in Poland, fled during the war, lost most of his family in the Holocaust, and was decisively stamped by these experiences, as well as by his underground fight against the British authorities, who pursued him as a terrorist. In contrast to his predecessors, Begin also had an openly displayed affinity for Jewish religious tradition. Even though he did not lead a life as an observant Jew, he tried to keep the Sabbath and to display his positive relationship towards Judaism in public.

This became clear on the evening of his election, when television viewers were witness to a rather unusual scene. In Likud headquarters a group played traditional Hassidic melodies and a bearded Jew blew the shofar. There was a messianic feel in the air.[47] Before asking the centrist Dash Party to join his coalition, Begin invited the ultra-Orthodox parties. In his first speech after the election he underlined that "the Jewish people have an eternal historic right to the Land of Israel, the land of our forefathers—an unassailable right."[48]

This was not just election rhetoric. When Begin traveled to see US President Jimmy Carter in Washington in the summer of 1977, he stopped first in New York to pay a publicly celebrated visit at 770 Eastern Parkway in Brooklyn, the home of the Lubavitcher Rebbe, a leader of the Hasidic movement, who would be celebrated as the messiah after his death by some of his supporters. And in 1982, Begin was instrumental in prohibiting the national carrier El Al from flying on the Shabbat and Jewish holidays.

Begin was convinced that the Jews were a unique people with a unique destiny. But by "uniqueness" he meant something quite different from Ben-Gurion's sense of the word. Ben-Gurion had combined prophetic teachings and socialist principles in his efforts to create a model state, and while biblical writings had influenced Begin as well, his heroes were not the prophets, but the ancient fighters—from Joshua to King David—associated with the Jewish return to the Land of Israel and the establishment of the kingdom of Israel. He was pro-

FIGURE 17. Newly elected Prime Minister Menachem Begin visits the Lubavitcher Rebbe on his way to meet with President Carter, July 17, 1977.

foundly attentive to the actions of the many enemies of the Jewish people mentioned in the Bible, from the Amalekites to Haman.

Begin regarded the Jewish state that had come to birth after the Holocaust as a continuation of the eternal tensions in Jewish history between triumph and tragedy. He regarded himself first as a Jew and only second as an Israeli. That is how his closest affiliates saw him as well. One of them, Yehuda Avner, who had worked with Golda Meir and Yitzhak Rabin before, said once that Begin was Israel's first "Jewish" prime minister.[49]

More than his predecessors, Begin cared about the relationship between Israel and Jewish communities around the world. In the early fifties, he suggested the creation of a new body consisting of representatives from Israel and from the Jewish diaspora that would decide critical issues for the entire Jewish people; such issues as for example the negotiations with post-war Germany, which Begin violently opposed.[50] Even

though no such body ever materialized, he and his successor
Yitzhak Shamir redefined in significant ways the meaning of
a Jewish state. It was no longer simply a state for the Jewish
people, or a state with a Jewish majority, but a state in which
Jewish religious values were cultivated and where the love for
the Land of Israel was elevated to prime importance. Occasionally, Begin's particularism could also become an expression of universalism. His first act as prime minister was to
grant asylum to Vietnamese boat refugees who were drifting
aimlessly in the Chinese Sea.

In general terms, however, the direction that the right now
took was toward a new collectivism that replaced the ideals of
the Israeli left. As a result of the decline of institutions such as
the kibbutz, the *Histadrut* (labor union), and the Labor Party,
the left was gradually embracing individualistic values and the
Americanization of Israeli society. Taking a path quite unlike
that in many other countries, where conservative political parties were identified with libertarian values and support for a
minimal role of the state as a guardian of public safety, the
Israeli right had always championed a strong state, while at
the same time advocating privatization of the economic sector.
The right's communitarian discourse circled around the motif
of the Jewish people's special mission and embraced Jewish
immigrants from the Arab world who had felt marginalized
by the ruling Labor Party elite.[51]

The 1960s had initiated a change in the social fabric. From
a society based almost exclusively on East and Central European traditions, there emerged an Israel increasingly composed of immigrants from Arab countries. Reflecting the
Yemenite and Iraqi immigrations in the early years of statehood and the North African Jewish immigration that culminated in the 1960s, Israeli society began to look less European.

This could be detected first, and on many levels, in popular culture. Falafel and hummus replaced gefilte fish and chopped liver as the national food of Israel and the public radio stations now played "Mizrahi music." The predominant popular music in the early decades of statehood had been the so-called "Songs of the Land of Israel," whose Eastern European tunes were unfamiliar to immigrants from North Africa and the Middle East. These were followed by pop and rock music from the English-speaking world and their Hebrew adaptations. Sephardi and Mizrahi songs from Greece to Yemen were at first mainly disseminated through tapes, then gradually gained legitimacy and were played on the state radio stations. By the turn of the century, they had become Israel's most popular music.[52]

In the 1960s, Israeli cinema depicted Jews from Arab countries as stereotypes, the most popular "Mizrahi" figure on the screen being Sallah Shabbati, a Moroccan immigrant and primitive male chauvinist, who walked funny and talked funny. He was played by an Ashkenazi actor, Topol (who later would play Tevye in *Fiddler on the Roof*), and the film was directed by Hungarian-born satirist Ephraim Kishon. In her seminal study on early Israeli cinema, Ella Shohat wrote in the late 1980s that Israeli cinema remained "Eurotropic."[53] But by then, the tide had already begun to turn. In the 1990s, Mizrahi movies were among the most successful, ambitious, and sophisticated of Israeli films, and they were written by members of the community itself. Films like Shmuel Hasfari's *Sh'hur* (1993), Savi Gabizon's *Lovesick on Nana Street* (1995), and Doron Tabari's *Shuli's Guy* (1997) dealt with Mizrahi identity politics and often contained religious motifs.[54]

It was on the political level, however, that the Mizrahi fight for integration and influence proved most successful. The Shas

Party was more than a religious party. Established in 1984 under the spiritual leadership of former Sephardic Chief Rabbi Ovadia Yosef, it provided assistance and material help, child-care, and religious services to all strata of the Mizrahi population. Most important, it gave them self-confidence and political empowerment. The party reached its peak in the late 1990s, when it received nineteen out of the 120 seats in the Knesset. "The traditional *Edot Ha mizrach*, now redefined as *Mizrahim*, were newly empowered under the common 'Judaic' denominator."[55] The triumph of Shas also marked the breakthrough of religious traditionalism into mainstream Israeli society. Unlike secular or ultra-Orthodox Ashkenazi Jews, many Jews from North Africa and the Middle East held fast to a set of religious beliefs and practices. They rejected the secular and often anti-religious ideology of early Zionism and viewed adoration of the state as idolatry. Instead, they brought religion back into the mainstream of Israel's political culture.

Jews in Arab countries could, theoretically, have become pioneers in the dialogue with Palestinian Israelis. Many of them shared the Palestinians' language, their food, and their music. But in politics, they often proved to be hardliners. They helped Likud to come to power and to stay in power.

Under Begin and his successor Yitzhak Shamir, the national-religious settler movement became a legitimate sector of society. The "settlers" (a term that was now used only for the Jewish settlements in the recently conquered territories) saw themselves as the new Zionist elite, replacing the old pioneers who had founded the kibbutz system and the Labor Party. Just as the earlier pioneers had drained the swamps and made the desert blossom while studying Marx, so these pioneers took possession of all religiously important places with Bibles in their hands. This is how Pinchas Wallerstein, a long-time spokesman for the settler movement, expressed this new self-understanding: "We followed Labor's ethos and used Labor's methods. In the last quarter of the twentieth century we did in Samaria what Labor did in the Valley of Harod in the first quarter of the twentieth century."[56]

The settler movement was inspired less by Herzl than by Rabbi Abraham Isaac Kook, Palestine's first Chief Rabbi, who in contrast to most Orthodox Jews of his generation interpreted the establishment of a Jewish state as the advent of the messianic age. Although he himself died in 1935 and did not live to see the founding of the state, his disciples, and especially his son Rabbi Zvi Yehuda Kook, invoked his legacy when referring to the holiness of the land. On the eve of the Six-Day War, the aged Zvi Yehuda Kook delivered a speech in which he recalled his emotional state after the UN partition decision of 1947:

> Where is our Hebron—are we forgetting it?! Where is our Shechem—are we forgetting it?! And our Jericho . . . our East Bank?! Where is each and every clod of earth? Every last bit, every four cubits of the Land Of Israel? Can we forego even one millimeter of them? God forbid! Shaken in all my body, all wounded and in pieces, I couldn't, then, rejoice.[57]

Just as Ahad Ha'am had felt like a mourner at a wedding party when attending the First Zionist Congress and as Ben-Gurion found himself thinking of the Jewish victims during the UN partition decision, so Kook suffered, albeit for very different reasons, when all around him were celebrating. This speech set the tone for the settler movement's notion of the holiness of the complete land of Greater Israel (*eretz yisrael ha-shlema*).

Only a few weeks after this speech, his vision became reality. Now Hebron, Shechem (Nablus), and Jericho were ruled by the Israeli army. Zvi Yehuda Kook became the spiritual father of the movement, which rebelled both against the passivity of traditional Orthodoxy and the secularism of the Zionist movement. In one dramatic action he draped himself in an Israeli flag in a synagogue and proclaimed: "This flag is no less holy than the velvet cloth covering the Torah ark behind me."[58]

The fundamental change in the character of the State of Israel after 1967 was very much related to the new territory of the Land of Israel now under Jewish control. The situation is aptly described by sociologist Baruch Kimmerling: "The establishment of the State of Israel alongside the sanctified territory of the 'Promised Land,' but not in this core territory, helped the Zionist sociopolitical system create a secular society and protect the state's autonomy in the face of pressure from religious and nationalist groups. With the conquest of the West Bank and its redefinition as 'Judea and Samaria,' the situation changed dramatically. The encounter between the sacred and the mundane provided several advantages for groups capable of exchanging 'holiness' for participation in the system, and these advantages continued to increase given the primordial components of the state's identity. . . . Thus, the settlers of 'Judea and Samaria' pushed Rabbi Abraham Isaac Kook's teachings to their logical extreme. The reunion of the 'People of Israel' with the whole 'Land of Israel' meant the termination of the first part of the redemption process. All that remained was to create a society based on halachic law: 'Israel's Torah,' in their terminology."[59]

The beginnings of the settler movement long predate Begin's tenure as prime minister. The government especially appreciated the strategic value of settling the land between Jordan and the Israeli core state. "More than deciding on settlement, the government drifted into permitting it. . . . It resulted not from strategy, but from a lack of it."[60] The first religiously motivated settlers arrived just after 1967. Thus, the later National Religious Knesset member Chanan Porat, who was expelled as a child from the area of Gush Etzion in 1948, returned to Kfar Etzion when it came under Israeli control in 1967. In Hebron, a small group of mostly Orthodox Jews around Rabbi Moshe Levinger, a graduate of Rabbi Kook's *yeshivat ha-rav*, took possession of an empty hotel in the center of the city, where all Jews had either been murdered or had left after the 1929 riots. The Hebron settlement was important in two ways: First, because it constituted one of the holiest sites in Judaism; according to Jewish (and Muslim) tradition it was in Hebron that the biblical patriarchs and matriarchs are buried. And second, because a Jewish presence reversed the violent termination of Jewish life in the city under the British Mandate. But the Israeli government was also aware of the potential for conflict that a Jewish settlement in the middle of an Arab city might present, and therefore allowed the settlers to live only outside the old city, in a new settlement called Kiryat Arba. In the late 1970s, under the Begin administration, Levinger and a small group of activists moved back into the old city and set up a small but highly contested Jewish presence there.

The combination of the triumphant victory of 1967 that evoked messianic expectations and the disillusionment of the almost-fiasco of the 1973 war turned the various supporters of settlements into a proper "movement." Gershon Shafat, one of the early activists and later a member of the Knesset, summarized their feelings: "We walked steadfast toward the light

of faith to escape the depression and despair that were prevalent after the Yom Kippur War, we walked toward hope and
fulfilment."[61]

In January 1974, a group of activists founded *Gush Emunim*,
the "Bloc of the Faithful," which would become the core organization of the settler movement. Its founders portrayed
themselves as an apotheosis of Zionism in that they took a
secular movement and recast it as religiously inspired.[62] While
the settlement of biblical Judea would begin in Hebron and
nearby Kiryat Arba, the area around the ancient town of Si-
chem (or Shechem, the Arabic Nablus) became the starting
point for settlers in Samaria. The aged rabbi Zvi Yehuda Kook
ruled that it was a religious commandment to settle all of the
land, even if this resulted in martyrdom. One day later, he
went together with the former general (and later prime minister) Ariel Sharon to express his solidarity with the group of
activists that constructed a new settlement in Elon Moreh near
Nablus.

While he was still labor minister under Golda Meir,
Yitzhak Rabin made it clear that he thought Jerusalem should
remain the indivisible capital of Israel, but that the rest of the
occupied territories are negotiable. To a settler who was concerned that the Etzion Block, already home to Jewish settlements before 1948, would not remain under Israeli control,
Rabin replied: "It won't be terrible if we go to Kfar Etzion with
a visa"; and to an Orthodox girl who asked him about the holiness of the biblical Land of Israel, his answer was: "For me the
Bible is not a land registry of the Middle East. It is a book that
provides education in values."[63] As Prime Minister Rabin sent
soldiers to prevent what he conceived as illegal settlements. In
an interview given in 1976 but only published in 2015, Rabin's
thoughts on the settlers movement are crystal clear: "I see

in Gush Emunim one of the gravest threats to the state of Israel. . . . It is not a settlement movement, it is a cancer in Israel's social and democratic fabric, a manifestation of an entity that takes law into its own hands." Elsewhere he warned that an annexation of the West Bank and Gaza and the resulting large number of Arabs in a Jewish state would lead to an apartheid state.[64]

But the settler movement received support from several members of the Knesset. Rabin's rival within the Labor Party, Shimon Peres, also expressed sympathy with their cause. The settlement of Elon Moreh was officially concluded under the government of Menachem Begin, who granted the right to build also in a nearby area in 1980. Shortly after his election, Begin went to see Rabbi Kook and to pay him tribute. Begin announced: "There will be many Elon Morehs!"[65]

The radicalization of the National Religious Party during the 1970s and 80s was another expression of Israel's political transformation. The party, a junior partner in many Labor-led governments, had been rather moderate under its leaders Haim Moshe Shapira and Yosef Burg. Now, a new generation in the party turned it into the political mouthpiece of the settlers and the main political forum for a messianic interpretation of Zionism. "Traditional Jewish theology suggested moral terms for messianic redemption: all Jewish people must become either fully observant or completely nonobservant. Upon fulfillment of this condition, the messiah will appear, the Jews will miraculously return to Zion, and the Temple will be rebuilt. Kook inverted the sequence of causality. The return to Zion became the first stage in God's grand design, and the secular Jews became God's messengers, even if unaware of their mission. According to Kook, redemption has already begun in the here and now. It is a process of reuniting the holy trinity—the Land of Israel, the People of Israel, and the Torah of Israel."[66]

The number of settlers rose considerably under the Likud-led governments of Menachem Begin and Yitzhak Shamir, from 3,500 in 1977 to 18,500 in 1982. By 1985 the number had reached 47,000. But Begin did not fulfill all the expectations of the settlers. His readiness to return the Sinai Peninsula after the peace agreement with Egypt especially disappointed Gush Emunim and its supporters. Some of them radicalized further and began to look for solutions outside the recognized party spectrum. The most extreme turned to violence and went underground. They planned and executed violent attacks against the mayors of Arab towns and against ordinary citizens. In 1984, the Israeli public was shocked to discover a plan by members of the right-wing Jewish underground to blow up the El-Aqsa mosque located on the Temple Mount. There was a fear that religious fundamentalism might pose a threat to Israel's democracy.[67]

Although the terrorists were arrested, convicted, and sentenced to prison, attacks against Israel's core understanding of a democratic state increased. Political parties came into being that questioned the equal status of the Arab population in a Jewish state. The Moledet Party of former general Rehavam Ze'evi (nicknamed "Gandhi") openly promoted a population transfer of Israeli Arabs, while the much more radical and openly racist Kach Party, led by American-born rabbi Meir Kahane, legitimized violence as a political means. Kach was outlawed by Israel's Supreme Court. Both Ze'evi and Kahane were later assassinated. Others continued their struggle for an exclusively Jewish state.

Only a few years after the Six-Day War the Jewish state was radically transformed. A unified Jerusalem was now its heart, and according to some of its new leaders "Judea and Samaria" was now an integral part of this new state, as were East Jerusalem and the Golan Heights. For these leaders, the Six-Day War had perfected what was before an imperfectly established state. As Baruch Kimmerling explained it, "The Gush Emunim subculture and ideology, as successful as it was, only partially overturned the original secular Zionist hegemony. It simply shifted the weight of already existing, or dormant, ideological and social components of secular Zionist socialist and *mamlakhti* culture. Nonetheless, the religious settler society movement's penetration into the center of the sociopolitical sphere created the social and political conditions necessary for even more far-reaching changes. This was accomplished mainly by overemphasizing the religious and primordial elements in the definition of nationalism. The state lost part of its autonomy and became merely a means of resource distribution and redistribution, rather than the central and monopolistic symbol of the collectivity. . . . The civil ideology of the secular Zionist segments was almost completely subordinated to Gush Emunim's religious interpretation of 'Judaism' at the expense of Israeliness."[68]

APOCALYPTIC NIGHTMARES

The new messianic vision of a Jewish state found fertile ground not only in Israel itself but also in America's Bible Belt. For evangelical Christians, the State of Israel was and is anything but a normal state. They have adopted it as the savior of the world. The connection between the return of the Jews to their historic land and apocalyptic Christian readings of the Bible in fact has a long history. According to this tradition, the restored Jewish sovereignty in the holy land and the rebuilding of the temple in Jerusalem will secure the end times. As a first step, the Antichrist will rule in Jerusalem; then there will be an apocalyptic war between the mythical powers of Gog and Magog; and ultimately Christ will appear on the Mount of Olives and initiate a new phase of peace.[69]

Already in Herzl's time there were millenarian Christians who regarded the founder of Zionism as a trail-blazer on the Christian road to salvation. Soon after he had published his *Jewish State*, Herzl received a letter from the Reverend William Hechler, chaplain of the British embassy in Vienna, who saw in Zionism a means to Christian fulfillment. Herzl characterized Hechler after his first meeting with him as a "naive visionary with a collector's quirks." He noted that there was "something charming about his naive enthusiasm"[70] but later he wrote in his diary: "Hechler is fine for the entrée, but afterwards one becomes a bit ridiculous because of him."[71] Herzl at first scorned Hechler's messianic zeal. When he learned that the chaplain had been hired by the Grand Duke of Baden as a private tutor for his children, however, he saw his chance to finally gain direct access to the German Emperor Wilhelm II, a nephew of the Grand Duke. By then, Herzl and Hechler needed each other for quite different reasons.

Later, both British and American Protestants would regard the possibility of Jewish statehood as a significant step toward the messianic age. This vision was expanded after the establishment of the state, but it was Israel's control over the holy sites in 1967 that spurred real messianic fervor among a segment of Protestant Christians. Nowhere did they carry more weight than in the United States, where Israel came to play an increasingly important role in the apocalyptic theories of American Christian fundamentalist preachers. Hal Lindsey, one of the most popular evangelicals, and the founder of the Campus Crusade for Christ, claimed in his popular book *The Late Great Planet Earth* (1970) that the nations of the world would be measured according to their treatment of Israel and that the return of Christ to earth could only happen after the Jews had established their state in Palestine.[72]

These voices became relevant in American politics alongside the increasing political influence of evangelical theology during the presidency of Ronald Reagan. During the eighties, the evangelical message was increasingly tied to the fate of Israel. The most influential Televangelist and founder of conservative Liberty University, Jerry Falwell, wrote in his influential book *Listen, America!* (1980), "To stand against Israel is to stand against God."[73] He also referred to May 14th, 1948, Israel's Independence Day, as the most important day for humankind after Christ's ascent to heaven.[74]

While some evangelicals disapproved of Israel's actions in the 1967 war and the subsequent occupation of East Jerusalem, others considered Israel's triumph part of a divine plan. Among the many voices who discerned God's work in the Six-Day War was premillenialist John Walvoord, president of the Dallas Theological Seminary: "Surely this is the finger of God indicating the approaching end of the age."[75] Many Christian bookstores sold out their prophetic books after Israel's victory, and preachers stressed that Israel should never return their "historic lands" conquered in 1967. Jerry Falwell characterized Israel's unique role in world history as follows: "God promises to bless those who bless the children of Abraham and curse those who curse Israel. I think that history supports the fact that he has been true to his word. When you go back to the Pharaos [*sic*], the Caesars, Adolf Hitler, and the Soviet Union, all those who dared to touch the apple of God's eye—Israel—have been punished by God. America has been blessed because she has blessed Israel."[76] It was hardly possible to characterize Israel's exceptionalism in more radical words.

For Menachem Begin, Falwell and his followers were welcome allies in Israel's time of greatest isolation. It is telling that after the widely condemned Israeli airstrike against the Osirak nuclear reactor in Iraq, Begin called Falwell before calling President Reagan. Falwell's statement that a possible return of "Judea and Samaria" by Israel to the Arabs would be as outlandish as a return of Texas by the United States to Mexico, and similar comments made him the first non-Jewish recipient of the Vladimir Jabotinsky Medal and a close friend of later Prime Minister Benjamin Netanyahu.

Evangelical support for Israel is often mixed with evangelical disdain for Islam and the Arabs. Pat Robertson, founder of the Christian Broadcasting Network (CBN) and a presidential contender in 1988, stressed Israel's role in humanity's final struggle. According to Robertson, Jerusalem had to remain under Jewish rule until the coming of Christ. He soundly rejected any concessions to the Palestinians, and regarded Islam as the eternal enemy of a Christian-Jewish alliance: "The struggle is whether Hubal, the Moon God of Mecca, known as Allah, is supreme, or whether the Judeo-Christian Jehovah God of the Bible is Supreme. If God's chosen people turn over to Allah control of their most sacred sites—if they surrender to Muslim vandals the tombs of Rachel, of Joseph, of the Patriarchs, of the ancient prophets—if they believe their claim to the holy land comes only from Lord Balfour of England and the ever fickle United Nations rather than the promises of Almighty God—then in that event, Islam will have won the battle. Throughout the Muslim world the message will go forth—Allah is greater than Jehovah. The promises of Jehovah to the Jews are meaningless."[77]

Millions of evangelical Christians in America share Robertson's belief. In their view, Israel is not just a state like any other, created because British politicians made certain promises and the United Nations decided to partition Palestine. It is rather a unique state that came into being as part of a divine plan with which humans should not interfere. Israel is for them the apple of God's eye (Zechariah 2:8), and the fate of the Jewish state directly impacts the fate of Christianity, playing a vicarious role in the apocalyptic struggle of humankind. It is up to Israel to retain control over the holy sites in Jerusalem, so that Christianity can fulfill its historical role.

A closer look reveals that the Jews and the State of Israel are for evangelicals only a means to a larger purpose. Many of the same activists who express their enthusiasm over Israel also hold that at the end of days Jews will be turned into Christians. Jerry Falwell, in the same book in which he stressed that standing against Israel meant standing against God, described the Jews as "spiritually blind and desperately in need of their Messiah and Savior."[78] Jewish reception of these voices varied considerably. While more liberal Jews rejected this support according to the motto, "God protect us from our friends" as just another modern conspiracy theory,[79] politically conservative Jews and right-wing Israeli governments embraced Fallwell, Robertson, and their ilk as Israel's most faithful allies. They lay emphasis on the massive support that evangelical organizations have summoned to the aid of Israel: evangelicals have organized mass demonstrations in Washington to promote Israel's "biblical borders," drummed up political support in Congress, and raised considerable sums in aid of Israel's settlement policy.

This group influences Republican policies on Israel much more than does the Jewish community. Less than 2 percent of the US population is Jewish, but about 25 percent are evangelical Protestants. They vary widely in their beliefs, and not all of them share the views of Israel delineated above. But a large segment of them, especially in America's Bible Belt, are open to theological scenarios that posit Israel's uniqueness and place it in many ways outside the regular laws of history and politics.[80] Their votes played an important role in Ronald Reagan's victories in the 1980s, and even more so in George W. Bush's victories twenty years later. According to a study by the Pew Institute, every third Bush voter identified as evangelical Protestant.[81] Right-wing Israeli governments can rely on more support from these Christians, two thirds of whom believe in Israel's role as a savior of humankind, than from American Jews who in their majority favor a more progressive Israel.[82]

PEACE ILLUSIONS

During the 1970s, those who had high hopes for peace also seemed to see Messianic times on the horizon. No one expected the hawkish Menachem Begin to make any progress toward peace with the Arabs, but a surprise visit to Jerusalem by Egyptian President Anwar el-Sadat on November 19th, 1977, changed history. The same Egyptian president who fought Israel on the battlefield four years earlier had now come to the conclusion that only an unprecedented historical gesture could bring peace to the region. He was ready and willing to be the first Arab leader to accept the legitimacy of Israel, if the Jewish state would return the Sinai Peninsula to Egypt and begin a process toward Palestinian autonomy. His dramatic speech in the Knesset made him many friends in Israel and in the West, but isolated him in the Arab world.

Israel gradually returned the Sinai to Egypt, but negotiations over Palestinian autonomy soon came to a halt. It would take more than another decade and much international involvement before Israel and the Palestinians, along with representatives from other states, would participate in a first peace conference, the Madrid Middle East Peace Conference, which convened in 1991. The fall of the Soviet Union and the rise of a new world order were decisive contributors to this development. When Russia and the East European states reestablished diplomatic ties with Israel, as did many African and Asian states, its isolation in the world lessened. In 1991, the UN officially declared the 1975 anti-Zionism resolution invalid, and a few years later, Israel was integrated into the UN's West European regional group.

There was political upheaval in Israel as well. In 1992, the Labor Party came back to power under its new old leader, Yitzhak Rabin. After negotiations that had started in the Norwegian capital, the Rabin government concluded the Oslo accords with the PLO and a peace treaty with its neighbor Jordan. Finally Herzl's vision of a Jewish state that would live in peace and prosperity with its neighbors seemed no longer utopian.

The signs of the new time were most clearly embodied in a person who had once represented the hawkish wing of Israel's Labor Party.[83] In the 1950s, Shimon Peres was the architect of Israel's nuclear arsenal, and in the 1970s he was a proponent of settlements. Now, emerging as the country's elder statesman, he drafted a vision of *The New Middle East*. In his book by this title, written in 1993, he expanded the classical Zionist idea of a model state into that of a model region. Peres argued against a narrow-minded nationalism that would isolate Israel in the region and instead pledged support for a new Jewish-Arab alliance. "In the early 1990s we had reached one of those rare critical junctures that enable discerning statesmen to make a quantum leap in their thinking—and perhaps to turn the tide of history."[84] Summarizing the Oslo talks and the new dialogue ongoing with Palestinian leaders, Peres outlined his new vision: "Peace between Israel and its Arab neighbors will create the environment for a basic reorganization of Middle Eastern institutions. Reconciliation and Arab acceptance of Israel as a nation with equal rights and responsibilities will sire a new sort of cooperation—not only between Israel and its neighbors but also among Arab nations. It will change the face of the region and its ideological climate. . . . Our ultimate goal is the creation of a regional community of nations, with a common market and elected centralized bodies, modeled on the European Community."[85]

Just as Germany and France were able to make peace and create new economic prosperity in Europe after centuries of war, Israel and its Arab neighbors could do the same in the Middle East. Peres looked to Europe as the model for his approach, recalling his meetings in the 1950s with the architect of the European Common Market, Jean Monnet. He saw himself as a modern-day Monnet but was also inspired by Theodor Herzl's dreams in his *Old New Land*: "At the end of the nineteenth century, it was fine to dream. At the end of the twentieth, it is time to transform the dream into reality," he wrote, referring to Herzl's original ideas, and more specifically to Herzl's vision of a Red Sea–Dead Sea Canal, which Peres now saw as within reach.[86] He laid out a blueprint for the future of a region anchored in economic cooperation, strategic security, and joint transportation and communication infrastructures. He called it boldly "A New Way of Thinking."[87]

Peres's Israel was no longer the pariah state excluded by many world organizations, nor was it the neighborhood bully described by Bob Dylan, but rather the model state envisioned by Theodor Herzl and his own mentor David Ben-Gurion. Like them, he admitted that the course of Jewish history was unique, as was the fate of the Jewish state: "The unusual, the paradoxical, and the extraordinary are our daily lot. Whether we be Jews or Israelis, we seem in some way to be a people apart, who always give rise to an endless number of complex questions, the likes of which we would be hard pressed to find in any other nation in the world."[88] In the midst of his enthusiasm over a new Middle East, he expressed confidence that the Palestinians, too, could become part of this unique constellation in the Middle East. They could partake of uniqueness: "I know that what happened to the Jews was unprecedented: A nation returned to its homeland and its ancient languages after centuries. I thought that something unprecedented could also happen to the Palestinians: a group that had never been a people could now be a people among peoples."[89] While the Palestinians would certainly dispute Peres's assumption that they had never been a people, Herzl might have been quite moved by Peres's statement. After all, in Herzl's *Old New Land* it was the "good Arab," Rashid Bey, who welcomed all the benefits that the Jews brought from Europe to the Middle East. But Peres might, in his enthusiasm, have followed Herzl just a bit too closely.

It was in fact at about this time that Peres discovered *Old New Land*—and in his next book, written five years later, he embarked on an imaginary voyage alongside the founder of Zionism to revisit his utopian novel. He begins *The Imaginary*

Voyage by admitting that it was only late in life that he had encountered Herzl's writings: "When I entered public life, I still knew nothing about him, and I made little or no effort to fill that gap."[90] But once he discovered Herzl he was so fascinated that he decided to bring him back to life to show him present-day (1998) Israel. In many ways, he says proudly, Israel constituted the fulfillment of Herzl's dreams. But in others it still fell far short of the founder's vision.

In this intensely personal book, written shortly after his temporary retreat into political opposition, Peres names as the greatest challenge to the survival of Israel as a Jewish state its need for reconciliation with the Arab population: "Indeed, to ensure that Israel remains a Jewish state, we must accept the existence of an adjacent Palestinian state. If we do not, Israel risks becoming bi-national—neither Jewish nor Palestinian— and condemned to chronic instability. The Palestinian question and the future of Israel, as Herzl had foreseen, are inseparable."[91]

Peres follows in Herzl's footsteps when he emphasizes that Israel must be a multiethnic society, and he painfully admits, in 1998, that extremist voices have been on the rise during the past few years. Again, he adopts the language of miracles for describing Israeli society: "Whatever our failings, we Israelis have tried to create a multiethnic democratic society in which those of all religions can enjoy the same rule of law and live together in peace. That is what I mean by 'Israeli miracle'— and that is why we must oppose those for whom the realization of Jewish national aspirations is synonymous with a policy of exclusion. That kind of thinking leads to 'ethnic purification' of the sort perpetrated in the former Yugoslavia. I painfully and regretfully had to acknowledge to Herzl that during these last few years voices favoring the latter policy

FIGURE 18. Yassir Arafat, Shimon Peres, and Yitzhak Rabin display their Nobel Peace prizes, 1994.

have been heard in Israel. We have seen the rise of groups and factions that revel in their minority status, and who would deny non-Jewish citizens fundamental rights—even call for their expulsion. The father of Zionism was the first to suspect that these hateful ideas, which run counter to Judaism's tradition of tolerance and sense of justice, might arise, and he denounced them with all his might."[92]

Peres strongly opposes exclusivist theories, as personified by the Orthodox rabbi Dr. Geyer, while his sympathies lie with the universalist vision in Herzl's novel: "As I read these lines again I became fully aware of Herzl's prophetic intelligence, his love of purity, his complete embrace of the biblical injunction from Isaiah for 'perfect peace'."[93]

During the five years that passed between the publication of *The New Middle East* and *The Imaginary Voyage*, the clock of peace had been turned back.[94] Prime Minister Rabin was assassinated in 1995 by an extremist from among his own people, just as Egyptian president Sadat had been killed fourteen years earlier. Waves of terror by Palestinian extremists brought the right-wing parties, which had vehemently opposed the Oslo accords and vilified Prime Minister Rabin, back to power in 1996, when Benjamin Netanyahu defeated Shimon Peres by a slim margin in the first (of only three) direct elections for prime minister. Israeli society was more split than ever before. During the following years, it would undergo yet another significant transformation as it searched for its identity.[95] When negotiations with the Palestinian leadership failed and a second Intifada broke out in September 2000, the new Middle East looked once again very much like the old Middle East.

GLOBAL ISRAEL

A STATE BEYOND BORDERS

The State of Israel is an endeavor—wholly understandable,
in many aspects admirable, perhaps historically inescapable—
to normalize the condition, the meaning of Judaism.

—GEORGE STEINER, "OUR HOMELAND, THE TEXT"

The so-called normalization of the Jew
was a tragic illusion from the start.

—PHILIP ROTH, *OPERATION SHYLOCK*

While the previous chapters of this book have dealt primarily
with the visionaries and leaders of mainstream Zionism and
the State of Israel, this chapter throws light on some of the
dynamics that were not predicted by the prophets of the
state. They neither foresaw the emigration of Jews from Israel, nor the immigration of non-Jews and recently converted
Jews from Africa and Asia to Israel. These developments have
been less prominent in the headlines about Israel, but they
are part of a changing Jewish state in the twenty-first century.
As intellectuals, novelists, and artists often sense such changes
more than politicians, they play a substantial role in this
chapter.

Israel was founded as a Jewish state in order to put an end
to what A. B. Yeshoshua called "the neurotic solution." Instead
of their existence as a minority among other nations, Jews

should finally have their own state and thus lead a "normal life," like all other peoples. If the wandering Jew would only settle, the Jewish diaspora would gradually dissolve.[1] And indeed, seventy years after the establishment of the Jewish state over 40 percent of all Jews call Israel their home. The majority, however, still live outside Israel—and alongside the traditional Jewish diaspora, there exists today a new Israeli diaspora.

Israel has gone global on many levels.[2] Politically, it holds the attention of the entire world, unlike any other state of its size. Economically, it is an important player in the high-tech sphere, boasting more start-up enterprises relative to its population than any other country. Demographically, its citizens have immigrated from over a hundred different countries. But they also emigrated to almost as many. Today, expat Israelis form a global community that extends between Los Angeles and Melbourne, they have established schools in New York and libraries in Berlin. The return of the descendants of immigrants from Germany and Poland to their ancestors' old homes, and the phantasies about Israelis settling in places like Argentina and Uganda have become frequent motifs for Israeli writers and artists. At the same time, there are new Israelis, whom nobody had expected when the state was founded. They are the self-declared descendants of the biblical "lost tribes," and they come from India and Nigeria, from Myanmar and South Africa. They join converts to Judaism from Uganda, guest workers from the Philippines, and refugees from Eritrea.

ISRAEL ABROAD

In the history of migration, the return of emigrants to their homelands is nothing exceptional. According to estimates, about one third of all emigrants from Europe between 1824 and 1924 returned at some point.[3] Patterns of immigration and emigration are characteristic of modern states. But when it comes to Israel, the issue of migration poses an insoluble dilemma in the face of the nation's claims to be aiming at normality. On the one hand, Zionist ideology demanded a state like all other states, which would entail accepting the fact that a good part of its citizens would leave the country. On the other hand, Zionism had only envisioned migration into one direction: into the Jewish state. Herzl's *Jewish State*, Israel's Declaration of Independence, the Law of Return—all of these foundational documents assumed that Jews would come to Israel, and not that they would leave it.

To be sure, the story of immigration to Israel is overall an unparalleled success story of a small country integrating over the course of decades many more new arrivals than the number of its actual inhabitants, providing them with living quarters and jobs, and making them full-fledged citizens. This was achieved by a country that was struggling economically during its first decades and was at war with its neighbors. But it would be a delusion to believe that, unlike all other countries, Israel would only experience immigration. In fact, a closer look reveals that the history of Jewish emigration from Palestine is as old as its history of Jewish immigration. There were years during the first modern waves of immigration in the late nineteenth and early twentieth centuries, when there were more immigrants leaving the Land of Israel—and this shortly after their arrival—than remaining there.[4] This tendency continued during the late twenties, when the mostly middle-class immigrants from Poland arrived during the so-called fourth Aliyah.[5] Even after the state was founded, there were recent *olim* (the Hebrew term for immigrants, which literally means "ascending"), who in the language of the day became *yordim* (those who are descending). Thus, between 1948 and 1967 about 184,000 Israelis left the country, approximately 13 percent of the immigrants who arrived during this period. During the early 1950s there were for a few years more emigrants than immigrants.[6]

The most significant destination of Israeli emigration was always the United States. In the first decade of the state, only just over 20,000 Israelis left for the US, a number that rose to over 30,000 in the 1960s and 70s, over 40,000 in the 80s and 90s, and over 50,000 in each of the last two decades.[7] The estimate of Israelis living in the US today is highly contested and depends on the definition of who is an Israeli: people born in Israel, people with an Israeli passport, or all descendants of Israelis. The vast majority of American Israelis live in the Greater New York and Los Angeles areas and have their own networks there. Some of them were recent immigrants to Israel from the former Soviet Union, who had family members in the US, others had professional reasons to come, and many simply wanted to exchange harsh living conditions for what they anticipated would be a more comfortable life in America.[8]

Western Europe has been another popular destination for Israelis, with London the main magnet, and Paris and Marseilles attractive alternatives for those of French-speaking North African background—while at the same time British and especially French Jews also move in the opposite direction, fleeing from an increasingly antisemitic climate in Europe. In recent years, Berlin has become a popular haven for young Israelis in search for more freedom, lower living costs, and the adventures offered by a multicultural European metropolis. In Berlin, there exists today a complete Israeli subculture, with Tel Aviv style "beach parties" and galleries of Israeli artists, Hebrew libraries and preschools for Hebrew-speaking children, and Hebrew magazines and websites.[9] Many of the young emigrants live in two worlds simultaneously, between "Berlin on the Yarkon" and "Tel Aviv on the Spree." Their home is neither here nor there, but in both places, which are separated only by a four-hour flight. For historian Fania Oz-Salzberger, this unique set of circumstances "prompts Israelis to trade their expensive, militant, nationalistic, and centralized homeland for the affordable, pacifist, liberal and globalized charms of Germany's capital city. . . . Today's Berlin Israelis are not 'descenders' . . . nor are they 'migrants' in the traditional sense. They are transnationals, a new and ephemeral concept of global citizenship. They reside, offline and online, in two places at the same time. Only a few have truly divorced Israel. Most might prefer to say that they and Israel are temporarily separated due to mutual disagreements."[10]

The Israeli diaspora in Germany is not a new phenomenon, even though it did reach unprecedented numbers in the last decade, so that today up to 25,000 Israelis live mainly in Berlin.[11] But already in the immediate years after the founding of the state, there were Israeli citizens relocating to Germany. A few thousands of East European Holocaust survivors who had made it to Israel actually returned to Europe and entered the last of the Displaced Persons Camps in Germany. There were also German-born Jews who returned to their country of origin.[12]

The perception of some observers in Israel only a few years after the nation's establishment was of a "mass exodus from Israel," a "mass psychosis," and a "tragedy."[13] No matter if their destination was Los Angeles or London, Paris or Berlin, the fact that Jews were leaving the Jewish state was neither sanctioned by official Israel nor by most Israelis. Leading politi-

FIGURE 19. Advertisement for the Hebrew web magazine *Spitz* in Berlin.

cians demanded a prohibition on emigration and even raised the possibility of forcibly "bringing up again" those who had "descended." A young Golda Meir thought in the 1950s that the Jewish people had to break their habit of wandering: "Where is it written that a person would go hither and thither and the . . . Jewish people would cover the expenses?"[14] In the 1960s, the Israeli paper *Yediot Aharonot* observed that "they are fleeing like rats from a sinking ship," and its rival *Ha'aretz* published a series of articles on the emigrants. It depicted them as characterless and unhappy even when they were economically successful. The two years before the Six-Day War saw a new surge of emigration, with emigrants once again outnumbering immigrants to Israel. As before, those who chose to go to Germany were singled out, as the ones who would "live in proximity to Fritz and Adolf, who a mere two decades ago were sending them to the crematoria."[15] The end of the post–Six-Day War euphoria after the Yom Kippur War and the widespread rejection of Israel's Lebanon War in the early 1980s prompted a growing number of young Israelis to leave the country, either temporarily or for good.

The huge wave of immigration from the former Soviet Union to Israel brought discussions of the "emigration problem" to a temporary halt. Within a few years, over a million people entered the country and changed its face. But after the outbreak of the second Intifada in 2000, when the number of emigrants again rose above that of immigrants, the discussion was revived. There was now talk of a "brain drain," with much of the academic elite leaving the country, partially because of a sheer lack of appropriate jobs in Israel. While immigration numbers reached a new low, with only 13,000 coming into the country in 2013, the number of emigrants remained stable at about 20,000 annually.[16]

According to Israel's Statistical Office, the total number of Israelis abroad increased from 300,000 in 1989 to 480,000 in 1999 and to 540,000 in 2006. If these numbers are correct, about 7 percent of all Israeli citizens live abroad. This was certainly not envisioned by the founders of Zionism and of the Jewish state, but in international perspective it is about the same percentage as in many other developed countries, such as Germany, Austria, Italy, Canada, and the Netherlands.[17]

There are many factors that push Israelis out of their country, but there can also be specific reasons that pull them toward another country. The pre-existence of a network of the Jewish community that will help them to integrate is a benefit that most other emigrants do not enjoy. Israelis are often welcomed by the Jewish communities, for in many places they improve the level of Jewish cultural life, and in some cases, especially in Europe, they receive financial assistance for helping in their areas of their expertise (which often might only be knowledge of the Hebrew language) and in religious life as well. And then there is the past: often new arrivals feel a cultural attachment to their new country, especially if their ancestors once lived there. They may also have the right to a passport from the country their families once fled. And one European passport grants them the right to live and work anywhere in the EU. In that sense, many Israeli Jews have a right of return to Europe, just as diaspora Jews have a right of return to Israel.

ISRAEL IMAGINED

The vast majority of Israeli emigrants leave the country for purely pragmatic reasons. Their homeland is too hot or too expensive or too dangerous for them. Their new home seems, at least on first glance, calm, affordable, and peaceful. Although many miss the Israeli style of life in their new diaspora and are open to return at some point, or at least want their children to return, most stay abroad. Among intellectuals, this phenomenon has raised the question of whether Israelis abroad threaten the normalization of Jewish history—or whether, on the contrary, they are actually living proof of normalization. For those who hold the latter view, the "normal" course of Jewish history is a history centered in the diaspora. Israeli historian Jacob Talmon once described the paradoxical existence of the State of Israel within the parameters of Jewish history as follows: "Israel has been seen as the fulfillment and ultimate denouement of Jewish history, but it has also been seen as the greatest deviation from the course of that history."[18]

On the one hand, there are Zionists who promote the concentration of all Jews in the Jewish state and brand emigrants as traitors to the Zionist cause. On the other, there are the defenders of the diaspora who argue that it has been a feature of Jewish existence since biblical times. According to them, the diaspora is no minor episode in Jewish history, but constitutes the very essence of Judaism.

The first position is most vehemently defended by the writer A. B. Yehoshua, according to whom "the *Golah* [exile] is the source of the problems the Jewish people have been struggling with for many generations, and especially during the last hundred years."[19] After three decades of emigration from Israel, Yehoshua noted that "disturbing signs of the Golah's recovery began already to appear. The world's most resilient people has already learned the laws of the new modern reality and is adapting its exilic being to it. The existence of a center allows it to strike deeper roots in the Golah, for it now has 'insurance.'"[20]

For Yehoshua, "the Holocaust is the final decisive proof of the failure of diaspora existence." He regards the Holocaust not as a singular episode in Jewish history, but as the culmination of centuries of antisemitism, the last nail in the coffin of diasporic existence: "The Holocaust proved to us the danger of our abnormal existence among the nations, the danger of the nonlegitimacy of our presence among the nations. . . . We were outside of history, we were not 'like all the nations.' Because of our ways of life we were 'other,' different from all others, it was easy to regard us as subhuman, and as subhuman our blood could be spilled freely. . . . The Holocaust bared the profound hazards of the Jew's situation in the world. The solution is not to change the world, to bring it into line with the special nature of our existence, but to change the nature of Jewish existence, to bring it into line with the world. The solution is normalization of Jewish existence."[21]

For Yehoshua there was only one path towards this normalization: the dissolution of the diaspora and the immigration of all Jews to Israel. As a first step, Jews—and Israelis—should give up their claims to difference: "Deep among the primary strands of our identity is the demand to be different, singular, unique, set apart from the family of nations. One of the fundamental elements of the Jewish religious conception is represented in the phrase 'You have chosen us.' It runs like a thread through all spiritual levels of Jewish religious-national activity. . . . The notion of being 'like all the other nations' has a clearly negative ring for the Jew."[22] Jews, he argued, had to learn again to become a people like all others. The best way to accomplish this was to regain their sovereignty: "I repeat the simple truth, that the Jewish people is a people like all other peoples, and am astonished to discover to what extent it does not appear simple to many. That is the first seed of trouble. I am amazed to see that the simple meaning of normality, the basic equality of the Jewish people with all other peoples, is not readily comprehensible to many Israelis. One cannot constantly insist on legal-political equality while not acknowledging our equal spiritual status with humanity as a whole."[23] Like Weizmann, Yehoshua too used Albania as a metaphor for a "normal state": "The uniqueness of the State of Israel is that it is a Jewish state with specific national content, in the same way that Albania is unique."[24]

While politicians like David Ben-Gurion and Golda Meir agreed with the traditional Zionist notion of the "negation of the diaspora," the defenders of a Jewish diaspora existence had deep roots in nineteenth-century Jewish thought. The Reform Movement turned the negative connotations of the destruction of the Second Temple and the end of Jewish statehood into a virtue: only in dispersion could the universal mission of Judaism develop and the idea of monotheism spread.[25] To be a minority among other nations had become a core element of Judaism.[26] In Eastern Europe, historian Simon Dubnov developed his theory of Jewish history centering around the idea of the Jews as a diasporic people. Palestine was just one of the centers of Jewish existence in history, followed by Babylonia, Spain, and Eastern Europe. What was "normal" in Jewish history for him was not the return to Palestine, but the coming into existence of ever-new centers of Jewish life.

It was the Holocaust that ultimately discredited the diaspora, at least in Europe. Only in a Jewish state would Jewish existence be safe. There was for a few decades far-reaching consensus among Jews that the Jewish state had a right to exist. But the ongoing conflict between Jews and Arabs, and the internal transformation of Israel had led to the development of a counter-ideology favored by a growing number of intellectuals. They do not necessarily deny Israel's right of existence, but they passionately defend the right of the diaspora to exist. Ironically, for some of them, instead of being the safe haven that it was founded to be, Israel has become a dangerous place to live, and even more ironically, a state that through its actions endangers Jewish existence worldwide.

At the opposite pole to A.B. Yehoshua among American Jewish writers is Philip Roth, or to be more precise, Philip Roth's fictional character named "Philip Roth." The doppelganger of the writer, the "other Philip Roth," appears in his novel *Operation Shylock* (1993) where he is the proponent of a new diasporism that aims to lead Jews of European origin back to Europe. Critical for Roth is the failure of the Zionist project of normalization: "The so-called normalization of the Jew was a tragic illusion from the start. But when this normalization is expected to flourish in the very heart of Islam, it is even worse than tragic—it is suicidal. . . . The time has come to return to Europe that was for centuries, and remains to this day, the most authentic Jewish homeland there has ever been, the birthplace of rabbinic Judaism, Jewish secularism, socialism—on and on. The birthplace, of course, of Zionism, too. But Zionism has outlived its historical function. The time has come to renew in the European Diaspora our preeminent spiritual and cultural role."[27]

In this fictional perspective, Zionism had a right to exist, but in the end, it proved to be a failed project: "In the immediate postwar era, when for obvious reasons Europe was uninhabitable by Jews, Zionism was the single greatest force contributing to the recovery of Jewish hope and morale. But having succeeded in restoring the Jews to health, Zionism has tragically ruined its own health and must now accede to vigorous Diasporism."[28] The "real Roth" initially opposes the "false

Roth" in the novel, and characterizes his diasporism as naïve and dangerous, but at the end of the novel the reader is confused as to the identity of the "real Roth" and confused also about the message of the novel. The fake Philip Roth's solution was the mass return of Jews to Europe: "Diasporism seeks to promote the dispersion of the Jews in the West, particularly the resettlement of Israeli Jews of European background in the European countries where there were sizable Jewish populations before World War II. Diasporism plans to rebuild everything, not in an alien and menacing Middle East, but in those very lands where everything once flourished."[29]

Roth paints in vivid colors the reception in Europe of the first returning Jews:

> You know what will happen in Warsaw, at the railway station, when the first Jew returns? There will be crowds to welcome them. People will be jubilant. People will be in tears. They will be shouting, "Our Jews are back! Our Jews are back!" The spectacle will be transmitted by television throughout the world.

Philip Roth's idea of return culminates ". . . in the year 2000, the pan-European celebration of the reintegrated Jews to be held in the city of Berlin."[30]

For Roth's protagonist, diaspora is the only authentic mode of Jewish existence. A diasporist, according to the novel, "is a Jew for whom *authenticity* as a Jew means living in the Diaspora, for whom the Diaspora is the normal condition and Zionism is the abnormality—a Diasporist is a Jew who believes that the only Jews who matter are the Jews of the Diaspora, that the only Jews who will survive are the Jews of the Diaspora, that the only Jews who *are* Jews are the Jews of the Diaspora."[31]

The borderlines between literature and political manifesto are blurred in *Operation Shylock*, and it is up to the readers to decide if they want to take the novel's diasporism seriously or regard it purely as fiction. In her review of the book, literary scholar Sidra DeKoven Ezrahi wrote: "When 'nomadism' competes with 'nativism' not only in the academy at large but among Jews who are increasingly ambivalent and puzzled over the uses and abuses of Israeli power, when 'narrativity' is the ascendant order of the imagination and the storyteller once again competes with the soldier for cultural privilege, 'Diasporism,' in its more sanitized versions, becomes as politically correct as Zionism was twenty-five years ago."[32]

Indeed, "diasporism" became politically correct within academia, just when Israel was turning into its whipping boy after the political developments that followed on the Six-Day War. A variety of Jewish scholars have produced theoretical writings defending diasporism. Unlike Jewish opponents of Israel, such as Noam Chomsky, Norman Finkelstein, and Judith Butler,[33] these intellectuals idealized the diaspora without necessarily opposing the existence of a Jewish state. The philosopher and literary critic George Steiner, to take a prominent example, is convinced that the Jews' home is a "portable home" (*portatives Vaterland*), an expression he borrows from the nineteenth-century German-Jewish poet Heinrich Heine.[34] In Steiner's view, it is the unique existence of the Jews, whose home is the book and not the soil that is responsible for their unusual creativity, which in turn has become an example for all humanity: "One need be neither a religious fundamentalist nor a mystic to believe that there is some exemplary meaning to the singularity of Judaic endurance, some sense beyond contingent or demographic interest to the interlocking constancy of Jewish pain and Jewish preservation. . . . I cannot shake off the conviction that the torment and the mystery of resilience in Judaism exemplify, enact, an arduous truth: that human beings must learn to be each other's guests on this small planet. . . . The State of Israel is an endeavor—wholly understandable, in many aspects admirable, perhaps historically inescapable—to normalize the condition, the meaning of Judaism. It would make the Jew level with the common denominator of modern 'belonging.' It is, at the same time, an attempt to eradicate the deeper truth of unhousedness, of an at-homeness in the world, which are the legacy of the Prophets and of the keepers of the text."[35]

For Steiner, the return of the Jews to a tiny state in the Middle East means the parochialization of a community that had bred a Freud and an Einstein and a Kafka, and from which 20 percent of Nobel Prize winners have emerged, even though it comprises less than one percent of the world's population. Thus, in his view, the ultimate home of the Jews is their homelessness.[36]

Steiner is not sparing of criticism toward Israel when he writes: "The virtues of Israel are those of beleagured Sparta. . . . Where it has traded its homeland in the text for one on the Golan Heights or in Gaza . . . Judaism has become homeless to itself," [37] but he also recognizes the Jewish state as a indispensable response to antisemitism, as a safe haven for "when it starts again, and it will start again."[38] In contrast to critics like Chomsky and Butler, he accepts, albeit painfully, the necessity for a Jewish state: "What mandarin fantasy, what ivory-tower nonsense, is it to suppose that alone among men, and after the unspeakable horrors of destruction lavished upon him, the Jew should not have a land of his own, a shelter in the night?"[39]

Postmodern scholars of Judaism were especially keen on the subject of an Israel-critical diasporism. Perhaps the most prominent champions were the brothers Daniel and Jonathan Boyarin, who are convinced that only the diaspora and not the Jewish state represents genuine Jewish values:

> We propose Diaspora as a theoretical and historical model to replace national self-determination. . . . The solution of Zionism—that is, Jewish state hegemony, except insofar as it represented an emergency and temporary rescue operation—seems to us the subversion of Jewish culture and not its culmination. It represents the substitution of a European, Western cultural-political formation for a traditional Jewish one that has been based on a sharing, at best, of political power with others and that takes on entirely other meanings when combined with political hegemony.[40]

In direct response to A. B. Yehoshua, Boyarin and Boyarin argue: "Reversing A. B. Yehoshua's famous pronouncement that only in a condition of political hegemony is moral responsibility mobilized, we would argue that the only moral path would be the renunciation of Jewish hegemony qua Jewish hegemony."[41]

Boyarin and Boyarin recall a history of the Jews that did not originate in the Land of Israel and that did not center on this land alone: "An alternative story of Israel, closer, it would seem, to the readings of the Judaism lived for two thousand years, begins with a people forever unconnected with a particular land, a people that calls into question the idea that a people must have a land in order to be a people. 'The Land of Israel was not the birthplace of the Jewish people, which did not emerge there (as most peoples have on their own soil). On the contrary it had to enter its own Land from without; there is a sense in which Israel was born in exile. Abraham had to leave his own land to go to the Promised Land: the father of Jewry was deterritorialized.'"[42] Ultimately, according to this view "Diaspora, and not monotheism, may be the most important contribution that Judaism has to make to the world."[43] For some observers, Israel is so closely related with the Jewish diaspora that it has become part of the larger diaspora itself. Thus, literary critic Christopher Hitchens noted: "Israeli Jews are *a part* of the Diaspora, not a group that has escaped from it."[44]

Is Israel still a safe haven for persecuted Jews—or has it instead become a source of danger for Jews around the world? This is a question posed by some Jewish intellectuals who argue that Israel's actions led to anti-Jewish violence in the diaspora, as Jewish communities are often identified with the State of Israel and serve as vicarious victims.

The late British (and New York based) historian Tony Judt has argued that Israel's actions take all Jews hostage, because they are all identified with its politics, whether they like it or not, and Israel has become the greatest threat to Jewish survival since the end of World War II.

In his vigorous criticism of Israel, Judt termed the Jewish state an "anachronism . . . and not just an anachronism, but a dysfunctional one." In contrast to the new nation-states that emerged after the First World War, Israel entered the political stage one world war later, when—according to Judt—the dawn of the age of nationalism had already broken. For Judt, Israel was—in many respects—an anomaly. Instead of normalizing Jewish history, Israel's policy achieved the exact opposite: "Today, non-Israeli Jews feel themselves once again exposed to criticism and vulnerable to attack for things they didn't do. But this time it is a Jewish state, not a Christian one, which is holding them hostage for its own actions. Diaspora Jews cannot influence Israeli policies, but they are implicitly identified with them, not least by Israel's own insistent claims upon their allegiance. The behavior of a self-described Jewish state affects the way everyone else looks at Jews. The increased incidence of attacks on Jews in Europe and elsewhere is primarily attributable to misdirected efforts, often by young Muslims, to get back at Israel. The depressing truth is that Israel's current behavior is not just bad for America, though it surely is. It is not even bad only for Israel itself, as many Israelis silently acknowledge. The depressing truth is that Israel today is bad for the Jews."[45] Judt predicted a further distancing between diaspora Jews and Israel. In one of his last interviews, Israeli journalist and later Knesset member Merav Michaeli asked Judt to define Israel's role and place in the history of the Jewish people. The NYU professor replied that, taking the long perspective, one would have "to say that Israel is behaving very much like the annoying little Judean state that the Romans finally dismantled in frustration. This classical analogy may be more relevant than we think. I suspect that in decades to come America (the new Rome) will abandon Israel as annoying, expensive, and a liability. This will leave Israel to its own resources or to making friends with anyone who will deal with it (as it once did with South Africa). That in turn will make it a very unpleasant place for Western liberals and democrats, who will loosen their ties with it. No doubt it will survive, but it will mean less and less to Jews elsewhere as people forget the original impulse and historical circumstances surrounding its founding. As to the future of Jews in the diaspora, they (we) will once again be the predominant community (once again as in classical times). I think Israel will grow increasingly marginal for most Jews, though I don't quite know what their Jewish life will look like either in a secularized world."[46]

In Israel itself there are growing voices demanding a change in the self-definition of the Jewish state. Beginning in the late 1980s, the so-called "New Historians" wrote a counternarrative to many facets of Israeli history. They questioned the role of the Zionist leadership with respect to possible rescue attempts during the Holocaust and pointed to Israel's responsibility in the flight or expulsion of the Palestinian population in 1948/49.[47]

In due course, more public intellectuals and even former politicians added their criticism. The former speaker of the Israeli parliament and former president of the Jewish Agency, Avraham Burg, called for a complete rethinking of the role of Zionism: "We seek to add humaneness and universalism to the old equations and new dimensions of value-based content and national existence. We propose a life of trust, not a reality composed of nothing but endless trauma."[48] He called for the cancellation of the Law of Return, and encouraged Israelis to obtain a second citizenship if they could meet the requirements.[49] His idea of Israel envisions several Jewish centers: "We were raised on the Zionism of Ben-Gurion, that there is only one place for Jews and that's Israel. I say no, there have always been multiple centers of Jewish life."[50]

The most radical view among Israeli "post-Zionist" intellectuals is that of Tel Aviv historian Shlomo Sand. By declaring the idea of a Jewish people a fiction (his book title is *The Invention of the Jewish People*), Sand undermines the very legitimacy of the State of Israel. If the Jews are no nation but only a religion, then they have no right to establish a national home. He proposed the following future path for Israel: "The Jewish supra-identity must be thoroughly transformed and must adapt to the lively cultural reality it dominates. It will have to forego a process of Israelization, open to all its citizens. It is too late to make Israel into a uniform, homogeneous nation-state. . . . To what extent is Jewish Israeli society willing to discard the deeply embedded image of the 'chosen people' and to cease isolating itself in the name of a fanciful history or dubious biology and excluding the 'other' from its midst?"[51] In a second book, published in 2012 under the title *The Invention of the Land of Israel*, he set out "to deconstruct the concept of the Jewish 'historical right' to the Land of Israel and its associated nationalist narratives, whose only purpose was to establish moral legitimacy for the appropriation of territory."[52] The provocative title of his following book seemed a logical next step in this development. He called it, *How I Stopped Being a Jew*. More interesting than the highly questionable arguments in his books was their reception. While almost all experts in the field rejected Sand's historical theories, such as the often mentioned but never proved mass conversion of Khazars to Judaism, as baseless, his books made it onto Israel's bestseller list and were translated into many languages. Despite their success, neither Burg nor Sand can claim a substantial following in Israel or, for that matter, in the Jewish diaspora.

In the age of globalization, "normality" means something entirely different for the Jewish state than what it meant half a century ago. If once the Jewish community was singled out as being global and spreading across the earth, today this is not a unique condition but a reality for many other peoples as well. In the eyes of many, it is precisely the diaspora, which once looked so "abnormal," that makes the Jews seem more "normal" today, while the nation-state has, at least in the eyes of some observers, an anachronistic ring to it.[53] It is crucial to be aware of the background of post-Zionist discussions on the Jewish state if one wants to understand the wave of novels about alternative Jewish states that washed over Israel in recent years.

"People, Brothers, Welcome to Neuland—a communal therapeutic space based on the principles of Benjamin Ze'ev Herzl." Thus reads the beginning of an informative brochure for guests at the farm founded by retired Zahal officer Meni Peleg in Argentina. In close vicinity to the agricultural settlement of Moisés Ville, which was founded by Baron Hirsch's Jewish Colonization Association in the late nineteenth century, Neuland serves as a safe haven for Israelis traumatized by war. "Neuland was not established to be a substitute for Altneuland, which is the State of Israel. Our goal, at the moment, is to challenge, to place a mirror, to bring people closer together, to be a miniature 'shadow state,' if you will, to remind the State of Israel what it was supposed to be. And what it can be."[54] In Neuland, there is no violence and complete equality between its Jewish and non-Jewish inhabitants. Telephones are forbidden, and visitors are allowed in only after thorough background checks.

Neuland is of course a fictitious settlement, and Meni Peleg a literary character in the novel of the same name by Israeli writer Eshkol Nevo. Nevo, who was born in 1971 as the grandson of Israel's third prime minister, Levi Eshkol, returns in this novel to the initial ideals of the Zionist movement and asks if and how those ideals were implemented in the Jewish state. Nevo also confronts the phenomenon of Israelis leaving their country. In *Neuland*—just as in reality—it is especially young Israelis who travel through the world after finishing their military service. South America is among their most popular destinations. While most return to Israel, Nevo imag-

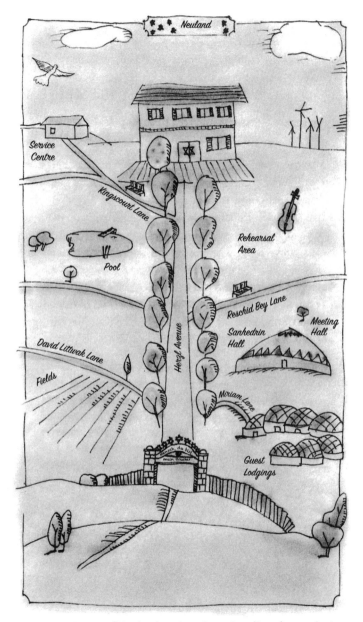

FIGURE 20. A map of Neuland, an imaginary Israeli settlement in Argentina, from Eshkol Nevo's novel *Neuland*.

ines a group of them building a Jewish collective settlement
in Argentina. He thus combines Herzl's utopian vision from
Altneuland with the real settlements of Baron Hirsch in Argentina and the kibbutz ideal of early Israel. Ironically, in
Nevo's vision it is young Israelis who revive the ideals of the
anti-Zionist Hirsch in order to build a better Israel in Argentina, a place Herzl had suggested as a possible alternative to
Palestine for his future Jewish state.

The leader of the colony is the charismatic visionary Meni
Peleg ("Señor Neuland"), who resembles Herzl himself or his
literary hero David Littwak, after whom a street in Neuland
is named (and there are other streets named after other characters in Herzl's novel). Peleg compares his project to Herzl's
imaginary ship, the *Futuro*, in which he assembles the bright-
est and fittest minds of the world to assess the Jewish state.

Just as in Altneuland, in Neuland too, the question arises
of whether it should serve as a model for all humankind. And
just as Herzl—and Ben-Gurion—clung to the idea of a model
society, the character Sarah in Neuland tells us, "we stop being
the persecuted Jews of the Holocaust and start being 'a light
unto the nations,' as Herzl envisioned it."[55] In Neuland too,
there are heated debates about who is to be allowed in as a
member of this "New Society." "Who is a Neulander?" Ironically, Israel, in Zionist imagination the destination of all emigrants, here becomes the country of origin, the "source country" for the emigrants to Neuland.[56] When the son of the
founder, Dori Peleg (Dori was also the short form of Theodor
Herzl's first name), asks his father why such a new foundation
was necessary, he replies: "A country cannot exist only to survive, Dori'nu. The original reason for the establishment of
Israel was to gather all the Jews of the Diaspora in a place
where they would not be persecuted. But that *was* the purpose,

past tense. A country needs a vision. A country without a vision is like a family without love. And if there's no love, why preserve the family?"[57]

In Nevo's novel, the protagonists are longing to fulfill Herzl's dream and establish a real *Altneuland*. Most of them want to return to Israel, but only to a changed Israel. One of the characters, reminded of the proverbial wandering Jew, disagrees; in his definition of a home he defies the Zionist idea of a return to Israel: "A home is not a place you live in; it's a place you know you can go back if you want. And you don't need more than one place like that."[58]

Nevo, however, has chosen to set his experiment of returning to Herzl's ideals outside Israel. And he is not the only Israeli writer with phantasies of an alternative Zion far from Palestine. Nava Semel's novel *I-srael (Isra-Isle)* ties in with Mordecai Noah's 1825 plan to establish a Jewish state on Grand Island in Buffalo, New York.[59] While Semel's novel is an encounter between Israeli and native American phantasies in the northern part of New York state, Yoav Avni's *Herzl Amar* (Herzl Said) describes a fictitious Jewish state in the heart of East Africa. In implementing Herzl's scheme (if only in a work of fiction), Avni describes a Jewish state that was actually established in Uganda (though the original Uganda Plan referred to an area in today's Kenya). In the novel, two friends decide, after finishing their army service in Jewish Uganda, to visit the historical home of the Jewish people in Palestine, where they find a mostly Arab population with smaller groups of German-speaking Templers and Yiddish-speaking Orthodox Jews.[60]

All three novels reverse Herzl's *Old New Land* and set out to establish a Jewish state in some of the places once considered alternatives to Zion: Grand Island in Buffalo, Argentina,

and Uganda. The same theme became popular in English-
language literature, when American-Jewish writer Michael
Chabon published his best-selling novel, *The Yiddish Policemen's Union*, in 2007, in which the State of Israel is destroyed
a few months after its establishment in 1948 and a Jewish home
is being built in Alaska.[61] One might dismiss these counterfactual novels as irrelevant phantasies, but it is significant that
they were all written within a few years of one another and
took up a theme that was very much discussed within Israeli
intellectual circles. It seemed a consolation for some Israelis
to dream for a moment of an alternative Jewish state, far away
and peaceful.

At the same time, other authors described the more real
destinations of Israelis. The Jewish and Israeli presence in Germany played a significant part in the writings of some of the
most respected Israeli writers, such as Yoram Kaniuk in *The
Last Berliner* (2002) and Chaim Beer in his *Bebelplatz* (2010).
Younger writers turned to the new Israeli community in Berlin, among them Ilan Goren, whose book *Where Are You,
Motek?* appeared in German. It deals critically with Berlin,
where Goren was a correspondent for an Israeli TV station, as
a new home for young Israelis. He describes the kinds of Israelis that tend to come to Berlin in an ironic fashion: There
was "an airlift between Tel Aviv and Berlin. Whole planes full
of film directors and screenwriters were brought in, their hair
carefully tousled, and their Israeli passports were accompanied
by recently issued EU documents. Besides the unkempt artists,
there were gold diggers in the real estate business and scholarship hunters of all colors, among them musicians, painters,
video artists and journalists, me being one of them. . . . The
creative ones went into the Eastern part of the city, the ones
with money into the Western part. It looked as if the video

artists had received an order to occupy Friedrichshain [in the East] and the real estate agents a marching order to Charlottenburg [in the West]."[62]

Other European cities also play a part in the imagination and reality of Israeli writers and artists. Etgar Keret, one of Israel's most celebrated writers, found a temporary home in Warsaw, where he lived in an art installation: The Keret House, designed by Polish architect Jakub Szczęsny, is reputed to be the narrowest house of the world. It occupies a tiny opening between two high rises. Besides providing a bed for its only occupant, Etgar Keret, it also has a study room, where he can entertain visitors.[63] The house is an escape from Israel, but it also represents Israel in its smallness and vulnerability.

The Jewish return to Poland is a central motif in the video art of Israeli artist Yael Bartana. Born in 1970, she belongs to the same generation as Eshkol and Keret, and like them she is intensively engaged in the thought of a fictitious return to the diaspora. Her video project "Europe Will be Stunned" is one of the most provocative Israeli works of art. It deals with a seemingly failed utopia. In the first part of the video trilogy (2007), a Polish activist stands in a huge decaying soccer stadium and gives a speech appealing to the descendants of three million Polish Jews to return to Poland. In the second part ("Wall and Power," 2009), a group of young pioneers builds a wooden settlement with barracks and a watchtower in the area of the former Warsaw ghetto, as a first sign of realizing the call of return. The place looks like a cross between a kibbutz and a concentration camp. In the third part ("Assassination"), which was the Polish contribution to the Venice Biennale in 2011, the young Polish activist who had called for a return of Jews to Poland is murdered and his body publicly displayed.

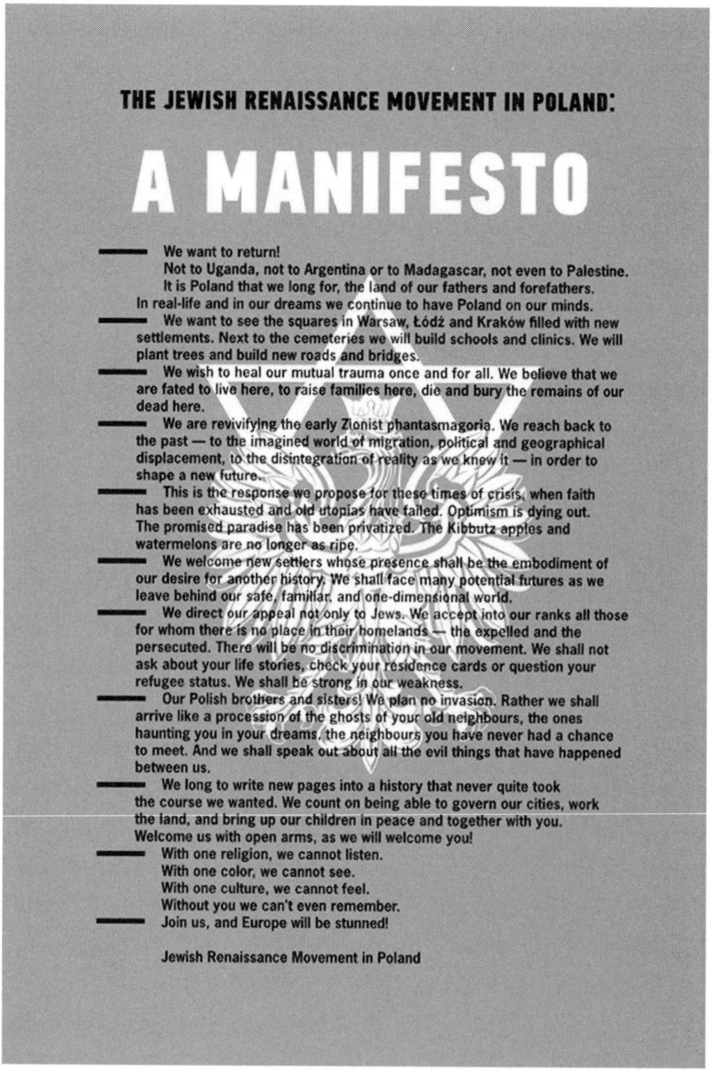

THE JEWISH RENAISSANCE MOVEMENT IN POLAND:

A MANIFESTO

—— We want to return!
Not to Uganda, not to Argentina or to Madagascar, not even to Palestine.
It is Poland that we long for, the land of our fathers and forefathers.
In real-life and in our dreams we continue to have Poland on our minds.

—— We want to see the squares in Warsaw, Łódź and Kraków filled with new
settlements. Next to the cemeteries we will build schools and clinics. We will
plant trees and build new roads and bridges.

—— We wish to heal our mutual trauma once and for all. We believe that we
are fated to live here, to raise families here, die and bury the remains of our
dead here.

—— We are revivifying the early Zionist phantasmagoria. We reach back to
the past — to the imagined world of migration, political and geographical
displacement, to the disintegration of reality as we knew it — in order to
shape a new future.

—— This is the response we propose for these times of crisis, when faith
has been exhausted and old utopias have failed. Optimism is dying out.
The promised paradise has been privatized. The Kibbutz apples and
watermelons are no longer as ripe.

—— We welcome new settlers whose presence shall be the embodiment of
our desire for another history. We shall face many potential futures as we
leave behind our safe, familiar, and one-dimensional world.

—— We direct our appeal not only to Jews. We accept into our ranks all those
for whom there is no place in their homelands — the expelled and the
persecuted. There will be no discrimination in our movement. We shall not
ask about your life stories, check your residence cards or question your
refugee status. We shall be strong in our weakness.

—— Our Polish brothers and sisters! We plan no invasion. Rather we shall
arrive like a procession of the ghosts of your old neighbours, the ones
haunting you in your dreams, the neighbours you have never had a chance
to meet. And we shall speak out about all the evil things that have happened
between us.

—— We long to write new pages into a history that never quite took
the course we wanted. We count on being able to govern our cities, work
the land, and bring up our children in peace and together with you.
Welcome us with open arms, as we will welcome you!

—— With one religion, we cannot listen.
With one color, we cannot see.
With one culture, we cannot feel.
Without you we can't even remember.

—— Join us, and Europe will be stunned!

Jewish Renaissance Movement in Poland

FIGURE 21. A fictitious call for the Jewish return to Poland from Yael
Bartana's art project.

Bartana's project was not restricted to the filming and screening of a video project. She designed and distributed posters in Polish, English, and Yiddish advertising a made-up "Jewish Renaissance Movement in Poland" (JRMiP), which claimed the right of Jews to return, not to Argentina, not to Madagascar, and not even to Palestine, but to Poland, in order "to heal our mutual trauma once and for all." Like Señor Neuland in Eshkol Nevo's novel, the movement claims to be the true heir to the Zionist experiment: "We are revivifying the early Zionist phantasmagoria. We reach back to the past—to the world of migration, political and geographical displacement, to the disintegration of reality as we knew it—in order to shape a new future."[64]

As the next and final step in Bartana's project, a congress convened in Berlin in May 2012, which was attended by a number of intellectuals, artists, and academics. They discussed three topics: First, how should the EU change in order to welcome "the Other"? Second, how should Poland change within a re-imagined EU? And third, how should Israel change to become part of the Middle East? Of course, the congress's suggestions were not to be taken literally. They included imposing a "reintegration" tax on all Polish citizens to pay for the immigration of three million Jews and making Hebrew an official language in Poland.[65] But the fact that Israeli, Palestinian, German, Polish, and American professors, museum directors, and writers took time to discuss such an imaginary project, shows how blurred the lines between an art project and political aspirations had become.

And indeed, the separation between fiction and reality is not always easy to draw when Hebrew is spoken by thousands of people in the immediate vicinity of Berlin's Wannsee Villa, where the "Final Solution of the Jewish Question" was planned in 1942; when an Israeli writer builds his home in the former Warsaw Ghetto; and when Israelis regularly commute between Paris or Budapest and Tel Aviv.

ISRAEL LOST AND FOUND

Just as the emigration of Israelis back into the diaspora was not part of the original "normalization program" of Zionism, the immigration of people from Africa and Asia, who at least until recently were not regarded as Jewish, was well beyond the imagination of Israel's founders. With very few Jews left in the former Soviet Union and Europe, no potential immigrants in Arab countries, and no realistic prospects of drawing masses of American Jews, Israel's future immigrants may well come from sub-Saharan Africa and South Asia. It is there that hundreds of thousands, perhaps millions of people are waiting to be officially recognized as Jews. British historian Tudor Parfitt, who is recognized as the world's leading scholar of this phenomenon, estimates that in today's world there are more "emerging Jews" than Jews who are Jewish by conventional definition. His Israeli colleague Shalva Weil believes that economic motives are one factor behind these sub-Saharan Africans' "rediscovery" of their Jewish roots and desire to immigrate to Israel.[66]

Israel's rise from a developing to a first-world country and the despair of many people in the poorest parts of the world certainly contribute to the sudden surge of interest in Jewish roots. But there are other reasons as well, such as the search for a new identity that distinguishes people from their surroundings, and the identification of their own suffering with the suffering of the Jews throughout history. In her study on the black Jews of Africa, Edith Bruder writes: "The groups under study seem to find in a Lost Tribes identity an important source for sustaining moral and political power."[67]

The first Jewish immigration wave from sub-Saharan Africa reached Israel in the 1980s, with the arrival of Ethiopian Jews. While their origins and their religious practices are disputed, the existence of this group, often called *falashas*, was known as early as in the nineteenth century.[68] When they first arrived in Israel, the Chief Rabbinate insisted that they would undergo a formal conversion ceremony, which caused an outcry not only among the immigrants but also among large segments of the Israeli public. In the end, the Chief Rabbinate had to give in and recognize them as Jews.

Thirty years later, many tribes in Africa have discovered what they consider their Jewish roots. Some, but not all of them, claim to be descendants of the ten lost tribes; i.e., of the northern kingdom of Israel that was destroyed by the Assyrians in 722 BCE.[69] In Nigeria, approximately 30,000 Igbo practice a form of Jewish religion and many of them are preparing for future immigration to Israel under the "Law of Return." The potential for "new Jews" is, however, much larger, as up to two million Igbos believe themselves to be descendants of the ancient Israelites.[70] In Zimbabwe and South Africa, 50,000 Lemba trace their origins to biblical Israel. They claim that part of the lost tribes migrated through Yemen into the southern part of Africa carrying the ark of the covenant with them. Most today practice a religion that combines elements of Judaism and Christianity.[71]

In Sefwi Wiawso in southwestern Ghana, there is a small new community that purports to be Jewish. Like the *Diaspora Jiosy Gasy* (Malagasy Jewish Diaspora) of Madagascar, the *Beth Yeshourun* (House of the Righteous) of Cameroon, and the Gogodala of Papua New Guinea, and like the better-known Lemba and Igbo, they claim descent from ancient Israel, and most openly and eagerly display their allegiance to Judaism and Israel. According to Tudor Parfitt, "on Israel Independence Day you see more Israeli flags in Port Moresby, the capital of Papua New Guinea, than you do in Tel Aviv."[72] In Mexico and other parts of Latin America, *anusim* (descendants of Jews who allegedly were converted to Catholicism by force centuries ago) now want to return to their ancestors' religion. In Uganda, the Abayudaya, who have a longer history of claiming Jewishness, are split into different Jewish denominations. They have today over two thousand members, maintain five synagogues, several Jewish schools, and—perhaps a sign of genuine Jewish vitality—there are fights between their Orthodox and Conservative congregations.[73] There were reports that the former Liberian dictator Charles Taylor adopted Judaism during his pretrial custody at the International Court in The Hague. According to one of his wives, he had planned to do so for many years.[74]

In the age of the Internet, the black Jews of Africa are increasingly connected with one another, and with the Black Hebrews in North America, who also trace their line to the ten lost tribes and compare their experience of persecution with that of the "white Jews." Since the 1990s, geneticists have tried to evaluate the validity of claims to Jewish ancestry by analyzing DNA. Though these analyses are highly disputed, they would seem to support the Lembas being genetically related to Jews in other countries.[75] "Subsequently many other groups, such as the Bene Menashe and the Bene Ephraim, have also tried to use genetics in support of their claims. The idea that Jewish authenticity has something to do with genetics has caught on. Even the vaguest whiff of a suggestion that there may be some genetic link has been sufficient grounds for some religious authorities to declare a group *zera Israel* (of Jewish origin)."[76]

The self-proclaimed descendants of the biblical Israelites are by no means restricted to Africa. In Northeast India, along the border to Myanmar, thousands of members of the Mizo, Kuki, and Chin peoples wait for their official recognition as Jews. After having studied Judaism for years and practiced the religion, they want to formally convert and, in many cases, to emigrate to Israel. Most of their ancestors were converted to Christianity in the early 19th century. It seems that Judaism was introduced to them by millenarian Welsh missionaries, and that they internalized some of the traditions that were taught by them about the ten lost tribes.[77] Other groups claiming to be Jewish are descendants of North African immigrants to the Amazon region, and the so-called "Inka Jews" in Peru, who do not claim biblical origins but converted to Judaism, just as did the residents of the Italian village of San Nicandro, who by now have almost all arrived in Israel.

Tudor Parfitt believes that we will see an expansion of this phenomenon of "emerging Jewish communities" in the future: "In Africa—in Ghana and Ivory Coast, in Nigeria, in Sierra Leone and Cameroon, in Zimbabwe, in South Africa, in Uganda and Kenya, in Malawi, in Cape Verde, in Ethiopia and Somalia, in Zambia, around the Great Lakes, in Congo, various groups have been constructed or have emerged into being, for a wide range of reasons, and now form part of differentiated cultures, which are increasingly linked one with the other. In the United States, Israel, Africa, and elsewhere, including Papua New Guinea where there are altogether millions of black Israelism, groups that exist increasingly consider themselves and may be considered by others as a completely legitimate, transnational, black Hebrew/Israelite community, with increasingly strong ties with other sections of the Jewish world."[78]

There is little historical credibility of the "lost tribe" stories. And even if there is a biological connection to Jews
around the world, it does not make a person Jewish. Jewishness is neither proven through DNA nor through practicing
vaguely biblical religious notions, often in combination with
Christian or Muslim practices. The Jewish religion as we know
it today developed only in the post-biblical period, long after
the disappearance of the "lost tribes" with the integration of
oral traditions that were gradually written down in the Talmud and rabbinical literature.[79]

While most Jews are skeptical about recognizing what
some scholars call "wannabe Jews," there are groups in Israel
whose mission it is to have them acknowledged as Jews and
to "bring them home" to Israel. When the state was founded,
a committee (*aguda le-ma'an nidhey Israel*) had already been
established, with the involvement of Israel's later president
Yitzhak Ben-Zvi, to search for the lost tribes of Israel. Today,
other institutions are active in Israel and the United States,
such as *Amishav* (My People Returns), founded by Rabbi
Elyahu Avichail in the 1980s with the goal of bringing as many
descendants of the lost tribes back to Israel as possible, and
Shavei Israel (Returners of Israel), an initiative by New York-
born Michael Freund, a former deputy communications director of the Netanyahu government and a correspondent for the
Jerusalem Post. Assisted by evangelical circles in the United
States, they have already brought thousands of people to Israel,
mainly from South East Asia.[80] In 2005, the Sephardic Chief
Rabbi Shlomo Amar declared the Mizo Jews from the Mani-
pur and Mizoram regions of Northeast India as Bnei Menashe
who needed only to go through an uncomplicated formal
conversion ceremony. After undergoing the procedure, they
would be eligible to immigrate to Israel under the Law of

FIGURE 22. A member of the Indian Bnei Menashe, who regard themselves as a lost tribe of Israel, stands in Israeli uniform beside his grandmother.

Return. Many of them were already settled in the occupied territories, including at Kiryat Arba, a stronghold of messianic radicals. This in turn led to debates in Israel about the political co-opting of these recent immigrants for the purpose of reinforcing the settlements. The Department for Diaspora Affairs established a committee to deal with groups that had "ties with Judaism and the Jewish communities."[81] In the meantime, the activism of these groups began to cause disruption in their native regions.

Besides these "emerging Jews" there are hundreds of thousands of recent non-Jewish migrants to Israel, who have come as guest workers from the Philippines, Thailand, India, Sri Lanka, Romania, and other countries. In 2012, over 200,000 foreign workers were officially employed in Israel.[82] The total number of foreign employees is probably much higher. They work principally in senior care, agriculture, and construction

and typically earn 40 percent less than their Israeli counter-
parts and 20 percent less than Palestinian workers from across
the Green Line.[83] Israel Drori, in his study about foreign workers in Israel, reports that "these workers are here to stay, and
in spite of setbacks, they gradually have embedded themselves
in the host society, especially within large urban centers."[84]
Here, again, it is not easy to judge if this process is part of the
"normalization" of the Jewish state. To be sure, every modern
Western state employs foreign workers; and in this respect, it
is a normal development. At the same time, it would seem
counter to the traditional Zionist ethos of *avoda ivrit* (Hebrew
labor), the idea that the Jews, once resettled in their own country, would be able to do all necessary labor themselves.

Another group of recent non-Jewish arrivals are the non-
Jewish family members of Jewish immigrants who were part
of the large immigration from the former Soviet Union. They
can enter and stay legally under a broad definition of the Law
of Return. While in the early 1990s, with the beginning of
Russian-Jewish immigration, more than 90 percent of immigrants from the former Soviet Union were Jewish according
to *halakha*, this number shrank to under 50 percent after 2000.
In other words, the majority of Russian and Ukrainian immigrants to Israel in more recent years were not Jewish.

Finally, there are African refugees without any claim to
Jewish descent who come in search for a new home, diversify-
ing Israeli society today. While most refugees from Africa tried
to get to Europe in recent years, some realized that the one
country with a Western living standard that they could get to
without crossing the Mediterranean was Israel. They had only
to cross Egypt's Sinai Peninsula. Between 1977 and 1979, newly
elected Prime Minister Menachem Begin took in 360 Vietnamese boat refugees as a humanitarian gesture. Many of their

descendants are today Israeli citizens. Their number was small and Begin's act largely symbolic, but, in the early 2000s, a much larger number of refugees from Eritrea, Congo, and Sudan poured across Israel's southern border. According to estimates, about 60,000 African refugees reached Israel between 2005 and 2015. Many of them settled in the poor neighborhoods of South Tel Aviv, where they found work in restaurants and other businesses. Their legal status is undefined, as Israel does not have asylum laws. When the state was founded, no one imagined that it would one day serve as an asylum for non-Jewish refugees.

As in most Western countries, so in Israel, this undocumented immigration evoked both gestures of welcome and expressions of resentment. A number of private organizations helped the new arrivals find places to live, learn the language, and get settled. Their support countered street protests and acts of violence against the refugees, who were often viewed in the context of fear of terrorists' infiltration. The Netanyahu government reacted by building a fence along the southern wall of Israel and by taking measures to return some of the refugees to their countries of origin.[85]

While Israelis leaving the country and newly emerging Jews and non-Jews coming to Israel made Israel a more diverse and complex society, there were profound changes taking place within Israel's core society. It is a demographic shift within the main groups of the Israeli population that presents the greatest challenge for Israel today, after the first seven decades of its existence. This is the phenomenon that Israel's President Reuven Rivlin has identified as Israel's New Order, and it will be discussed in the concluding chapter.

ISRAEL'S NEW ORDER

How to deal with the Palestinians and ongoing
wars is just foreground. In the background is a
contest over what kind of state Israel must be.[1]

—BERNARD AVISHAI

At the fifteenth annual Herzliya conference in June 2015, Israeli
President Reuven Rivlin made the following remarks:

Israeli society is undergoing a far-reaching transformation.
This is not a trivial change, it is a transformation that will
restructure our very identity as "Israelis," and will have a
profound impact on the way we understand ourselves and
our national home; there is no escape from this change.
These changes may well stir up, for some of us, nostalgia
for "the old and much loved Israel," but those experiences
of togetherness sitting around an imaginary Israeli campfire will not return.

I am standing here today, because I have identified a
very real threat in our collective suppression of the transformations that Israeli society has been undergoing in recent decades; in neglecting to confront what I call the
"new Israeli order," the significance of which I want to deal
with today.

The "new Israeli order" is not an apocalyptic prophecy.
It is the reality. A reality that can already be seen in the
composition of the first grade classes in the Israeli educa-

tion system. In the 1990s, Israeli society comprised a clear and firm majority, with minority groups alongside it. A large secular Zionist majority, and beside it three minority groups: a national-religious minority, an Arab minority, and a Haredi minority. Although this pattern remains frozen in the minds of much of the Israeli public, in the press, in the political system, all the while, the reality has totally changed.

Today, the first grade classes are composed of about 38% secular Jews, about 15% national religious, about one quarter Arabs, and close to a quarter Haredim. While it is true that numbers and definitions are dynamic, neither identities nor birth-rates remain static over time. But one thing is clear, the demographic processes that are restructuring or redesigning the shape of Israeli society, have, in fact, created a "new Israeli order." A reality in which there is no longer a clear majority, nor clear minority groups. A reality in which Israeli society is comprised of four population sectors, or, if you will, four principal "tribes," essentially different from each other, and growing closer in size. Whether we like it or not, the make-up of the "stakeholders" of Israeli society, and of the State of Israel, is changing before our eyes.

This was not just another speech by another Israeli president. Rivlin was delivering a wake-up call to those secular middle-class, mainly Tel Aviv-based Israelis who live in a bubble, either unaware of the changes around them or in denial of them. The New Israeli order that Rivlin describes still knows divisions between right and left, between rich and poor, between Jews with origins in Europe and in the Arab world, but all of these differences are in constant flux. People change their political outlooks, rise and decline in the economic order, and marry partners whose ethnic origins are different from their own. The rifts between the four groups mentioned by Rivlin, however, reach deeper. Members of these groups cleave to their respective school systems, walk in their own social circles, marry within their group, and share distinct ideas of what a Jewish state should be. Rivlin's nostalgic notion of "the old and much loved Israel . . . around an imaginary campfire" is still very much alive, especially among outside observers. For many Israelis, however, life in an extremely fragmented society is a daily reality.

Israel's Central Bureau of Statistics projects that by 2019 only 40 percent of Israel's elementary school children will study in the national public school system (which includes both secular and national-religious schools), while the majority will attend either *haredi* (ultra-Orthodox) or Arab schools. Once out of school, most will *not* serve in the army, unless the country's laws and these groups' attitudes change. The Israeli army will thus cease to be a unifying factor in a society divided by ethnicity, religion, class, and politics. When Israel's first prime minister, David Ben-Gurion, agreed to a compromise to exempt ultra-Orthodox yeshiva students from obligatory military service, it applied to four hundred Talmud students. Seventy years later, their number is in the tens of thousands.[2]

Anyone wishing to observe the various Israels of today would be well advised to take a trip from Tel Aviv to Jerusalem. The two cities are only forty miles apart, and a new fast-speed train makes the journey in half an hour. But in many ways the two cities could not be further apart. Tel Aviv is a secular, hedonistic Mediterranean city famous for its gourmet (non-kosher) restaurants, dance clubs, and a vibrant LGBT scene. Sun-tanned bodies in shorts and bikinis, IT managers in business suits, and twenty-first-century flaneurs fill its lively boulevards and the beachside cafés. In Jerusalem, religion dominates street life. In the shadow of the Western Wall, the Dome of the Rock, and the Church of the Holy Sepulchre, black-clad Hassidic Jews with side locks and fur hats, Muslim women in their hijabs, and Christian monks in robes of all colors and denominations cross one another's paths. On Friday, people in the Muslim parts of town gather for prayer in the many mosques of the city. On the Sabbath, in the Jewish parts of town, most of the restaurants are closed, no busses are on the streets, and a sacred atmosphere prevails. On Sunday, church bells can be heard in the Christian quarters. The thirty-minute ride from Tel Aviv to Jerusalem is a ride not only to a different city but into a different world. Tel Aviv is a worldly metropolis, a small Manhattan or Paris, Berlin or Buenos Aires. Jerusalem is a unique city, which gave birth to two religions and is held holy by a third. Tel Aviv is also a rather homogenous secular Jewish city, while Jerusalem boasts of a diversity of *haredim*, national-religious Jews, Arab Muslims, and Christians, alongside a secular minority. Tel Aviv wants to be a "normal" Western city, while Jerusalem is a sacred space and unquestionably a part of the Middle East.

The contrast between these two cities was visible even more than usual during the fall of 2013, when two very special burials occurred within a few weeks of each other. On November 27, 2013, thousands of mourners assembled at the historical Trumpeldor Cemetery in central Tel Aviv. In close proximity to the graves of the erstwhile rivals in the Zionist movement, Max Nordau and Ahad Ha'am, and alongside the bodies of the national poets Hayim Nahman Bialik and Shaul Tchernichovsky, Israel's most beloved pop singer, Arik Einstein,

FIGURE 23. Jerusalem, center of religious Israel.

FIGURE 24. Tel Aviv, center of secular Israel.

found his eternal rest. As Chemi Shalev wrote in *Ha'aretz*: "He was our Frank Sinatra, our Elvis Presley, our Bruce Springsteen—all rolled into one. Einstein was the embodiment of the new, liberal, secular Israel that we once thought we would be."[3] His colleague Ari Shavit's obituary of Einstein was a eulogy not just of a generation's idol but of the old Israel in its entirety. He entitled it "The Singer of a Lost Israel."[4]

The mourners who followed the funeral from rooftops around the cemetery felt as if they were burying the old Israel. They listened to the singer Shalom Chanoch, the actor Chaim Topol, and Prime Minister Netanyahu. And they also listened to Einstein's old companion, the film director and actor Uri Zohar, who more than anyone else embodied the change the observers sensed in the air. Many years ago, the erstwhile stand-up comedian and singer who had once been sentenced to community service for the possession of marijuana, had become an ultra-Orthodox Jew and rabbi. He was a conspicuous figure at this rather secular funeral, with his long white beard and his black coat. Zohar was not only a family friend, but a family member. Two of his sons had married two of Einstein's daughters—who both turned to Orthodoxy as well.

Zohar had been less exposed at the funeral he had attended just a few weeks earlier. On October 7, 2013, the former Sephardic Chief Rabbi Ovadia Yosef had died, at age ninety-five, in Jerusalem. He was an iconic figure among the Sephardic Jews in Israel. His burial took place the evening of his passing, and even at such short notice over 800,000 took part in the mourning procession through the city. It was the largest assembly of people Israel had ever seen, and as some observers noted, probably the most populous Jewish crowd ever assembled since the destruction of the Second Temple almost two thousand years earlier. Police feared that roofs might collapse under the weight of the people who had climbed to the tops of buildings for a better view. Traffic in Jerusalem came to a complete halt. In contrast to the melancholy comments about Israeli society made after Einstein's funeral, no one spoke here of the death of the old Israel or the decline of Orthodox Judaism. Unlike Einstein's daughters, who had left secular life behind, Uri Zohar's eleven children had remained faithful to Orthodox Judaism. Rabbi Yosef's Israel was self-confident and sure that the future belonged to it. Between Ovadia Yosef's and Arik Einstein's funerals there was a time span of six weeks—and the ever-growing distance between Jerusalem and Tel Aviv.

This episode exemplifies the enormous transformation Israeli society had undergone in just one generation and illuminates the rather abstract picture drawn by President Rivlin. Each group designated by Rivlin stands for a different concept of what kind of a state Israel should become in the future. There are the Haredi (ultra-Orthodox) Jews, who envision a state according to the rules of *halakha*. There is the national-religious populace, who in their vast majority are adamant about holding on to the West Bank and granting more weight to religious laws that favor the Jewish part of the state. There is the Arab-Palestinian society, which demands a "state of all its citizens" and an end to the favoring of Jewish interests in the state's symbols and actions. And there is the shrinking secular group, which wants to live in a modern Western society, with a clear separation between state and religion. Just as there are many more ways of living than in Jerusalem and Tel Aviv, these four segments of society are also divided into many more sub-segments: Hasidic and non-Hasidic ultra-Orthodox; radical and moderate national-religious; Muslim, Christian, and secular Palestinians; and left-wing and right-wing secular Jews, to mention but a few of these subdivisions.

The fastest growing among these groups are the *haredim*. Their proportional increase within Israel's population was only delayed in the 1990s and early 2000s due to the immigration of one million Jews from the former Soviet Union, who were almost in their entirety secular. Today, the *haredi* community is increasing at a rate of 6 percent a year, which is more than three times the 1.8 percent growth rate of Israeli society over all. Even though there has been a slight decrease in recent years, the average *haredi* family still has more than six children.[5] By 2039 they are projected to constitute close to 20 percent of Israel's total population (compared to 11 percent in 2015).[6]

This change is not only of a quantitative, but also of a qualitative nature. Over the decades, Orthodox Jews in Israel have modified their position towards the Jewish state. The *haredim* have gone from total rejection of the idea of a Jewish state to various degrees of accommodation. In order to enhance their interests, such as support for their schools and other institutions, and to compensate for their exemption from military service, they participate in their majority (although not in their entirety) in state institutions, including the government, and a small but growing number even join the army voluntarily. Originally a purely Ashkenazi phenomenon, they have succeeded in recruiting a substantial following among the descendants of immigrants from Muslim countries. Even with increasing acceptance of the State of Israel and the knowledge that no other state would support their institutions as much as Israel, their Israeli identity is marginal compared to their Jewish identity. When asked, if they were Jewish or Israeli first, 91 percent of *haredim* answered Jewish, as compared to only 20 percent of secular Israelis. Only one third identified themselves as Zionists.[7]

This stands in high contrast to the national-religious camp, which today regards itself as the vanguard of Zionism. When the *Mizrahi* movement was founded as a small national-religious element within a mostly secular Zionist movement in 1902, it subordinated the Orthodox belief that only the messiah could lead the Jews into the holy land to the conviction that a Jewish state would save lives in times of persecution. Its support for political Zionism was pragmatic rather than ideological. For decades, even after the establishment of the State of Israel, the National Religious Party was a relatively moderate force that went along with the left-wing Zionist majority. After 1967, with the conquest of the holy sites in Jerusalem and on the West Bank of the Jordan River, vital segments within the national-religious camp shifted their ideology from a pragmatic position that regarded the State of Israel as at best compatible with conflicting messianic views to a theological position that turned the secular Zionist enterprise itself into a messianic endeavor. To this way of thinking, the State of Israel by its very existence enhances the coming of the messiah. As a result, the national-religious population, and among them a large part of the settler movement, sees itself no longer as a bystander but rather as the new spearhead of Zionism and views the Jewish state as the harbinger of the messianic age.

For both national-religious and *haredi* Jews, the internationally recognized borders of the State of Israel have ultimately as little meaning as the land swaps suggested by several secular politicians, which would exclude some of the holiest sites of Judaism. There is a strong consensus among Orthodox Jews of all creeds that it is necessary to annex the West Bank, as suggested by the political leader of the national-religious camp, education minister Naftali Bennett. In a 2016 poll, 99 percent of all Orthodox Jews (as compared to 31 percent of secular Jews) claimed that Israel was given to the Jewish people by God. Once a theological argument is granted as legitimate reason for Israel's existence, no rational logic can define its borders.[8]

The State of Israel means two fundamentally different things to its secular founders and to their religious heirs. For the former, Israel was meant to be a Jewish state with respect to the composition of its majority population, its function of a safe haven for all Jews, its Hebrew language, and its symbols (the flag, the national anthem, and the Jewish holidays). Ultimately, they regarded the Jewish state as a revolt against the last two millennia of Jewish history. A Jewish state and its creation of a new secular Israeli identity that would "normalize" Jewish history were their ultimate goals. For the Orthodox Jews, on the other hand, the state symbolized continuity; not a break with Jewish history, but its ultimate culmination. For them, the establishment of a Jewish state served no purpose by itself, but only as a vehicle toward their ultimate messianic goals.

A third element in Israel's New Order is the rising prominence of the Palestinian Arab sector, which has been gradually increasing its numbers in relation to Israel's total population—from 10 percent in the 1950s to over 20 percent today. The Arabs were never part of the imaginary Israeli campfire, to adopt President Rivlin's term, but there were at least serious efforts to make them a more integral part of larger Israeli society after the lifting of the martial laws to which most of them had been subjected until 1966. This hope was crushed when only half a year later, as a result of the 1967 war, an even larger number of Palestinians were brought under Israeli control, with an uncertain legal status. There was a historic irony in the fact that the civic freedom gained by Israel's Arab population after the lifting of military rule in 1966 was almost immediately followed by Israeli military rule over an even larger Palestinian population.

The Six-Day War resulted also in renewed relations between Israeli Arabs and the Palestinians across the Green Line. The two groups, no longer separated by a border, shared a growing sense of a larger Palestinian identity, a process of "Palestinization." Land Day in 1976, when six Israeli Palestinians were killed in protests against the Israeli government's announcement that it would expropriate land for the sake of security and settlement, marked a new phase and set off violent protests. The Lebanon War of the early 1980s led to a further fraying of Jewish-Arab coexistence, and the outbreak of the First Intifada in the West Bank and the Gaza Strip in December 1987 saw Israeli Arabs in widespread solidarity with the Palestinian population beyond the Green Line.

The Palestinian citizens of Israel, as they now prefer to be called, have a complex identity. Haifa University scholar Sami al-Mar'I describes them as "Palestinians (by peoplehood), Arabs (by nation), and Israelis (by citizenship)."[9] Alongside the process of Palestinization there was a process of Israelization. Sociologist Sammy Smooha came to the conclusion that "Israeli Arab citizens are a nondominant, nonassimilating, working-class minority. They are also considered by the Jews as a dissident and enemy-affiliated minority which rejects Israel's national consensus on Zionism and potentially threatens its national security."[10] He observed that since the 1980s many among Israel's Arab-Palestinian population were highly educated, committed to the values of democracy, and accepted the existence of Israel, but also felt deprived and were willing to fight hard for their equality. It was "this new Israeli Palestinian Arab who [presented] a serious challenge to the status quo and [demanded] to negotiate new terms of coexistence."[11]

There can be no doubt that Israel's Palestinian citizens have made many advances in terms of their economic life, their infrastructure, and also in the area of education.[12] They are formally equal citizens, who enjoy both active and passive voting rights, have their own political parties, and have had an occasional ambassador, Supreme Court justice, and government minister. But most lead lives separate from Jewish Israelis, whom they meet only at the university and in the workplace. They do not serve in the army for reasons agreed to by both groups. The army, though, serves an important means of integration into Israeli society, and the Arabs' exclusion is therefore seen as a major obstacle to integration. There is also a conspicuous inequality when it comes to land ownership, the distribution of local administrative services, and access to higher education. After decades of what they conceive as a second-class existence, Arab Israelis have become increasingly politicized and more vocal in their solidarity with the Palestinians beyond the Green Line. In the words of political scientist Amal Jamal of Tel Aviv University, "Palestinians in Israel, given the identity and the policies of the state, are not, and, it seems, cannot become Israeli patriots. Instead, they are increasingly becoming Palestinian patriots, attached to the land and the nation of Palestine and identified with its aspirations."[13] Still, although a majority of Israeli Palestinians support the establishment of an Arab state, an even greater majority would prefer to continue living in Israel after such a state is established.[14]

As historian Elie Rekhess remarked, besides their Palestinization and their Israelization, there is also an accelerating process of Islamization, which parallels in some ways the growing tendency of Orthodoxy among Israel's Jews. Since the 1970s, there has been an Islamic revival among Israel's Muslim population, first under the influence of the Islamic Brotherhood and in later decades also influenced by Hamas, following its rise to power in Gaza and its growing political importance in the West Bank. In Israel, Muslim associations have had considerable success in influencing the cultural life of its Palestinian citizens, its educational and its medical institutions. As a result, the mixing of young men and women in public has been restricted in some areas. Politically, the Islamic Movement in Israel splits into a more moderate southern section willing to participate in Israel's political process and a more radical northern faction that rejects the state and its institutions.[15]

The bold and optimistic visions of a harmonious coexistence have been in constant decline since the failed peace process of the 1990s. While in 2013, almost 80 percent of Israeli Arabs still expressed hope in a peaceful two-state solution, only three years later that number had shrunk to 50 percent.[16] On the Jewish side, support for the "Clinton parameters" (a demilitarized Palestinian state without settlement blocs and full Palestinian security control of the West Bank, and a Jerusalem divided and serving as the capital of both states), has steadily declined from 59 percent in 2005 to 29 percent in 2017.[17] Acceptance of Arab equality among Jewish Israelis has also dropped, with the greatest rejection of Arab equality coming from the Orthodox. In 2016, 97 percent of Orthodox Jews believed that Jews deserved preferential treatment in Israel, and a majority of Orthodox Jews in Israel were in favor even of expelling or transferring Arabs from Israel.[18]

The growing radicalization of Israel's Arab population led to a series of stabbings of Israeli Jews in the fall of 2015 and the subsequent outlawing of the northern branch of the Islamic Movement. During the same year, the Arab parties merged for the first time into one list for the Israeli elections. This "Joint List" became Israel's third-largest party with fifteen Knesset mandates.

Since the beginning of the new century, Israel's Palestinian Arabs have formulated visions of their own about their place in a future Israel and about the nature of such a state. Their theories find expression in three documents, known as "future vision papers" and published in 2006 and 2007. They include a collection of research papers (by the National Committee for the Heads of Arab Local Authorities), a classical visionary document (the "Haifa Declaration"), and a legal proposal (the Democratic Constitution), which rejects the legitimacy of an ethnic democracy that favors Jewish rights, and pleads instead for a "state of all its citizens." One document reads: "Defining the Israeli State as a Jewish State and exploiting democracy in the service of its Jewishness excludes us, and creates tension between us and the nature and essence of the State. Therefore, we call for a Consensual Democratic system that enables us to be fully active in the decision-making process and guarantees our individual and collective civil, historic, and national rights."[19]

In order to achieve equal status, the documents demand that the State of Israel acknowledge responsibility for the expulsion of Palestinians in 1948, recognize the Palestinians as the indigenous population of the land, grant them far-reaching administrative and cultural autonomy, acknowledge that Israel is the homeland of both Palestinians and Jews, refrain from adopting policies that favor the Jewish majority, and yield control over holy Christian and Muslim sites. In general, the call is for far-reaching collective rights in addition to individual rights.[20]

The documents were received with skepticism, even among the left wing of established Israeli politicians, among whom there is broad consensus about the nature of Israel as a Jewish and a democratic state and support for a future two-state solution. By contrast, the Palestinian documents call for a binational state in Israel and therefore for an end to the Jewish state. They essentially propose "a 'one and a half state solution' (a Palestinian state in the West Bank and Gaza, and a Jewish-Palestinian state in Israel), which, as far as Israeli Jews are concerned, is no solution at all."[21]

Finally, as the fourth population sector mentioned by President Rivlin, there is the once dominant group of predominantly secular Jews. Their ancestors stem from Europe, North America, North Africa, and the Middle East. They maybe left- or right-leaning. Some follow religious traditions, while others are vehemently anti-religious. But they all favor some degree of separation between state and religion, regard Israel as a society with Western values, and are the main drivers of Israel's transformation into a consumerist society. In the words of sociologist Uri Ram, "from the austerity of the 1950s and modesty of 1960s, Israel developed to an affluent, hedonistic, and globalized consumer's society in the 1990s and 2000s."[22]

Characteristics of this consumer society are the increasing proportion of multinational corporations in relation to Israeli companies, the privatization of state-owned enterprises, and the rise of new economic oligarchies. By 2005, 75 percent of all shopping in Israel was done in malls. The consumer revolution is especially pronounced in contrast to the early decades of Israel's existence, when cars, private telephones, and travel were luxuries available only to a small minority. In 1970, only 15 percent of all Israeli households owned one car; by 2010 that same percentage owned two or more cars, and more than half the population commuted to work in their own car. While installing a regular phone line was still a major achievement in the 1970s, by 2010 the average household had 2.1 cell phones (and they seem to be in constant use).[23] The number of Israelis who traveled abroad at least once a year had reached 2.3 million in 2008, almost one third of the country's population. The total number of departures to destinations abroad was 4.2 million that year. In 1990, the number of departures had still been fewer than one million.[24]

Instead of oranges, microchips symbolize the Israeli economy of today. The most global of media, the Internet, is more a part of Israeli society than of any other. Proportionally more households in Israel own computers than in nearly all of the European countries. The new narrative of Israeli society centers in its high tech sector, and its new heroes are neither the kibbutz pioneers nor the army's paratroopers of former decades, but the *startupistim* and *hightechistim*, as the Hebraized version of the new high-tech elite in the "start-up nation" is called.[25] In 2012, *Ha'aretz* estimated that between 3,500 and 5,000 start-ups operated in Israel.[26] No other country, perhaps with the exception of India, has been as successful and so much defined by developments in the high-tech arena.

Gaps between various groups within Israeli society are especially noticeable when it comes to the role of women, a role that secular and Orthodox, Jewish and Arab Israelis define in quite different ways. In recent years, the gap between the more traditional and the modern sectors began to close somewhat, as more Arab and Orthodox Jewish women joined the workforce.[27] In terms of women's political representation, the beginning of the twenty-first century marked a watershed. The number of women in the Knesset rose gradually from nine in 1996 to 18 in 2003, and reached a record number of 28 in the 2015 elections. With respect to personal status legislation, however, there is still no gender equality. Israel does not enable civil marriage (even though it recognizes civil marriages contracted abroad), which not only makes interfaith marriages in Israel impossible, but also implies gender inequalities and entails discrimination against non-Orthodox Jewish denominations.

Israel is a Jewish and democratic state, but it is not as democratic as the defenders of its democracy wish it to be, and it is not as Jewish as the defenders of Orthodox Judaism or of more nationalist values would like it to become.[28] The concept of a Jewish and democratic state was first spelled out in the Biltmore Program of 1942, which speaks of a "Jewish Commonwealth integrated in the structure of the new democratic world."[29] While Israel's Declaration of Independence does not contain the word democratic, it clearly encompasses the concept of a democratic state. "The phrase *Jewish and democratic* is not simply a slogan," writes Bernard Avishai. "It appears in something like constitutional law in Israel and has become as iconic as *life, liberty, and the pursuit of happiness.*"[30]

The Basic Laws, which took the place of Israel's constitution, began to include the model of a "Jewish and democratic state" from the mid-1980s. Thus, an amendment to the *Basic Law*, adopted by the Knesset in 1985, reads as follows: "A list of candidates shall not participate in the Knesset elections if its goals or acts explicitly or implicitly include one of the following: 1) denial of the existence of the State of Israel as the state of the Jewish people; 2) negation of the democratic character of the State; 3) incitement to racism." The implications of this law are clear: It bans any party or representative defined as racist or anti-democratic from campaigning for the Knesset, as well as those who question Israel's existence as "the state of the Jewish people."[31] For Arab politicians, this means walking a fine line between their integration to Israeli society and their preservation of a national and cultural Palestinian identity.[32]

Two Basic Laws of 1992 (*The Government* and *Freedom of Occupation*) specify the Jewish *and* democratic nature of the State of Israel. The 1992 *Basic Law: Human Dignity and Liberty* speaks of the "values of the State of Israel as a Jewish and democratic state," a phrase that since then has been repeated again and again.[33] There is no agreement, though, as to what the two principles mean, whether one principle should be valued higher than the other, or what happens when the two principles come into conflict with each other. The long-time president of Israel's Supreme Court, Aharon Barak, interpreted Jewish values as universal values and defined the Jewish character of the state "in the sense that Jews have the right to migrate there, and that their national being is reflected in the being of the state (the matter finds expression, inter alia, in language and in days of rest). The fundamental values of Judaism are the fundamental values of the state—namely, love of man, the sanctity of life, social justice, doing what is good and right, preserving human dignity, the rule of law, etc.—values bequeathed by Judaism to the entire world. These values must be approached on a universal level of abstraction that befits the democratic character of the State. Hence, the values of the State of Israel as a Jewish State cannot be identified with Jewish Law. One must not forget that a sizeable non-Jewish population lives in Israel."[34]

While Barak defined Jewish mainly in ethnic and cultural terms, some of his colleagues, such as Justice Menahem Elon, demanded a stronger role for *halakha* and the religious meaning of Jewishness. And indeed, in recent years the Jewish component has been cited more often in public discussions than the democratic one, and often with a religious undertone. In the words of historian Fania Oz-Salzberger, Israeli public discourse "has been steadily fattening the concept of Jewish and thinning the concept of democratic."[35] In 2014, Prime Minister Netanyahu's push for a new basic law on Israel as a Jewish nation-state caused his governing coalition to tumble and triggered new elections. If passed, such a law would indeed strengthen the Jewishness of the state at the expense of its democratic character. In 2017, more than 70 percent of Israelis believed that the condition of a future Palestinian state should be conditional upon Palestinian recognition of Israel as a Jewish state.[36]

In all polls, the vast majority of Israelis have over time defended both the democratic and the Jewish character of their state. But if one scratches the surface, it becomes clear that for many, "democratic" is sometimes reduced to rules. They defend elections, majority rule, and free speech, but they do not necessarily mean by those words full equality and minority rights. The definition of what Israeli democracy means varies from group to group. Israel's Palestinian citizens define it differently from its Jewish citizens, as do ultra-Orthodox from secular Israelis, Russian immigrants from American immigrants, and so on.[37]

For these and more reasons, University of Haifa Law Professor Eli Salzberger notes that "Israel's democracy should be an enigma. In light of the fact that Israel has been in a constant state of emergency since its establishment, that it is one of the few countries in which there is no written constitution limiting the powers of government, that it inherited a non-democratic colonial legal system, and that most of its founding fathers, as well as its immigrant citizens, came from countries lacking democratic traditions, how did Israel manage to establish and more importantly, maintain and develop a liberal democracy?"[38] In his view, it is public legal institutions, and above all the Supreme Court, that guarantee Israel's democratic values. His colleague Yedidia Stern agrees with Salzberger's assessment but warns of threats to Israel's democratic substance. Because of competing sources of authority (among them Jewish religious laws), the complex composition of its population, continuous existential threats from outside, and the absence of a tradition of sovereignty in Jewish history, Israel's democracy is constantly endangered and must protect itself.[39]

Some scholars stated already many years ago that Israel's democracy is limited by the Jewish character of the state and all the consequences of that character. Thus, the sociologist Sammy Smooha described Israel as an "ethnic democracy." In this model, all citizens are granted equal individual rights, while the minorities enjoy some collective rights but do not participate in ruling or power-sharing, which is exclusively left to the "core ethnic nation." Israel does not grant the same collective rights to its Palestinian citizens, who in the eyes of many Israelis are perceived as a security threat and as cultural aliens to the Zionist enterprise.[40] And indeed, among Palestinians in particular and Arabs in general, despite peace agreements and interim solutions, despite decades of negotiations and changes in leadership, there is still widespread resistance to the recognition of a Jewish state, and calls for its destruction come from as nearby as Gaza and as far away as Iran.

There is one other threat to Israeli society as a whole, which is independent of both internal divisions and external threats, and which is often overlooked in the heated debates over ethnic and religious conflicts. The growth of the Israeli population both due to large immigration numbers and high fertility poses an enormous challenge to the sustainability of a future Israel. Early Zionists warned that not more than half a million, or a million, or at best two million people could live in this small territory. Today, Israel counts more than eight million inhabitants, it still openly invites mass Jewish immigration, and both its Jewish and Arab politicians favor high birth rates either for political reasons or out of religious motivations. If this demographic pattern persists, the projected number of people living in Israel in four or five decades will be about fifteen million, even without the previous rate of increase by immigration. This would undoubtedly result in a serious deterioration in the quality of life and in an ecological disaster.[41]

Seventy years have passed since Israel was established, and a hundred-and-twenty years since it was first conceived. During this period, many different definitions of what a Jewish state means in the modern age have been floating around—with respect to Jewishness and to statehood, regarding its borders and its sovereignty, and concerning its concepts of democracy and minority rights. As the State of Israel enters its eighth decade of existence, different segments of its population offer very different paths into the future. Will there be two states west of the Jordan River or one state? Will it be a democracy with equal rights for all its citizens or an ethnocracy that favors one group over another? Will the society remain a dominantly secular one, or will religious groups make more inroads?

Today, most Israelis are no longer first-generation immigrants. They, and often their parents and grandparents too, have grown up in the first Jewish state of the modern age. They do not get up in the morning and ask themselves if they live in a state like any other state or in a unique state. They are concerned with the issues of everyday life: where to send their kids to school, when to go to the beach, which soccer team to support, how to improve their neighborhoods and lower their taxes. For them, their country is just as normal or abnormal a state as France to the French or Turkey to the Turkish. Still, the vast majority of Israelis have strong doubts that Zionism has achieved its goal of turning the Jews into a people like any other people in a state regarded by the world as just like any other state.[42]

If Theodor Herzl were alive in Israel today, he would have to study Hebrew, confront the strong role of the army in "his" state, and come to terms with the fact that the religious element is steadily growing. This was not his vision. Herzl hoped to found a miniature version of Europe in the Middle East. He would probably be shocked to learn that the existence of Israel did not lead to the end of antisemitism, but rather formed the basis for its recrudescence, often masquerading as anti-Zionism. He might regret that there is no seven-hour working day, smile at the numerous street signs that misspell his name, and wonder why it took sixty years to bury the remains of his children next to his own on Mt. Herzl. He would, however, most certainly take delight in sitting in a Viennese-style coffee house, visiting a modern opera house, and strolling through the world-class collections of the Israel Museum and the Tel Aviv Museum. He would be amazed by Israel's thriving economy and technology; its vibrant society, composed of immigrants from more than one hundred nations; its flourishing agriculture; and its highly developed urban life. All this was far from what he saw when he visited Palestine at the turn of the twentieth century.[43] Of course, it is not possible to really answer this question. Were Theodor Herzl alive today, he would not be Theodor Herzl. What is certain, though, is that his legacy is being claimed today by a variety of political camps, and that he is interpreted by the right as a nationalist and by the left as a cosmopolitan.

In its eighth decade, the State of Israel is both a better and a worse place than its founders had envisioned. It is a vibrant and dynamic society, but still it searches for peace and harmony. It is the only democracy in the Middle East, but it is not a democracy without flaws. It is a place of hope and a place of despair. It is unique and it is normal. It is a state like any other state and it is a state like none other.

INTRODUCTION: A STATE (UN)LIKE ANY OTHER STATE

1. For Zionists, Albania served as an example of a small state that was not of much concern to the rest of the world. In 1924, for example, the Zionist Revisionist Abba Ahimeir concluded his dissertation at the University of Vienna with a remark on Albania. Aba Gaissinowitsch (=Ahimeir), "Bemerkungen zu Spenglers Auffassung Russlands," 86–87. I am grateful to Peter Bergamin, Oxford, for this reference. For an intellectual biography of Berlin, see Arie M. Dubnov, *Isaiah Berlin*. On the Weizmann anecdote, see Martin Sieff, "Isaiah Berlin and Elie Kedourie: Recollections of Two Giants," in *Covenant: Global Jewish Magazine*, 1/1 (November 2006), 3.

2. David Nirenberg, *Anti-Judaism*, 1.

3. Zygmunt Bauman, "Allosemitism," 143. He credits the Polish-Jewish literary critic Artur Sandauer with the original use of the term.

4. Ibid., 150, 153.

5. Israel I. Mattuck, *What Are the Jews*, 249–51.

6. Joseph Heller, *The Zionist Idea*, 71.

7. British historian A.J.P. Taylor considered National Socialism the result of the peculiar path of German history; Helmuth Plessner created the term "belated nation;" Fritz Stern, George Mosse, and Hans Kohn emphasized the illiberal traditions and anti-modernism in German history; Michael Stürmer regarded the geographical location of Germany as unique; and Hans-Ulrich Wehler noted the gap between rapid industrialization and slow political and social reforms. For a much-discussed polemic against the thesis of the "peculiar way" (*Sonderweg*) of German history, see David Blackbourn and Geoff Eley, *The Peculiarities of German History*, which also contains references to the works of the above-mentioned authors.

8. C. Vann Woodward, "The Comparability of American History," 3.

9. See e.g., the classical study by Martin Seymour Lipset, *American Exceptionalism*. See also Godfrey Hodgson, *The Myth of American Exceptionalism*.

10. Todd Gitlin and Liel Leibovitz, *The Chosen Peoples*, xiv.

11. Daniel Elazar, *Israel*, 1.

12. Uri Bialer, *Between East and West*, 1.

13. Todd Gitlin and Liel Leibovitz, *The Chosen Peoples*, 58.

14. Yedidia Stern, "Israel: A Jewish Democracy," 199.

15. Michael N. Barnett, "The Politics of Uniqueness," 7–8. See also his reference to other scholars, ibid., 13. For a different perspective, see Alexander Yakobson, "Jewish Peoplehood and the Jewish State, How Unique?" 1–27. See also Emanuel Adler, ed., *Israel in the World*.

16. Jerold S. Auerbach, *Jewish State*, 5.

17. Edward Said, "An Ideology of Difference," 40, 43.

18. M. Shahid Alam, *Israeli Exceptionalism*, 20.

19. "What is Normalization?" accessed March 31, 2017: https://972mag.com/what-is-normalization/31368/. For a different Palestinian view favoring normalization with Israel, see Mohammed S. Dajani, "Why Palestinians Should Support 'Normalization' with Israel," accessed 31 March, 2017: {URL missing here}. In general, see Mahmoud Mi'ari, "Attitudes of Palestinians Toward Normalization with Israel," 339–48.

20. In Hebrew, it is usually referred to as *or la'goyim*, although the original references in the book of Isaiah (42:6, 49:6, 60:3) speak of *am le'or goyim*.

21. The speech is on the website of the Israeli Ministry of Foreign Affairs, accessed March 31, 2017: http://www.mfa.gov.il/mfa/pressroom/2010/pages/pm_netanyahu_herzliya_conference_3-feb-2010.aspx.

22. Todd Gitlin and Liel Leibovitz, *The Chosen Peoples*, 60.

23. See http://izionist.org/eng/120-years-of-zionism-ben-gurion-airport/.

24. See the classical study by Georges Canguilhem, *The Normal and the Pathological*.

25. This book is set apart from the classical studies on Zionist ideology, which were mostly written and published in the 1960s, and only addressed pre-state ideological foundations. These important studies include Arthur Hertzberg's *The Zionist Idea* (a source reader with a long and valuable introduction), Ben Halpern's *The Idea of the Jewish State* (a study grounded in the theoretical framework of the 1960s), Gideon Shimoni's *The Zionist Ideology* (an overview of the thought of impor-

tant Zionist thinkers and factions before the state was founded), and Walter Laqueur's magisterial *History of Zionism* (written in the 1960s as a straightforward history rather than an intellectual inquiry into the different state models). For overall histories of the State of Israel, see most recently, Anita Shapira's *Israel: A History* and Daniel Gordis's less dense *Israel*. Interestingly the Hebrew title of Shapira's book is: *Like Every Nation: Israel 1881–2000*. Ari Shavit's *My Promised Land* is a highly personal account, in the form of short essays, by a *Ha'aretz* journalist; it depicts the dilemmas of Israeli society and the Arab-Israeli conflict and centers around diverse characters in both pre-state Palestine and the State of Israel. Moshe Berent's *A Nation Like All Nations* (first published in Hebrew in 2009, an English edition appeared with Israel Academic Press in 2014) deals with some of the same ideas as this book, but it concentrates mainly on the separation of religion and nationality and has a specific political agenda.

CHAPTER 1. THE FIVE SEASONS OF 1897: SHAPING THE JEWISH FUTURE

1. On the protracted process of emancipation, see Michael A. Meyer, ed., *German-Jewish History in Modern Times*, vols. 2 and 3.
2. Rathenau was mentioned in Theodor Lessing's study of a phenomenon he called Jewish self-hatred. See his *Der Jüdische Selbsthaß*, 80–100. See also Sander Gilman, *Jewish Self-Hatred*, and Paul Reitter, *On the Origins of Jewish Self-Hatred*.
3. Walther Rathenau, "Höre Israel!" 1. An English translation can be found in: Walter Rathenau, "Hear, O Israel!" accessed February 26 2017: http://germanhistorydocs.ghi-dc.org/pdf/eng/234_Walther_ Rathenau_Hear%20Israel_47.pdf. For the reference to the earlier manuscript versions, see Shulamit Volkov, *Walther Rathenau*, 45.
4. Walther Rathenau, "Höre Israel!" 4, 10. Translation: http://germanhistory docs.ghi-dc.org/sub_document.cfm?document_id=717.
5. Quoted in Shulamit Volkov, *Rathenau*, 20.
6. Walther Rathenau, "Staat und Judentum," 188–89.
7. Quoted in Shulamit Volkov, *Rathenau*, 142.
8. Fritz Stern, "The Burden of Success: Reflections on German Jewry," 97–113.
9. For a systematic comparison between the two, see Rudolf Kallner, *Herzl und Rathenau*.

10. Carl E. Schorske, *Fin-de-Siècle Vienna*, 74.

11. The references can be found in Jens Malte Fischer, "Gustav Mahler und das 'Judentum in der Musik,'" 84, 132, and 141. See also Fischer's biography, *Gustav Mahler*.

12. See Johann Freiner, *Herrgott von Wien*, and Albert Lichtblau, ed., *Als hätten wir dazugehört*, 97.

13. Theodor Herzl, *The Complete Diaries of Theodor Herzl*, vol. 2, 244.

14. Adolf Hitler, *Mein Kampf*, vol. 1, 55–56.

15. Stefan Zweig, *World of Yesterday*, 100–101.

16. Freud saw Herzl's play *The New Ghetto* in 1898, and related to Herzl in his dream, "My Son, the Myops," without mentioning him by name. See Sigmund Freud, *The Standard Edition of the Complete Psychological Works*, vol. 4, 442. The dream is included in his *Interpretation of Dreams*, which he sent to Herzl in 1902, "as a token of the high esteem in which for years now I like so many have held the writer and fighter for the human rights for our people." Yosef H. Yerushalmi, *Freud's Moses*, 12.

17. Stefan Zweig, *World of Yesterday*, 105.

18. Theodor Herzl, *The Jewish State*, 28 and 33.

19. The two standard biographies of Herzl are Amos Elon, *Herzl*; and Ernst Pawel, *The Labyrinth of Exile*. The latest addition to the rich literature on Herzl is Shlomo Avineri, *Herzl*. On his childhood in Budapest, see Andrew Handler, *Dori*; and on his formative period in Vienna, Jacques Kornberg, *Theodor Herzl*. See also Gideon Shimoni and Robert S. Wistrich, eds., *Theodor Herzl*.

20. Theodor Herzl, *The Complete Diaries of Theodor Herzl*, vol. 1,196.

21. March 16, 1897, Herzl to Harden, in Theodor Herzl, *Briefe und Tagebücher*, vol. 4, p. 205.

22. Theodor Herzl, *The Complete Diaries of Theodor Herzl*, vol. 2, 105.

23. Stefan Zweig, *World of Yesterday*, 103

24. Karl Kraus, "Eine Krone für Zion," 308.

25. Theodor Herzl, *The Complete Diaries of Theodor Herzl*, vol. 1, 285.

26. Ibid., 305.

27. Theodor Herzl, *Briefe und Tagebücher*, vol. 2, 269.

28. Theodor Herzl, *The Complete Diaries of Theodor Herzl*, vol. 1, 327

29. Michael Brenner, "Warum München nicht zur Hauptstadt des Zionismus wurde," 39–52.

30. Theodor Herzl, *The Complete Diaries of Theodor Herzl*, vol. 2, 525.

31. Theodor Herzl, *Briefe und Tagebücher*, vol. 2, 266.

32. Theodor Herzl, *The Complete Diaries of Theodor Herzl*, vol. 1, 12.

33. Christoph Schulte, *Psychopathologie des fin de siècle*, 23. For another interpretation of Nordau, see Michael Stanislawski, *Zionism and the Fin-de-Siecle*.
34. Theodor Herzl, *The Complete Diaries of Theodor Herzl*, vol. 2, 581. Still the best account of the road leading to the first congress is David Vital's *The Origins of Zionism*. See also Lawrence J. Epstein, *The Dream of Zion*.
35. Ben Halpern, *The Idea of the Jewish State*, 30–31.
36. Jeremy Dauber, *The Worlds of Sholem Aleichem*, 111.
37. Moses Hess, *Rome and Jerusalem*. See also Shlomo Avineri, *Moses Hess*.
38. Jacob Katz, "The Forerunners of Zionism," 33–45.
39. For an overview of the East European background of Jewish nationalism, see Israel Bartal, *Letaken Am*; see also his *The Jews of Eastern Europe*.
40. Leon Pinsker, "Auto-Emancipation," 81.
41. Ibid., 77.
42. Dimitry Shumsky, "Leon Pinsker and Autoemanciation!'" 53.
43. Michael Heymann, ed., *The Uganda Controversy*, vol. 1, 16.
44. Theodor Herzl, *The Complete Diaries of Theodor Herzl*, vol. 2, 581.
45. On the founding of the Bund, see Henry Tobias, *The Jewish Bund in Russia*, 65–69; cf. also Nora Levin, *While Messiah Tarried*, 258–60, and the important works by Ezra Mendelsohn, *Class-Struggle in the Pale* and Jonathan Frankel, *Prophecy and Politics*.
46. On the complex relationship between the Bund and Polish Zionists, cf. Joshua D. Zimmerman, *Poles, Jews, and the Politics of Nationality*.
47. Zvi Gitelman, "A Century of Jewish Politics in Eastern Europe," 8.
48. Henry Tobias, *The Jewish Bund in Russia*, 65.
49. Sai Englert, "The Rise and Fall of the Jewish Labour Bund," accessed 26 February 2017: http://isj.org.uk/the-rise-and-fall-of-the-jewish-labour-bund/.
50. Jonathan Frankel, *Prophecy and Politics*, 207–209.
51. Yoav Peled, *Class and Ethnicity in the Pale*, 69.
52. Henry Zvi Margoshes, quoted in Ehud Manor, *Forward*, 9.
53. Ibid., 18
54. Ibid., 18–20.
55. Steven J. Zipperstein, *Elusive Prophet*, 68.
56. Ibid., 71.
57. Simon Dubnow, *Buch des Lebens* 1, 341.
58. On diaspora nationalism and minority rights in general, see Allon Gal, Athena S. Leoussi, and Anthony D. Smith, eds., *The Call of the Home-*

land. On the specific Jewish context, see Simon Rabinovitch, *Jewish Rights, National Rites*; and David H. Weinberg, *Between Tradition and Modernity*.

59. The best brief overview of Dubnow's life is Jonathan Frankel, "S. M. Dubnov: Historian and Ideologist," 1–33. See also Robert Seltzer, *Simon Dubnow's "New Judaism."* On his historiography, see Anke Hilbrenner, *Diaspora-Nationalismus*.

60. Simon Dubnow, *Buch des Lebens* 1, 442.

61. Ibid., 345. On Dubnow's relationship to Zionism, see Dimitry Shumsky, "Tzionut be-merkavot kefulot: Ha-im haya Dubnov lo-tzioni?" 369–84.

62. Simon Dubnow, *Buch des Lebens* 1, 335.

63. Ibid., 343.

64. Simon Dubnow, "On Nationalism: Letters on Old and New Judaism," 97.

65. Simon Dubnow, *Grundlagen des Nationaljudentums*, 57–58.

66. See Michael Brenner, *Prophets of the Past*, 93–105.

CHAPTER 2. THE SEVEN-HOUR-LAND: A LIGHT UNTO THE NATIONS

1. Theodor Herzl, *The Jewish State*, 34.

2. Elon Gilad, "Why is Israel called Israel?" accessed February 26, 2017: http://www.haaretz.com/israel-news/.premium-1.652699.

3. Theodor Herzl, *The Jewish State*. 40.

4. Ibid., 61.

5. Theodor Herzl, *The Complete Diaries of Theodor Herzl* 1, 105.

6. Theodor Herzl, *The Jewish State*, 50.

7. Ibid., 34.

8. Ibid., 58.

9. Ibid., 37.

10. Ibid., 54.

11. Theodor Herzl, *The Complete Diaries of Theodor Herzl* 1, 213.

12. Both Revisionist Zionist and anti-Zionist historians have used this diary entry against Herzl. See the excellent discussion in Derek Penslar, "Historians, Herzl, and the Palestinian Arabs," 51–61. For a reading of *Altneuland* in a colonialist light, see Muhammad Ali Khalidi, "Utopian Zionism or Zionist Proselytism?" 55–67.

13. This theme is explored in detail in Dimitry Shumsky's forthcoming book, *Beyond the Nation State*.

14. Among Herzl's biographers, this change is stressed especially by Joseph Adler, *The Herzl Paradox*. Adler, however, analyzes this shift exclusively in the context of Herzl's contribution to European political and economic thought.

15. Theodor Herzl, *The Jewish State*, 28.

16. Alex Bein, *Thedore Herzl*, 14. He told this story to the Russian-Jewish writer Reuven Brainin shortly before his death.

17. Theodor Herzl, *Old-New-Land*, 72.

18. Ibid., 64.

19. Theodor Herzl, *Old-New-Land*, 210–11.

20. Ibid., 62.

21. Amos Elon, *Herzl*, 348–49.

22. Theodor Herzl, *Old-New-Land*, 164.

23. Ibid., 129.

24. Ibid., 53.

25. Ibid., 109.

26. Ibid., 86.

27. Ibid., 100.

28. Ibid., 108.

29. The fictional protagonists in Herzl's novel are easily recognizable in real life. *Marmor* means marble, and *Stein* means stone, hence Marmorek and Steineck. Herzl shaped his hero David Littwak after his closest associate in the Zionist movement (and later successor), David Wolffsohn, who was a "Litvak," a Lithuanian Jew, and like Herzl's Littwak had grown up in a poor traditional Yiddish-speaking family.

30. Ernst Pawel, *The Labyrinth of Exile*, 471.

31. Yoram Hazony, *The Jewish State*, 144–45.

32. Theodor Herzl, *The Complete Diaries of Theodor Herzl*, vol. 4, 1357.

33. Ibid., 1358.

34. Peter Beinart, *The Crisis of Zion*, 12.

35. Rachel Elboim-Dror, *Ha-mahar shel ha-etmol*. The works mentioned are Menachem (Edmund) Eisler, *Ein Zukunftsbild*; Jacques Bachar, *L'Antigoyisme à Sion*; Elchanan Leeb Lewinsky, *Masa le'eretz-yisrael bi-shnat T"'T*; and Sholem Aleichem, *Meshuga'im*.

36. Rachel Elboim-Dror, *Ha-mahar*, 104–107.

37. Ibid., 104.

38. On Ahad Ha'am, see Steven Zipperstein, *Elusive Prophet*, and Yossi Goldstein, *Ahad Ha-am*. On the relationship between Herzl and Ahad Ha'am: Yossi Goldstein, *Ahad ha-am ve-Herzl*.

39. Simon Dubnow, *Buch des Lebens* I, 342. See Ahad Ha'am, "The First Zionist Congress," 30.

40. Ahad Ha'am, "The First Zionist Congress," 26.

41. Ahad Ha'am, "The Jewish State and the Jewish Problem," 76–77.

42. Ahad Ha'am, "Emet me-erets yisrael." See the commentary in the translated edition by Alan Dowty, "Much Ado About Little," 154–81.

43. Ahad Ha'am, "Altneuland."

44. Max Nordau, "Ahad-Haam über 'Altneuland.'" *Die Welt*, 7/11 (13 March 1903), 1–5.

45. Theodor Herzl, *The Jewish State*, 36.

46. Karl Emil Franzos, *Aus Halb-Asien: Culturbilder aus der Bukowina, Südrußland und Rumänien*, 2 vols., Leipzig: Duncker & Humblot, 1876.

47. Theodor Herzl, *The Complete Diaries of Theodor Herzl*, vol. 2, 741.

48. Jonathan Gribetz, "An Arabic-Zionist Talmud," 1–30.

49. Ahad Ha'am, "The Jewish State and the Jewish Problem," 74.

50. Ahad Ha'am, "Hamusar ha-leumi," 159–61.

51. Zvi Hirsch Jaffe, ed., *Ma'amar ha-yahadut ve-ha-tzionut*.

52. Jakob Klatzkin, *Krisis und Entscheidung im Judentum*, 190.

53. Anita Shapira, *Yosef Haim Brenner*, 194–95.

54. *Stenographisches Protokoll der Verhandlungen des V. Zionisten-Kongresses in Basel*, 102/108, 109. Vienna: Eretz Israel, 1901.

55. Aaron David Gordon, "Labor," 51–52.

56. Ber Borochov, "The Socialism of Poale Zion Here," 160.

57. Matityahu Mintz, "Ber Borokhov," 132.

58. See the detailed account by Gershon Shafir, *Land, Labor, and the Origins of the Israeli-Palestinian Conflict*. For the mandate period, cf. Deborah Bernstein, *Constructing Boundaries*.

59. Yehudah Mirsky, *Rav Kook*, 65.

60. Arthur Koestler, *Promise and Fulfilment*, 313.

61. The most comprehensive survey is Henry Near, ed., *The Kibbutz Movement*.

62. See Yael Zerubavel, *Recovered Roots*, 41.

63. Gideon Reuveni, "Sports and the Militarization of Jewish Society," 54–56.

64. Derek Penslar, *Jews and the Military*, 80–82.

65. Margalit Shilo, "The Double or Multiple Image of the New Hebrew

Woman," 73–94; Deborah Bernstein, *The Struggle for Equality*; Bernstein, *Nashim be-shulayim*.

66. Deborah S. Bernstein, "Introduction," 16.

67. On the changing role of women in early Israeli society, see Julie Grimmeisen, "Halutzah or Beauty Queen?" 27–52.

68. Hillel Cohen, *Army of Shadows*, 260.

69. Rashid Khalidi, *Palestinian Identity*, 19. See also Baruch Kimmerling and Joel S. Migdal, *The Palestinian People*.

70. Khalidi, *Palestinian Identity*, 28–29. On the role of the press in the process of Palestinian nation-building, see Michelle Campos, *Ottoman Brothers*.

71. For an overview see Benjamin Brown, "Orthodox Judaism," 311–33.

72. Joseph Salmon, *Religion and Zionism*; Salmon, *Im ta'iru ye-im te'oreru: Ortodoksia bi-metzarey ha-le'umiut*. Shmuel Almog, Jehuda Reinharz, and Anita Shapira, eds., *Zionism and Religion*. Ehud Luz, *Parallels Meet*. Nadav G. Shelef, *Evolving Nationalism*.

73. Bacon, *Politics of Tradition*; Mittleman, *The Politics of Torah*; Morgenstern, *Von Frankfurt nach Jerusalem*.

74. Ravitzky, *Messianism, Zionism, and Jewish Religious Radicalism*, 15.

75. Daniel Mahla, "Orthodoxy in the Age of Nationalism," 210; Moses Burstein, *Self-Government of the Jews in Palestine Since 1900*, 65–184; Neil Caplan, *Palestine Jewry and the Arab Question*, 13–46.

76. Daniel Mahla, "Orthodoxy in the Age of Nationalism," 31.

77. Menachem Friedman, "The State of Israel as a Theological Dilemma," 171–72.

78. Ravitzky, *Messianism, Zionism, and Jewish Religious Radicalism*, 87; Yehudah Mirsky, *Rav Kook*, 49.

79. Daniel Mahla, "Orthodoxy in the Age of Nationalism," 86; Isaac Breuer, *The Jewish National Home*; Asher D. Biemann, "Isaac Breuer: Zionist against His Will?" 129–46; Alan L. Mittleman, *Between Kant and Kabbalah*.

80. Robert S. Wistrich, "In the Footsteps of the Messiah," in *Theodor Herzl: Visionary of the Jewish State*, Gideon Shimoni and Robert S. Wistrich, eds., Jerusalem: Magnes Press, 1999, 321–38.

81. Reuven Brainin, *Hayei Herzl*, 17–18. Alex Bein, *Thedore Herzl*, 14.

82. Both quotes appear in Todd Gitlin and Liel Leibovitz, *The Chosen Peoples*, 39.

83. See in more detail: Eliezer Don-Yehiya and Charles S. Liebman, "The Symbol System of Zionist-Socialism," 121–48.

84. For a modern theological (and problematic) interpretation of Zionism, see David Novak, *Zionism and Religion*, 171. Novak claims that secular Zionists distorted an originally highly religious concept. He suggests that we should look at the declaration of independence of the State of Israel as a "cultural ornament, that is, a relic that played its necessary role in the past, but that has no authority in the present and no authority for the future."

CHAPTER 3. THE NATIONAL HOME: A STATE IN THE MAKING?

1. Vladimir Ze'ev Jabotinsky, "Ekronot manhim li-ve'ayot ha-sha'a," 75.
2. On the history of the Balfour Declaration, see Jonathan Schneer, *The Balfour Declaration*.
3. *The League of Nations. Mandate for Palestine, together with a Note by the Secretary-General relating to its application to the Territory known as Trans-Jordan, under the provisions of Article 25, Cmd. 1785* (1923). See James Renton, "Flawed Foundations," 16.
4. The term "national home" appeared in connection with Armenian ideas of self-determination at the Lausanne peace talks, but was immediately dropped. See Uwe Feigel, *Das evangelische Deutschland und Armenien*, 260.
5. *Palestine Royal Commission Report (Peel Report)*, accessed March 3, 2017: http://unispal.un.org/pdfs/Cmd5479.pdf, 24.
6. *Peel Report*, 34.
7. Article 2 of the Mandate. The complete text can be found at: *The Palestine Mandate*, accessed March 3, 2017: http://avalon.law.yale.edu/20th _century/palmanda.asp.
8. Nahum Sokolow, *History of Zionism*, xxiv–xxv.
9. See for example Howard Grief, *The Legal Foundation and Borders of Israel*, 81–82.
10. Zentralbüro der Zionistischen Organisation, *Der XII. Zionisten-Kongress Karlsbad 1.–14. September 1921*, 72.
11. Adolf Böhm, *Die zionistische Bewegung*, 343.
12. Ibid., 121.
13. On Weizmann, see Jehuda Reinharz, *Chaim Weizmann: The Making of a Zionist Leader*; and Reinharz, *Chaim Weizmann: The Making of a Statesman*.

14. Zentralbüro der Zionistischen Organisation, *Der XII. Zionisten-Kongress Karlsbad*, 79.

15. Quoted in Shumsky, "Tzionut u-medinut ha-le'um: Ha'arakha mehadash," 227.

16. A detailed discussion of these plans can be found in Yosef Gorny, *From Binational Society to Jewish State*, 44–94.

17. Ben Halpern, *Idea of a Jewish State*, 35.

18. Efraim Karsh und Inari Karsh, *Empires of the Sand*, 255.

19. Zentralbüro der Zionistischen Organisation, *Der XII. Zionisten-Kongress Karlsbad*, 77.

20. On the changes in Labor Zionism's visions of a future Jewish homeland, see Nadav G. Shelef, *Evolving Nationalism*, 25–49.

21. See Nadav G. Shelef, "'Both Banks of the Jordan' to the 'Whole Land of Israel,'"125–48.

22. Emma Lundgren Jörum, *Beyond Syria's Borders*, 14. In general see Isaiah Friedman, *The Question of Palestine*.

23. Hillel Cohen, *Army of Shadows*.

24. Roberto Mazza, "Transforming the Holy City," 179–96.

25. Hillel Cohen, *Army of Shadows*, 26.

26. Meir Chazan, "Mapai and the Arab-Jewish Conflict," 28–51.

27. Hermann Cohen, *Deutschtum und Judentum*, accessed March 3, 2017: http://sammlungen.ub.uni-frankfurt.de/freimann/content/titleinfo/181866.

28. Bernard Wasserstein, *Herbert Samuel*, 230–70.

29. Reuven Snir, "Double Exclusion and the Search for Inessential Solidarities," 147.

30. Moses Burstein, *Self-Government of the Jews in Palestine*, 98–109.

31. S. Zalman Abramov, *Perpetual Dilemma*, 90. See also Yehudah Mirsky, *Rav Kook*, 161.

32. Burstein, *Self-Government*, 162–72.

33. See Liora Halperin, *Babel in Zion*.

34. For different overviews of this period, cf., Tom Segev, *One Palestine Complete*; and Aviva Halamish, *Mi-bayit le'umi le-medina ba-derekh*.

35. Yaacov Shavit, *Jabotinsky and the Revisionist Movement*, 185.

36. Daniel Mahla, "Orthodoxy in the Age of Nationalism," 211.

37. Burstein, *Self-Government*, 170.

38. Vladimir Ze'ev Jabotinsky, "Building," *Hadshot Ha'aretz*, October 27, 1919, 13.

39. The question of national autonomy, both in the diaspora and in Pales-

tine, has been the topic of several important recent studies. See e.g., David N. Myers, *Between Jew and Arab*; Noam Pianko, *Zionism and the Roads Not Taken*; Simon Rabinovitch, *Jews and Diaspora: Nationalism Writings on Jewish Peoplehood in Europe and the United States*; and James Loeffler, "Between Zionism and Liberalism," 289–308.

40. Arie M. Dubnov, "Notes on the Zionist passage to India," 198.

41. One of the few scholars to point to the similarities in Zionist concepts of a future Jewish national home is Dimitry Shumsky. See his "Brith Shalom's Uniqueness Reconsidered," 339–53.

42. Hans Kohn, "Nationalismus," 679.

43. Ernst Simon, "Das palästinensische Ghetto." *Jüdische Rundschau*, July 7, 1929.

44. Hans Kohn insisted that there would always be an equal representation of Jews and Arabs, whereas most members of Brit Shalom preferred to make parliamentary representation relative to the changing demographics. For more detail, see Anja Siegemund, "Utopia in Palästina?"

45. Shmuel Hugo Bergmann, quoted in Shalom Ratzabi, *Between Zionism and Judaism*, 265.

46. Michael Stanislawski, *Zionism and the Fin-de-siècle*, 218–19.

47. Quoted in Hillel Halkin, *Jabotinsky*, 82.

48. Colin Shindler, *The Rise of the Israeli Right*, 130–32.

49. Joseph B. Shechtman, *Rebel and Statesman*, 60

50. Vladimir Jabotinsky, "Hartza'a al ha-historia ha-yisra'elit," 159–168.

51. Vladimir Jabotinsky, *Ha-mivta ha-ivri*, 8–9.

52. Hillel Halkin, *Jabotinsky*, 207.

53. *Peel Report*, 561.

54. Vladimir Jabotinsky, "Jewish Needs vs. Arab Claims," in Paul R. Mendes-Flohr and Jehuda Reinharz, eds., *The Jew in the Modern World*, 611.

55. Vladimir Jabotinsky, "Ba-derekh le-medina"; see also Reuven Shoshani, "Ha-basis ha-metodologi," 191.

56. Yaacov Shavit, *Jabotinsky and the Revisionist Movement*, 189–90.

57. Colin Shindler, *The Rise of the Israeli Right*, 85. The Jabotinsky quote is on the same page.

58. During a visit to South Africa's Jewish community, where he had many supporters, Jabotinsky said, in 1931, that there was one truth for the whites and another truth for the blacks. See Shoshani, "Ha-basis ha-metodologi," 199. See also Joseph Heller, "Emdotei'hem shel Ben-Gurion, Weizman ve-Jabotinsky ba-she'ela ha-aravit," 203–41.

59. Vladimir Jabotinsky, "The Iron Wall," accessed March 3, 2017: http://en.jabotinsky.org/media/9747/the-iron-wall.pdf.
60. Dimitry Shumsky, "Tzionut u-medinat ha-le'om," 224.
61. Vladimir Jabotinsky, "Mimshal atzmi shel mi'ut le'umi," in Jabotinsky, *Le'umiut liberalit*, 198–243.
62. Yosef Gorny, *From Binational Society to Jewish State*, 20–35. On this topic, see the review by Samuel Moyn, "Fantasies of Federalism," 145–51.
63. For a refreshing analysis of Jabotinsky's political theories, cf. Dimitry Shumsky, *Beyond the Nation State*, chapter 4.
64. Arye Naor, "Ha-mitve ha-hukati shel Ze'ev Jabotinsky le-medina ha-yehudit be-eretz yisrael," 58–60.
65. It is remarkable that most of Jabotinsky's biographers do not relate to his last book. This includes the latest biography by Hillel Halkin.
66. Vladimir Jabotinsky, *The War and the Jews*, 116. The British edition appeared earlier under the title *The Jewish War Front*.
67. Vladimir Jabotinsky, *The Jewish War Front*, 215.
68. For a discussion of Jabotinsky's bi-nationalism, see Yosef Gorny, *From Binational Society to Jewish State*; Aryeh Naor, "Ha-mitve ha-hukati;" Colin Shindler, *The Rise of the Israeli Right*, 127–48. See also Eran Kaplan, *The Jewish Radical Right*.
69. Vladimir Jabotinsky, *The War and the Jews*, 215–17.
70. Ibid., 213.
71. Shumsky, "Tzionut u-medinut hale'um: Ha'aracha me-hadash," 229. Just as is the case with Sokolow, some scholars also argued with respect to Jabotinsky that his federal state vision was a tactical attempt to convince the British and Americans to establish a Jewish army. See Arye Naor, "Ha-mitveh ha-hukati," 80. There is, however, little evidence for such an approach.
72. Vladimir Jabotinsky, *The War and the Jews*, 215.
73. See N. A. Rose, *The Gentile Zionists*, chapter 4; Paul Mulvey, *The Political Life of Josiah C. Wedgwood*; Joshua Stein, *Our Great Solicitor*. Arthur Koestler still discusses the possibility of this idea in his *Promise and Fulfillment*, published in 1947.
74. Hillel Halkin, *Jabotinsky*, 80.
75. Reuven Shoshani, "Ha-basis ha-metodologi," 195–196. See also Vladimir Jabotinsky, "Ra'ayon ha-yovel," 173–80. This idea was influenced by the utopian book by Frederick Edwin Smith, aka Lord Birkenhead, *The World in 2030*.

76. Quoted in Hillel Halkin, *Jabotinsky*, 137.

77. Quoted in Michael Stanislawski, *Zionism*, 214–15.

78. For a detailed account of the Zionist attitude towards the Arabs during these years, see Anita Shapira, *Land and Power*, 219–76; and Neil Caplan, *Palestine Jewry and the Arab Question*.

79. *Peel Report*, 142.

80. *Peel Report*, 377.

81. Itzhak Galnoor, *The Partition of Palestine*, 96.

82. Ibid., 132.

83. Vladimir Jabotinsky, *Der Judenstaat*.

84. Yossef Fund, *Perud o-hishtatfut*, 207.

85. Mahla, "Orthodoxy," 321. For Grodzinki's halakhic ruling, see Shulamit Eli'ash, "Ha-emda ha-datit, tzionit ve-lo-tzionit, le-tokhnit halukat eretz-yisra'el, 1937–1938," 59.

86. Menachem Friedman, "The State of Israel as a Theological Dilemma," 175.

87. Shulamit Eli'ash, "Ha-emda ha-datit," 55–74. See also, Mahla, "Orthodoxy," 326–27.

88. Quoted in Itzhak Galnoor, *The Partition of Palestine*, 199.

89. Quoted in ibid., 208.

90. See Yossi Katz, *Medina ba-derekh*. An earlier and shorter version appeared in English; see his *Partner to Partition*.

91. Gil Shalom Rubin, "The Future of the Jews."

92. Nur Masalha, *Imperial Israel and the Palestinians*, 57.

93. Allon Gal, *David Ben-Gurion and the American Alignment for a Jewish State*, Jerusalem: Magnes Press, 1991, 186–208.

94. Bruce Hoffman, *Anonymous Soldiers*, 101–201.

95. Joseph Heller, *The Birth of Israel*, 164 and 177.

96. On Territorialism, Adam Rovner, *In the Shadow of Zion*; on Noah and his plans, 15–43.

97. Vladimir Jabotinsky, *The Jewish War Front*, 152.

98. Theodor Herzl, *The Complete Diaries of Theodor Herzl*, vol. 1, 134.

99. On the Uganda Plan, see Yitzhak Conforti, "Searching for a Homeland," 36–54; Gur Alroey, *Zionism without Zion*, 161–70.

100. Michael Heymann, *The Uganda Controversy*, vol. 2, 180.

101. Yossi Lang, "Tzion o Uganda?" accessed 3, March 2017: http://cms.education.gov.il/NR/rdonlyres/2537B23B-4773-4951-BBC9-AC157DE4E542/118410/tzion_uganda.doc. See also Yitzhak Conforti, "Searching for a

Homeland," 41; Gur Alroey, *Zionism without Zion*, 184–93; and Arieh
B. Saposnik, *Becoming Hebrew*, 44–51.

102. *Die Welt*, December 25, 1903, n. 52, 1–3.

103. *New Liberal Review*, Dec. 1901, p. 615.

104. Quoted in Joseph Udelson, *Dreamer of the Ghetto*, 165. For earlier references, see Albert Hyamson, "British Projects for the Restoration of
Jews to Palestine," 140.

105. Udelsohn, 186.

106. Ibid., 175.

107. Ibid., 175.

108. Israel Zangwill, "A Land of Refuge," 243. Quoted in Adam Rovner, *In
the Shadow of Zion*, 89.

109. Allan Laine Kagedan, *Soviet Zion*, 30–32.

110. On Rosen and the Agro-Joint, L. Dekel-Chen, *Farming the Red Land*.

111. Laine Kagedan, *Soviet Zion*, 100.

112. Magnus Brechtken, *Madagaskar für die Juden*. See also Tara Zahra, *The
Great Departure*, especially chapters 3 and 4.

113. Alfred Döblin, "Jüdische Erneuerung," 41.

114. Alfred Döblin. Letter to Thomas Mann, 23 May 1935, in Döblin, *Briefe*,
ed. Heinz Graber, 207–208.

115. Alfred Döblin, "Der allgemeine Territorialismus," 348.

116. Chaim Ya'akov (Eugenio) Villa, *Eretz Yehuda*, n.p.

117. Adam Rovner, *In the Shadow of Zion*, 154.

118. Isaac Nahum Steinberg, *Australia*, 37.

119. Ibid., 116.

120. On both see Adam Rovner, *In the Shadow of Zion*, 149–218.

121. Isaac Nahum Steinberg, *Australia*, 8.

122. Adam Rovner, *In the Shadow of Zion*, 215.

123. Anshel Pfeffer, "Theodor Herzl's only grandson reinterred in J'lem
cemetery," *Haaretz*, Dec. 5, 2007.

124. Ilse Sternberger, *Princes without a Home*; and Andrea Livnat, *Der
Prophet des Staates*.

CHAPTER 4. ORIGINAL ISRAEL:
A STATE DEFINING ITSELF

1. "Spielt nie mehr die Herren," Interview with Claude Lanzmann, *Der
Freitag*, accessed March 20, 2017: https://www.freitag.de/autoren/der
-freitag/spielt-nie-mehr-die-herren.

2. Elon Gilad, "Why is Israel Called Israel?" *Ha'aretz*, 20 April, 2015, accessed March 20, 2017: http://www.haaretz.com/israel-news/.premium -1.652699.

3. David Ben-Gurion, *Yoman-Milhama*, 416.

4. Anita Shapira, *Israel*, 163.

5. The groundbreaking study on the subject is Benny Morris, *The Birth of the Palestinian Refugee Problem Revisited*. See also Yoav Gelber, *Palestine 1948*.

6. The State of Israel, "Proclamation of Independence," accessed March 20, 2017: https://www.knesset.gov.il/docs/eng/megilat_eng.htm.

7. David Ben-Gurion, "Netzah Yisrael," 147.

8. Joseph Heller, *The Birth of Israel*, 97–98.

9. Joseph Heller, *The Zionist Idea*, 184. It should be noted that the author of this book is not the same Joseph Heller as the one quoted in the previous footnote.

10. John D. Rayner, *A Jewish Understanding of the World*, 69.

11. Interview on CBS, (5 October 1956). In Robert Andrews, *The Columbia Dictionary of Quotations*, New York: Columbia University Press, 1993, 477.

12. Shimon Peres, *The Imaginary Voyage*, 3.

13. Nahum Goldmann, "The Creation of Israel," 89.

14. Jeffrey K. Salkin, ed., *A Dream of Zion*, 120 and 190.

15. David Grossman, "Looking at Ourselves," in the *New York Review of Books*, January 11, 2007. It can be found on the internet: http://www .nybooks.com/articles/2007/01/11/looking-at-ourselves/.

16. A. B. Yehoshua, "The Holocaust as Junction," 7–8.

17. The State of Israel, "Proclamation of Independence," accessed March 20, 2017: https://www.knesset.gov.il/docs/eng/megilat_eng.htm.

18. Elyakim Rubinstein, "The Declaration of Independence as a Basic Document of the State of Israel," 195–210; Ilan Troen, "Conclusion: Imagination and Reality in the Imagination of Israel's Future," 273.

19. The State of Israel, "Proclamation of Independence," accessed March 20, 2017: https://www.knesset.gov.il/docs/eng/megilat_eng.htm. On the American influence on the Declaration of Independence, see Yoram Shahar, "Jefferson Goes East," 589–618. See also his "Early Drafts of the Israeli Declaration of Independence," 523–600.

20. In the rich literature on this question, see especially Amnon Rubinstein and Barak Medina, *Ha-mishpat ha-konstitutzyoni shel medinat yisrael*; Ruth Gavison, *Ha-mahapekha ha-hukatit*; Gavison, "The Contro-

versy over Israel's Bill of Rights," 113–54; Shlomo Aronson, "Huka le'yisrael," 9–30; Philippa Strum, "The Road Not Taken," 83–104; Ilan Peleg, "Israel's Constitutional Order and Kulturkampf," 230–50.

21. Akiva Eldar, "Border Control Getting in a State over the UN Vote," *Ha'aretz*, September 13, 2011.

22. Menachem Friedman, "The State of Israel as a Theological Dilemma," 183–84.

23. Zvi Jonathan Kaplan, "Rabbi Joel Teitelbaum, Zionism, and Hungarian Ultra-Orthodoxy," 165–78.

24. Anita Shapira, "Ben-Gurion and the Bible," 654. See also Ben Gurion's writings: *Medinat yisrael ha-mehudeshet* and *Netzah yisrael*, where this speech is printed.

25. David Ben Gurion, *Le-mefakdim tze'irim*.

26. The discussion between Ben-Gurion and the intellectuals is reprinted in: David Ohana, *Meshihiut u-mamlakhtiut*, 73.

27. Nir Kedar, "Ben-Gurion's View of the Place of Judaism in Israel," 158.

28. Joel Peters, *Israel and Africa*, 15–16.

29. Gil Troy, "Israel in World Opinion," 155–156.

30. Anita Shapira, *Israel*, 656.

31. Ariel L. Feldestein, *Ben Gurion, Zionism and American Jewry*, 103.

32. Ibid., 106.

33. Ibid., 110.

34. Itzhak Navon, "Preface," iv.

35. David Ben-Gurion, *Like Stars and Dust*, 6.

36. Ibid., 72.

37. Ibid., 202.

38. Ibid., 299–300.

39. David Ben-Gurion, "Yisrael be-amim," 86.

40. Ibid., 133.

41. Nahum Goldmann, "The Road Towards an Unfulfillable Ideal," 141–42.

42. Nahum Goldmann, *Israel muß umdenken!* 19.

43. Ibid., 65.

44. Simon Rawidowicz, "Jerusalem and Babylon," 229–239. On Rawidowicz, see David M. Myers, ed., *Between Jew and Arab*.

45. David Ben-Gurion, *Like Stars and Dust*, 209.

46. Simon Rawidowicz, "Excerpts from a Correspondence between David Ben-Gurion and Simon Rawidowicz," 197.

47. Simon Rawidowicz, "Israel," 182–93.

48. Simon Rawidowicz, "Excerpts from a Correspondence between David Ben-Gurion and Simon Rawidowicz," 197.

49. Ehud Ben Ezer, *Unease in Zion*, 80.

50. Ibid., 79.

51. Ibid., 80.

52. David Ben-Gurion, "Sitting 160 of the First Knesset," 611. Quoted in *Major Knesset Debates, 1949-1981: The Constituent Assembly–First Knesset 1949-1951*, Netanel Lorch, ed. Landham: University Press of America 1993, 611.

53. From a national religious perspective, see Zerah Wahrhaftig, *Huka le'yisrael*, 38–40.

54. Oscar Kraines, *The Impossible Dilemma*, 3–9.

55. Eliezer Ben-Rafael, *Jewish Identities*, 278–79

56. Ibid., 152.

57. Ibid., 314.

58. Ibid., 166–67.

59. Ibid., 154–56.

60. Ibid., 171–72.

61. Ibid., 350.

62. Ibid., 182.

63. Reprinted in Kraines, *The Impossible Dilemma*, 97.

64. On the legal and political background of the case, see Michael Stanislawski, "A Jewish Monk?"

65. Asher Felix Landau, *Selected Judgments of the Supreme Court of Israel*, 10.

66. On the court proceedings and Margalit's interpretation, see Michael Walzer, Menachem Lorberbaum, and Noam J. Zohar, eds., *The Jewish Political Tradition*, 424–35.

67. Walzer, *The Jewish Political Tradition*, 295–309. Since 2005 Israeli identity cards no longer have a visible entry for nationality, but the category remains (marked by an asterisk) and it is registered with the administration. In 2013, linguist Uzzi Ornan tried to legalize his entry as "Israeli" under nationality in his ID. The Supreme Court, however, confirmed a previous decision from 2007, when it denied a group of prominent left-wing Israeli intellectuals, among them Uri Avnery, Shulamit Aloni, and Yehoshua Sobol, the right to register their nationality as "Israeli." The court argued that there was no Israeli nationality but only an Israeli citizenship; the nationality would be Jewish, Arab, Druze, or some other existing category. See Revital Hovel, "Supreme

Court Rejects Citizens' Request to Change Ethnicity from 'Jewish' to 'Israeli,'" in *Ha'aretz*, October 3, 2013, accessed March 20, 2017: http://www.haaretz.com/israel-news/.premium-1.550241.

68. Zalman Abramov, *Perpetual Dilemma*, 316. Ben-Gurion's granddaughter had to undergo an Orthodox conversion in order to marry in Israel. The matter of who was a Jew came up again periodically in Israeli legislation and political debate. Often, the national and religious categories were confused. Thus, the question of converts from non-Orthodox rabbis and their rights as new immigrants were hotly debated both by rabbis and state officials. Here, the decision by a religious body (a rabbinical court) had direct implications on the Interior Ministry's decision. Should Jews who converted outside Israel, especially with non-Orthodox rabbis, be recognized as Jews in terms of nationality and thus be able to move to Israel in the sense of the Law of Return? In 1989, the Israeli Supreme Court ruled that Reform and Conservative conversions had to be recognized by the ministry and that any immigrant who came to Israel after having converted to Judaism abroad—even in non-Orthodox ceremonies not recognized by the Israeli Chief Rabbinate—would be able to enter Israel under the provisions of the Law of Return. This caused much debate both among Orthodox Jews and in the government coalitions that often depended on the support of the religious parties. It led to several government crises and to the installation of official committees to resolve the issue, but no accepted results have been obtained to date. See David Ellenson, "'Jewishness in Israel,'" 269–74.

69. Tom Segev, *1949*, 45–46.

70. Shira Robinson, *Citizen Strangers*, 47.

71. One of the first to use this phrase was the French-Jewish Marxist scholar Maxime Rodinson, in the wake of the Six-Day War. See his essay "Israel, fait colonial" in Jean-Paul Sartre's journal *Les Temps Modernes*, in June 1967, and in his later book, *Israel*.

72. Shira Robinson, *Citizen Strangers*, 3. See also Nadim N. Rouhana and Areej Sabbagh-Khoury, "Palestinian Citizenship in Israel," 32–61.

73. "Survival of the Fittest." Interview with Benny Morris, *Ha'aretz Friday Magazine*, January 9, 2004, accessed March 20, 2017: http://www.haaretz.com/survival-of-the-fittest-1.61345.

74. De Gaulle called the Jews "a self-righteous people, sure of itself and domineering" ("peuple d'élite, sûr de lui-même et dominateur"). See Jean-Pierre Filiu, "France and the June 1967 War," 261.

75. On this topic, see the thoughtful essay by Derek J. Penslar, "Is Zionism a Colonial Movement?," 90–III.

76. Isaac Deutscher, "On the Israeli-Arab War," 30.

77. Ian Lustick, *Arabs in the Jewish State*, 8.

78. See Adia Mendelson Maoz, *Multiculturalism in Israel: Literary Perspectives*, West Lafayette: Purdue University Press, 2014, 53–60. The text is reprinted as: https://genius.com/Mahmoud-darwish-identity-card-english-version-annotated.

79. Nadim N. Rouhana, *Palestinian Citizens in an Ethnic Jewish State*, 67.

80. Hillel Cohen, *Army of Shadows*, 7.

81. This is described in detail in Ian Lustick's *Arabs in the Jewish State*.

82. A useful recent overview of the Canaanite movement and some of its modern implications is Klaus Hofmann, "Canaanism," 273–294. The classical studies on Canaanism are Yaacov Shavit, *The New Hebrew Nation*, revised translation of *Me-ivri 'ad kena'ani*, and J. S. Diamond, *Homeland or Holy Land?*

83. Quoted in Shavit, *The New Hebrew Nation*, 63.

84. Quoted in Colin Shindler, *The Rise of the Israeli Right*, 222.

85. Ehud Ben Ezer, *Unease in Zion*, 202.

86. Ibid., 205–206.

87. Ibid., 175.

88. Ibid., 278.

89. Ibid., 288–89.

90. Benny Morris, *Israel's Border Wars*, 396.

91. S. Yizhar, "Al pney ha-noar." See Nitza Ben-Ari, "Hero or Anti-Hero," 98; and Michael Keren, *The Pen and the Sword*, 45. The term was originally created by Arthur Koestler.

92. Orit Rozen, *The Rise of the Individual in 1950s Israel*; on the Miss Israel competition, see Julie Grimmeisen, "Halutzah or Beauty Queen," 27–52; and her Ph.D. diss., "Pionierinnen und Schönheitsköniginnen." On the Wadi Salib unrest, see Yfaat Weiss, *A Confiscated Memory*.

93. Nir Kedar, *Mamlakhtiyut*.

94. For the first twenty years, the one Israeli television station only broadcast in black and white, with the exception of Egyptian president Sadat's visit to Jerusalem in 1977 and the 1979 Eurovision song contest, which took place in Israel. On Israeli TV, see Tasha G. Oren, *Demon in the Box*.

95. For an English biography, see Shlomo Aronson, *Levi Eshkol*.

96. On the early years of the Herut party, see Yehiam Weitz, *Ha-tza'ad ha-rishon le-khes ha-shilton*, and Colin Shindler, *The Rise of the Israeli Right*, 229–73. On Kastner, see Yehiam Weitz, "The Herut Movement and the Kasztner Trial," 349–71.

CHAPTER 5. GREATER ISRAEL:
A STATE EXPANDING

1. A systematic treatment of this topic is still a scholarly desideratum. For an analysis of the matter from the viewpoint of Israeli officials see: Avi Beker, *The United Nations and Israel*. This book contains an appendix with most of the relevant UN resolutions concerning Israel. See also Yehuda Z. Blum: "Israel and the United Nations," 69–77. It is telling that several former Israeli ambassadors to the United Nations published critical accounts of the relationship between Israel and the UN after their tenure. See e.g., Yehuda Z. Blum, *For Zion's Sake* and Dore Gold, *The Tower of Babble*.

2. Amy L. S. Staples: *The Birth of Development*, 148. See also: http://apps.who.int/iris/bitstream/10665/130505/1/EB15_81_eng.pdf.

3. 44th General Conference of UNESCO Resolution on Protection of Cultural Property in Jerusalem–20 November 1974, accessed March 20, 2017: http://www.mfa.gov.il/mfa/foreignpolicy/mfadocuments/yearbook2/pages/44%20general%20conference%20of%20unesco%20resolution%20on%20prot.aspx.

4. GA Resolution ES-7/4 of April 28, 1982, article 11, p.6, accessed March 20, 2017: http://www.un.org/en/ga/search/view_doc.asp?symbol=A/RES/ES-7/4.

5. In 2000 Israel became first a temporary and four years later a permanent member of the "Western European and Others" group.

6. Alan M. Dershowitz, "Israel," 129–36.

7. Saul Bellow, *To Jerusalem and Back*, 26.

8. Among the numerous books on the Six-Day War, see e.g., Michael B. Oren, *Six Days of War* and Tom Segev, *1967*.

9. See Arthur Hertzberg, *The Jews in America*, 375. Among American intellectuals see Saul Bellow, *Mr. Sammler's Planet*, which was an expression of his changing attitude towards Israel.

10. See Peter Novick, *The Holocaust in American Life*, 148–51.

11. Lawrence Grossman, "Transformation Through Crisis," 27–54.

12. André Nehér, "Jerusalem, notre lumière," 52. Quoted in Katharina Hey, "Ein Schritt gen Messias," 45–56.

13. "Frieden und Sicherheit für Israel," *Süddeutsche Zeitung*, June 7, 1967.

14. Ehud Ben Ezer, *Unease in Zion*, 295.

15. Moshe Unna, "Oz ve-Shalom," 75.

16. Ehud Ben Ezer, *Unease in Zion*, 115. The conversations with Buber took place between 1961 and 1965, the others in 1966.

17. Ibid., *Unease in Zion*, 190.

18. Ibid., 321.

19. Ehud Ben Ezer , *Unease in Zion*, 338.

20. Amos Oz, *In the Land of Israel*, 239.

21. Saul Bellow, *To Jerusalem and Back*, 136.

22. Ehud Ben Ezer, *Unease in Zion*, 263.

23. "Manifesto of the Land of Israel Movement, August 1967," trans. In Rael Jean Isaac, *Israel Divided*, 171.

24. Daniel Gordis, *Israel*, 286.

25. Gershom Gorenberg, *The Accidental Empire*, 38.

26. Noam Zadoff, "From Mishmar Ha'emek to Elon Moreh."

27. Ibid.

28. Yeshayahu Leibowitz, "Forty Years After," 243.

29. Yehoshua Leibowitz, *Tora u-mitzvot ba-zeman ha-ze*, 1954.

30. Arieh Bruce Saposnik, "Wailing Walls and Iron Walls," 1653–81.

31. A. B. Yehoshua, *Ha-kir ve-ha'har*.

32. Tom Segev, *1967*, 433.

33. Yitzhak Rabin, "Address to the Knesset by Prime Minister Rabin on Jerusalem, 29 May 1995," accessed March 20, 2017: http://www.mfa.gov .il/MFA/Foreign+Relations/Israels+Foreign+Relations+since+1947 /1995-1996/Address+to+the+Knesset+by+Prime+Minister+Rabin+on +Jerusalem.htm.

34. Meron Benvenisti, *Jerusalem*, 305.

35. Eliezer (Elie) Wiesel, Yedioth Aharonoth, 16 June 1967. Quoted in: Edith Zertal, "From the People's Hall to the Wailing Wall," in *Representations 69*, Winter 2000.

36. David Landau, "70.000 at Western Wall; little mourning observed," *The Jerusalem Post*, August 1 1971.

37. Ibid., 160.

38. Jacob L. Talmon, *The Six Day War*, 62.

39. Ibid., 83–85.

40. Amos Oz, *In the Land of Israel*, 120.

41. Todd Gitlin and Liel Leibovitz, *The Chosen Peoples*, 48.

42. Amos Oz, "Sar ha-bitahon u-merhav ha-mehiya," *Davar*, August 22, 1967.

43. *Ha'aretz*, 18th July, 1967, 1.

44. She was preceded by Sirimavo Bandaranaike of Ceylon (Sri Lanka) and Indira Gandhi of India, but they followed their husband or father.

45. Hanna Herzog, *Interests, Identities, and Institutions in Comparative Politics*.

46. The word used, *mahapakh*, literally means reversal, but it is also closely related to the word *mahapekha*, which means revolution.

47. Avi Shilon, *Menachem Begin*, 258.

48. Ibid., 269.

49. Daniel Gordis, *Menachem Begin*, 154.

50. Ibid., 177–78.

51. Joel Migdal, *Through the Lens of Israel*.

52. For an overview, see Motti Regev and Edwin Seroussi, *Popular Music and National Culture in Israel*.

53. Ella Shohat, *Israeli Cinema*, 272.

54. See Yaron Peleg, *Directed by God*, 53–79.

55. Baruch Kimmerling, *The Invention of Israeliness*, 110–11.

56. Ari Shavit, *My Promised Land*, 221.

57. Yehudah Mirsky, *Rav Kook*, 226.

58. Yossi Klein Halevi, *Like Dreamers*, 119.

59. Baruch Kimmerling, *The Invention of Israeliness*, 82, 127.

60. Gershom Gorenberg, *The Accidental Empire*, 160.

61. Gershon Shafat, *Gush Emunim*, 7.

62. Gideon Aran, *Kookism*, 14.

63. Itamar Rabinovich, *Yitzhak Rabin*, 100.

64. Ibid., 126–27.

65. Ian S. Lustick, *For the Land and the Lord*, 37; Yehudah Mirsky, *Rav Kook*, 228.

66. Baruch Kimmerling, *The Invention of Israeliness*, 109.

67. Gideon Aran, "Jewish Zionist Fundamentalism," 265–344; Charles S. Liebman, "Jewish Fundamentalism and the Israeli Polity," 68–87; Ehud Sprinzak, "Three Models of Religious Violence," 462–90; Sprinzak, "The Genesis of Zionist Fundamentalism," 8–27; Michael Feige, *Settling*

in the Hearts; Motti Inbari, *Jewish Fundamentalism and the Temple Mount*; Inbari, *Messianic Religious Zionism Confronts Israeli Territorial Compromises.*

68. Baruch Kimmerling, *The Invention of Israeliness*, 110–11.

69. For the historical background, see David S. Katz, *Philo-Semitism and the Readmission of the Jews to England*, and Jill Hamilton, *God, Guns and Israel.*

70. Theodor Herzl, *The Complete Diaries of Theodor Herzl*, vol. 1, 312.

71. Theodor Herzl, *The Complete Diaries of Theodor Herzl*, vol. 2, 655.

72. Lindsey and Carlson, *The Late Great Planet Earth*, 42–43.

73. Jerry Falwell, *Listen, America!*, 113.

74. Stephen Spector, *Evangelicals and Israel*, 27.

75. Eric. R. Crouse, *American Christian Support for Israel*, 102. Crouse also mentions the different opinions expressed in various evangelical publications at the time.

76. Caitlin Carenen, *The Fervent Embrace*, 199–200.

77. Pat Robertson, "Why Evangelical Christians Support Israel," accessed March 20, 2017: http://www.patrobertson.com/speeches/israellauder .asp.

78. Jerry Falwell, *Listen, America!* 113.

79. See Michael Lind, "Rev. Robertson's Great International Conspiracy Theory," *New York Review of Books*, February 2, 1995.

80. Timothy P. Weber, "American Evangelicals and Israel."

81. Victoria Clark, *Allies for Armageddon*, 196.

82. Jonathan Rynhold, *The Arab-Israeli Conflict in American Political Culture*, 95–115.

83. Guy Ziv, *Why Hawks Become Doves.*

84. Shimon Peres, *The New Middle East*, 2–3.

85. Ibid., *The New Middle East*, 61–62.

86. Ibid., 141–142.

87. Ibid., 75.

88. Shimon Peres, *The Imaginary Voyage*, 1.

89. Shimon Peres, *The New Middle East*, 15.

90. Shimon Peres, *The Imaginary Voyage*, 10.

91. Ibid., 114.

92. Ibid., 117.

93. Ibid., 119–120.

94. A French version of Peres's *Imaginary Journey with Theodor Herzl* was

already published in 1998: *Le Voyage imaginaire: Avec Théodore Herzl en Israël*, Paris: Éditions, 1998.

95. Yoram Peri, *Yad ish be-ahiv*, 252–290.

CHAPTER 6. GLOBAL ISRAEL:
A STATE BEYOND BORDERS

1. For a thorough analysis of Zionism's attitude toward exile and diaspora, see Amnon Raz-Krakotzkin, "Galut mitokh ribonut," 6–23, 113–132, and Oz Almog, *The Sabra*.

2. Uri Ram, *The Globalization of Israel*.

3. Mark Wyman, "Emigrants Returning," 16–31.

4. Gur Alroey, "The Jewish Emigration from Palestine in the Early Twentieth Century," 112–31. See also his book, *An Unpromising Land*.

5. In 1927 there were 2,713 Jewish immigrants to Palestine, but 5,071 Jewish emigrants from Palestine. In 1928, the number of emigrants equaled the number of immigrants. Magdalena M. Wróbel Bloom, *Social Networks and the Jewish Migration between Poland and Palestine, 1924–1928*, 223.

6. Ori Yehudai, "Forth from Zion," 7. See also: Nir Cohen, "From Legalism to Symbolism," 19–26.

7. 2012 Yearbook of Immigration Statistics, Office of Immigration Statistics, Homeland Security, Table 2 page 6.

8. On the divergent numbers of the Israeli diaspora, see Uzi Rebhun and Lilakh Lev Ari, *American Israelis*, 16–17; Steven J. Gold, *The Israeli Diaspora*, 22–25.

9. See e.g., the magazine *Spitz*: http://spitzmag.de/. Tal Hever-Chybovski founded a Hebrew journal, intending to connect to a tradition that began in the eighteenth century with philosopher Moses Mendelssohn's journal *kohelet musar* and culminated in the Hebrew activities in the Berlin of the 1920s and early 30s. See also http://mikanve.net /wp/. The writer Michal Zamir opened a Hebrew library in Berlin, which serves as a social meeting point for Hebrew speakers in the German capital: http://www.botschaftisrael.de/2014/01/16/eine-hebraeische -buecherei-in-berlin/.

10. October 26, 2014, http://www.i24news.tv/en/opinion/48688-141026-the -new-generation-of-wired-hebrew-nomads.

11. Dani Kranz, *Israelis in Berlin*, Gütersloh: Bertelsmann, 2015, 11, believes

this number is exaggerated and estimates about 11,000 Israelis living in Berlin. This estimate seems, however, just as arbitrary as the higher numbers.

12. Michael Brenner, ed., *Geschichte der Juden in Deutschland von 1945 bis zur Gegenwart*, 167–68.

13. Ori Yehudai, "Forth from Zion," 251.

14. Ibid., 259.

15. Quoted in Tom Segev, *1967*, 131.

16. Uri Ram, *The Globalization of Israel*, 84–85. As a result of anti-Jewish actions in Europe, immigration to Israel, especially from France, rose again in 2014 to a total of 26,500. Omri Efraim, "2014 a Record Breaking Year for Aliyah," accessed March 20, 2017: http://www.ynetnews.com /articles/0,7340,L-4609941,00.html.

17. Ynon Cohen: "Israeli-born Emigrants," 45–62, 47–51.

18. Jacob L. Talmon, *The Six Day War*, 8.

19. A. B. Yehoshua quoted in: Gilead Morahg, "A. B. Yehoshua: Fictions of Zion and Diaspora," 125.

20. A. B. Yehoshua, "The Holocaust as Junction," 62.

21. Ibid., 12–14.

22. Ibid., 51.

23. Ibid., 64.

24. Ibid., 63.

25. See for example Abraham Geiger, *Das Judentum und seine Geschichte*, 167–68.

26. A good example is the writer Stefan Zweig, who stressed in a letter to Martin Buber that he never wanted the Jews to become a nation again, and that he loves the diaspora as the essence of his Jewishness. Martin Buber, *Briefwechsel aus sieben Jahrzehnten*, 462–64 and 499. See also Mark Gelber, *Stefan Zweig Reconsidered*, 68–70.

27. Philip Roth, *Operation Shylock*, 32.

28. Ibid., 44.

29. Ibid.

30. Ibid., 45–46. There is an almost literal precursor for this scene in the popular Austrian dystopian novel by Hugo Bettauer of 1922, *Die Stadt ohne Juden*, 98–100.

31. Philip Roth, *Operation Shylock*, 170–71.

32. Sidra DeKoven Ezrahi, "The Grapes of Roth," 148.

33. See Alvin Rosenfeld, *Progressive Jewish Thought and Antisemitism*.

34. Heinrich Heine, "Geständnisse," 58.

35. George Steiner, "Our Homeland, the Text," 326.

36. "According to Steiner, the true mission of the Jews is to be found in exile: It is to be 'guests' among the nations, aliens who live as refugees, restless and dispossessed. Only when they are outside of their homeland, Steiner argues, have the Jews served as the cultural vanguard and moral conscience of the nations, as prophets of a lofty and profound human ideal." Assaf Sagiv, "George Steiner's Jewish Problem."

37. George Steiner, "Our Homeland, the Text," 324.

38. See Steiner's speech on receiving the Börne Prize in 2003. Ulrich Rüdenauer, "Im Dialog mit den Klassikern," accessed March 20, 2017: http://www.literaturkritik.de/public/rezension.php?rez_id=6122&ausgabe=200306; see also: Assaf Sagiv, "George Steiner's Jewish Problem.

39. George Steiner, "Our Homeland, the Text," 325.

40. Daniel Boyarin and Jonathan Boyarin, "Diaspora: Generation and the Ground of Jewish Identity," 711–12.

41. Boyarin and Boyarin, "Diaspora," 713.

42. Ibid., 718.

43. Ibid., 723. See also Alan Wolfe, *At Home in Exile.*

44. Roane Carey, " 'A Non-Jewish Jew', Hitchens Welcomed He Was Jewish—But Not Zionism," *Forward*, December 21, 2011, accessed March 20, 2017: http://forward.com/articles/148355/a-non-jewish-jew-hitchens -welcomed-finding-h/.

45. Tony Judt, "Israel: The Alternative," *New York Review of Books*, September 25, 2003, accessed March 20, 2017: http://www.nybooks.com/articles /archives/2003/oct/23/israel-the-alternative/.

46. See "Tony Judt's Final Word on Israel," *The Atlantic*, September 14, 2011. On disillusion with Israel among other British Jews, see Jacqueline Rose, *The Question of Zion*, and Antony Lerman, *The Making and Unmaking of a Zionist.*

47. On the New Historians, see Weitz, *Beyn hason le-revisia.* In English there is a special issue of *History and Memory*, vol. 7/1 (1995) under the title *Israeli Historiography Revisited.* For a different assessment, see also Yoav Gelber, *Nation and History*, and Ephraim Karsh, *Fabricating Israeli History.*

48. Avraham Burg, *The Holocaust Is Over*, xv.

49. Ari Shavit, "Burg: Defining Israel as a Jewish State Is the Key to Its End," *Ha'aretz*, June 7, 2007, accessed March 20, 2017: http://www .haaretz.com/news/burg-defining-israel-as-a-jewish-state-is-the-key-to -its-end-1.222491.

50. J. J. Goldberg, "Avraham Burg's New Zionism" *Forward*, June 15, 2007, accessed March 20, 2017: http://forward.com/opinion/editorial/10943 /avraham-burg-s-new-zionism/.

51. Shlomo Sand, *The Invention of the Jewish People*, 312–13.

52. Shlomo Sand, *Invention of the Land of Israel*, 29.

53. See e.g., Diana Pinto, *Israel Has Moved*.

54. Eshkol Nevo, *Neuland*, 514.

55. Ibid., *Neuland*, 547.

56. Ibid., 543.

57. Ibid., 551.

58. Ibid., 557.

59. Nava Semel, *I-srael*. An English translation appeared in 2016: *Isra-Isle*, trans. Jessica Cohen, Simsbury, Conn., 2016.

60. Yoav Avni, *Herzl amar*, 2011.

61. Michael Chabon, *The Yiddish Policemen's Union*, New York: Harper Collins, 2007. Another example of this kind of counterfactual history is the dystopian novel *Judenstaat* by Simone Zeitlich, New York: Tor Books, 2017, which locates a Jewish state after the Holocaust in East German Saxony. See also Walter Laqueur's imaginative essay "Disraelia: *A Counterfactual History, 1848–2008*," in his collection *Harvest of a Decade: Disraelia and Other Essays*," (New Brunswick: Transaction, 2012).

62. Ilan Goren, *Wo bist du, Motek? Ein Israeli in Berlin*, 83.

63. See http://kerethouse.com/.

64. http://yaelbartana.com/.

65. For a video of the conference proceedings, see: http://www.berlinbien nale.de/blog/en/events/and-europe-will-be-stunned-a-congress-by -jrmip-and-yael-bartana.

66. Judy Maltz, "Secret Jewish Majority?" *The Jewish Daily Forward*, November 8, 2014, accessed March 20, 2017: http://forward.com/articles/208769 /shadow-jews-outnumber-recognized-members-of-tribe/.

67. Edith Bruder, *The Black Jews of Africa*, 193.

68. David Kessler, *The Falashas*; Tudor Parfitt, *Operation Moses*.

69. The first legends of this kind appeared in the Middle Ages among Europeans, and were often revived by the colonial powers. See Tudor Parfitt, *Black Jews in Africa and the Americas*, 65. See also Tudor Parfitt and Netanel Fisher, eds., *Becoming Jewish*.

70. Daniel Lis, *Jewish Identity Among the Igbo of Nigeria*; Lis, "Igbo," and Lis, "Israeli Foreign Policy towards the Igbo," 87–162. Parfitt, *Black Jews*,

112–13. Daniel Lis, William F.S. Miles, and Tudor Parfitt, eds., *In the Shadow of Moses.*

71. Tudor Parfitt, *Journey to the Vanished City.*

72. Tudor Parfitt, "What Will the Worldwide Explosion of New Israelite Communities and Judaizing Movements Mean for the Jewish State?"

73. Melanie Lidman, "In Uganda, Conservative prayer services with an African lilt," *Times of Israel*, November 13, 2014, accessed March 20, 2017: http://www.timesofisrael.com/in-rural-uganda-conservative-prayer-services-with-an-african-lilt/.

74. Haviv Rettig Gur, "Charles Taylor is 'now a Jew,' Wife Says," *Jerusalem Post*, June 7, 2009, accessed March 20, 2017: http://www.jpost.com/International/Charles-Taylor-is-now-a-Jew-wife-says. Despite his reported conversion he said he still believed in Jesus.

75. Nicholas Wade, "DNA Backs a Tribe's Tradition of Early Descent from the Jews," *New York Times*, May 9, 1999, accessed March 20, 2017: http://www.nytimes.com/1999/05/09/us/dna-backs-a-tribe-s-tradition-of-early-descent-from-the-jews.html.

76. Tudor Parfitt, "What Will the Worldwide Explosion of New Israelite Communities and Judaizing Movements Mean for the Jewish State?"

77. Shalva Weil, "Lost Israelites from North-East India," 219–33. See also Hillel Halkin's account in *Across the Sabbath River.*

78. Tudor Parfitt, *Black Jews*, 169–70.

79. See e.g., Alan F. Segal, *Rebecca's Children.*

80. "'Lost' Indian Jews Come to Israel Despite Skepticism Over Ties to Faith," *Ha'aretz*, October 20, 2013, accessed March 20, 2017: http://www.haaretz.com/jewish-world/jewish-world-news/1.553350.

81. Judy Maltz, "New Diaspora Ministry Initiative Could Open Israel's Gates to Millions of Non-Jews with Jewish Links," *Ha'aretz*, August 17 2015, accessed March 20, 2017: http://www.haaretz.com/jewish/news/.premium-1.671594.

82. Billie Frenkel, "How many Foreigners Work in Israel," *Ynet*, August 2, 2013, accessed March 20, 2017: http://www.ynetnews.com/articles/0,7340,L-4412537,00.html. A smaller number is given by: http://www.oecd.org/migration/mig/IMO%202012_Country%20note%20Israel.pdf.

83. Uri Ram, *The Globalization of Israel*, 103.

84. Israel Drori, *Foreign Workers in Israel*, xi.

85. See Karin Fathimath Afeef, "A Promised Land for Refugees?" In *New Issues in Refugee Research, Research Paper No. 183, United Nations High*

Commissioner for Refugees Policy Development and Evaluation Service, December 2009; and Haim Yacobi " 'Let Me Go to the City.' "

CONCLUSION: ISRAEL'S NEW ORDER

1. Bernard Avishai, *The Hebrew Republic,* 5.
2. Yedidia Stern, "Religion, State and the Jewish Identity Crisis in Israel," 16.
3. Chemi Shalev, "Arik Einstein, 74: The Voice of the Good Old Israel We Still Dream Of," *Ha'aretz,* November 27, 2013.
4. Ari Shavit, "Arik Einstein, the Singer of a Lost Israel," *Ha'aretz,* November 28, 2013.
5. Alon Tal, *The Land Is Full,* 131–33.
6. Israel Democracy Institute, *Statistical Report on Ultra-Orthodox Society in Israel,* 7.
7. Pew Research Center, *Israel's Religiously Divided Society,* 26 and 81.
8. Pew Research Center, *Israel's Religiously Divided Society,* 165.
9. Jacob M. Landau, *The Arab Minority in Israel,* 168.
10. Sammy Smooha, *Arabs and Jews in Israel,* 218.
11. Ibid., 223.
12. See for example the rapid rise of Arab students enrolled in Israeli universities: Amal Jamal, *Arab Minority Nationalism in Israel,* 211.
13. Amal Jamal, *Arab Minority,* 106. See also Azmi Bishara, "Al she'elat ha-mi'ut ha-falastini be-yisrael," 7; Ahmad Tibi, "Medinat kol le'umeha," *NRG Website,* May 10, 2005: http://www.nrg.co.il/online/1/ART/932/352.html.
14. Jacob M. Landau, *The Arab Minority in Israel, 1967–1991,* 173. For a good and brief overview, see Elie Rekhess, "The Arab Minority in Israel, 187–217.
15. Elie Rekhess, "Resurgent Islam in Israel," 189–206.
16. Pew Research Center, *Israel's Religiously Divided Society,* Washington DC: 2016, 184.
17. Jerusalem Center for Public Affairs: "New Poll: Survey of Israeli Jewish Attitudes on Future Peace Agreeement," accessed March 28, 2017: http://jcpa.org/article/new-poll-survey-israeli-jewish-attitudes-future-peace-agreement/ (page 1).
18. Pew Research Center, *Israel's Religiously Divided Society,* 159–61.
19. The National Committee for the Heads of Arab Local Authorities

in Israel, *The Future Vision of the Palestinian Arabs in Israel*, Nazareth 2006, 5.

20. Ibid., 11.
21. Dov Waxman, "Israel's Other Palestinian Problem," 214–29. For a Palestinian criticism of the future vision documents, see Mohammed S. Wattad, "A Vision of Citizenship," 185–207.
22. Uri Ram, *Globalization*, 71.
23. "Census figures: 2.2 kids, 2.1 cell phones per family," accessed March 31, 2017: http://www.ynetnews.com/articles/0,7340,L-3884633,00.html; http://www.cbs.gov.il/www/mifkad/mifkad_2008/profiles/rep_e_000000.pdf.
24. http://www.cbs.gov.il/www/statistical/touris2008e.pdf.
25. Dan Senor and Paul Singer, *Start-up Nation: The Story of Israel's Economic Miracle*, New York: Twelve, 2009.
26. Orr Hirschauge, "Israel's Start-up Forecast: Geo-tag Flurries with a Chance of Cash Flow," *Ha'aretz*, June 6, 2012.
27. Calvin Goldscheider, *Israeli Society in the 21st Century*, 134–53.
28. Sammy Smooha, "Is Israel Western?"
29. Printed in Jehuda Reinharz and Itamar Rabinovich, eds., *Israel in the Middle East*. For the background, see Yehuda Bauer, *From Diplomacy to Resistance*.
30. Bernard Avishai, *The Hebrew Republic*, 17.
31. The law and its amendments are to be found at: http://www.knesset.gov.il/elections16/eng/laws/basic_knesset_eng.htm, accessed March 31, 2017.
32. Elie Rekhess, "Identity Dilemmas of the Palestinian-Arabs in Israel."
33. knesset.gov.il/laws/special/eng/BasicLawLiberty.pdf.
34. Aharon Barak, "Ha-mahapekhah ha-hukatit: zekhuyot yesod muganot" in *Mishpat u-mimshal* 1 (1993), 30. An English version can be found at http://www.jewishvirtuallibrary.org/values-of-a-jewish-and-democratic-state.
35. Fania Oz-Salzberger, "Democratic First, Jewish Second: A Rationale," 67.
36. Jerusalem Center for Public Affairs: "New Poll: Survey of Israeli Jewish Attitudes on Future Peace Agreeement," March 28, 2017, 8: http://jcpa.org/article/new-poll-survey-israeli-jewish-attitudes-future-peace-agreement/.
37. Bernard Avishai, *The Hebrew Republic*, 40.

38. Eli Salzberger, "The Law of Politics and the Politics of Law."
39. Yedidia Stern, "Israel: A Jewish Democracy," 195–96.
40. Sammy Smooha, "Ethnic Democracy: Israel as an Archetype," *Israel Studies* 2/2 (1997), 198–241. For a critique of this model claiming a contradiction between the concepts of "demos" and "ethnos," see As'ad Ghanem, Nadim Rouhana and Oren Yiftachel, "Questioning 'Ethnic Democracy': A Response to Sammy Smooha," *Israel Studies* 3/2, (1998), 253–67.
41. Alon Tal, *The Land Is Full*, xviii. See also 131–67 for Tal's analysis of Orthodox population growth.
42. Jerusalem Center for Public Affairs: "New Poll: Survey of Israeli Jewish Attitudes on Future Peace Agreement," March 28th, 2017, 14. 85 percent of Jewish Israelis were convinced that the world would remain critical of Israel, no matter if a settlement were found for the Palestinians. http://jcpa.org/article/new-poll-survey-israeli-jewish-attitudes-future-peace-agreement/.
43. Among the many attempts to make Herzl come back to life, see Shimon Peres, *The Imaginary Voyage*, Walter Laqueur, "My Dear Doctor Herzl," and Doron Rabinovici and Natan Sznaider, *Herzl Reloaded*.

BIBLIOGRAPHY

Abramov, Zalman. *Perpetual Dilemma: Jewish Religion in the Jewish State.* London: Associated University Presses, 1976.

Adler, Emanuel, ed. *Israel in the World: Legitimacy and Exceptionalism.* Abingdon: Routledge, 2013.

Adler, Joseph. *The Herzl Paradox: Political, Social and Economic Theories of a Realist.* New York: Hadrian Press and Herzl Press, 1962.

Ahad Ha'am. "Altneuland." In *Ha-shiloah* 10/6 (1902) and *Ost und West* 4 (1903), 227–44.

———. "The First Zionist Congress." In *Ten Essays on Zionism and Judaism*, Leon Simon, trans., 25–31. New York: Arno Press, 1973.

———. "Hamusar ha-leumi [National morality]." In *Kol kitvei Ahad Ha'Am*, 159–161. Tel Aviv: Dvir, 1956.

———. "The Jewish State and the Jewish Problem." In *Nationalism and the Jewish Ethic*, Hans Kohn, ed., 66–89. New York: Herzl Press, 1962.

Alam, M. Shahid. *Israeli Exceptionalism: The Destabilizing Logic of Zionism.* New York: Palgrave Macmillan, 2009.

Almog, Oz. *The Sabra: The Creation of the New Jew.* Berkeley: University of California Press, 2000.

Almog, Shmuel, Jehuda Reinharz, and Anita Shapira, eds. *Zionism and Religion.* Hanover: University Press of New England, 1998.

Alroey, Gur. "The Jewish Emigration from Palestine in the Early Twentieth Century." *Journal of Modern Jewish Studies* 2/2 (2003): 111–31.

———. *An Unpromising Land: Jewish Migration to Palestine in the Early Twentieth Century.* Stanford: Stanford University Press, 2014.

———. *Zionism without Zion: The Jewish Territorial Organization and Its Conflict with the Zionist Organization.* Detroit: Wayne State Organization, 2016.

Aran, Gideon. "Jewish Zionist Fundamentalism: The Bloc of the Faithful in Israel (Gush Emunim)." In *Fundamentalism Observed*, Martin Marty and R. Scott Appleby, eds., 265–344. Chicago: Chicago University Press, 1991.

———. *Kookism: Shoreshei Gush Emunim, tarbut hamitnahalim, teologia tzionit, meshihiut bi-zmanenu* [The roots of Gush Emunim, Jewish settlers' subculture, Zionist theology, contemporary messianism]. Jerusalem: Carmel, 2013.

Aronson, Shlomo. "Huka le'yisrael: Ha-degem ha-briti shel David Ben-Gurion" [A constitution for Israel: David Ben-Gurion's British model]. *Politika* 2 (1998): 9–30.

———. *Levi Eshkol—From Pioneering Operator to Tragic Hero—A Doer.* London: Mitchell, 2010.

Auerbach, Jerold S. *Jewish State—Pariah Nation: Israel and the Dilemmas of Legitimacy.* New Orleans: Quid pro, 2014.

Avineri, Shlomo. *Herzl: Theodor Herzl and the Foundation of the Jewish State.* London: Weidenfeld & Nicolson, 2014.

———. *Moses Hess. Prophet of Communism and Zionism.* New York: New York University Press, 1985.

Avishai, Bernard. *The Hebrew Republic: How Secular Democracy and Global Enterprise Will Bring Israel Peace at Last.* Orlando: Harcourt, 2008.

Avni, Yoav. *Herzl amar* [Herzl said]. Or Yehuda: Zmora Bitan, 2011.

Bacon, Gershon C. *The Politics of Tradition: Agudat Yisrael in Poland, 1916–1939.* Jerusalem: Magnes Press: 1996.

Barak, Aharon. "Ha-mahapekha ha-hukatit: zekhuyot yesod muganot" [The constitutional revolution: protected human rights]. *Mishpat u-mimshal* 1 (1993): 9–35.

Barnett, Michael N. "The Politics of Uniqueness: The Status of the Israeli Case." In *Israel in Comparative Perspective: Challenging the Conventional Wisdom*, Michael N. Barnett, ed., 3–28. Albany: SUNY Press, 1996.

Bartal, Israel. *Letaken am: Ne'orut ve-le'umiut be-mizrah Europa* [To redeem a people: enlightenment and nationalism in Eastern Europe]. Jerusalem: Carmel, 2013.

———. *The Jews of Eastern Europe, 1772–1881*, Chaya Naor, trans. Philadelphia: University of Pennsylvania Press, 2005.

Bauer, Yehuda. *From Diplomacy to Resistance: A History of Jewish Palestine, 1939–1945.* Philadelphia: Jewish Publication Society, 1970.

Bauman, Zygmunt. "Allosemitism: Premodern, Modern, Postmodern." In *Modernity, Culture, and "the Jew,"* Bryan Cheyette and Laura Marcus, eds., 143–56. Cambridge: Polity Press, 1998.

Bein, Alex. *Thedore Herzl: A Biography*, Maurice Samuel, trans. Philadelphia: Jewish Publication Society, 1940.

Beinart, Peter. *The Crisis of Zionism*. New York: Times Book, 2012.

Beker, Avi. *The United Nations and Israel: From Recognition to Reprehension*. Lexington, Mass.: Lexington Books, 1988.

Bellow, Saul. *To Jerusalem and Back: A Personal Account*. New York: Viking, 1976.

Ben-Ari, Nitsa. "Hero or Anti-Hero? S. Yizhar's Ambivalent Zionism and the First Sabra Generation." In *Struggle and Survival in Palestine/Israel*. Mark Levine and Gershon Shafir, eds., 85–104. Berkeley/Los Angeles: University of California Press, 2012.

Ben Ezer, Ehud. *Unease in Zion*. New York: Quadrangle, 1974.

Ben-Gurion, David. *Le-mefakdim tze'irim* [To young officers]. Hotza'at sherut tarbut shel tzava hagana le-yisrael, 1949, 16–17. Library of Congress, Hebraic Section, pamphlet collection.

———. *Like Stars and Dust: Essays from Israel's Government Year Book*. Sede Boqer: Ben Gurion Research Center, 1997.

———. *Medinat yisrael ha-mehudeshet* [The renewed state of Israel], vol. 1. Tel Aviv: Am Oved, 1969.

———. "Netzah yisrael" [Eternity of Israel]. In *Kochavim ve-efer. Maamarim mi-tokh shnaton ha-memshala be-hotza'at merkaz ha-hasbara*, 110–56. Givatayim/Ramat Gan: Massada, 1976.

———."Yisrael be-amim" [Israel among the nations]. In *Netsah yisrael*, Tel Aviv: Ayanoth 1964.

———. *Yoman-Milhama* [War diary], *1948–1949*, vol. 1, Gershon Rivlin and Elhanan Oren, eds. Tel Aviv: Ministry of Defense, 1982.

Ben-Rafael, Eliezer. *Jewish Identities: Fifty Intellectuals Answer Ben-Gurion*. Leiden: Brill, 2002.

Benvenisti, Meron. *Jerusalem: The Torn City*. Minneapolis: University of Minnesota Press, 1976.

Berent, Moshe. *A Nation Like All Nations: Towards the Establishment of an Israeli Republic*. London: Israel Academic Press, 2014.

Berkovitch, Nitza. "Motherhood as a National Mission: The Construction of Womanhood in the Legal Discourse in Israel Berkowitz." *Women's Studies International Forum* 20 (1997): 605–19.

Bernstein, Deborah. *Constructing Boundaries: Jewish and Arab Workers in Mandatory Palestine*. Albany: State University of New York Press, 2000.

———. "Introduction." In *Pioneers and Homemakers*, Bernstein, ed., 1–28. Albany: State University of New York Press, 1992.

Bernstein, Deborah. *Nashim be-shulayim: Migdar ve-le'umiut be-Tel Aviv ha-mandatorit* [Women at the edge: gender and nationalism in Tel Aviv during the Mandate]. Jerusalem: Yad Ben Zvi, 2008.

———. *The Struggle for Equality. Urban Women Workers in Prestate Israeli Society.* New York: Praeger, 1987.

Bettauer, Hugo. *Die Stadt ohne Juden. Ein Roman von übermorgen.* Vienna: Metroverlag, 2008.

Bialer, Uri. *Between East and West.* New York: Cambridge University Press, 1990.

Biemann, Asher D. "Isaac Breuer: Zionist against his Will?" *Modern Judaism*, 20/2 (2000): 129–46

Bishara, Azmi. "Al she'elat ha-mi'ut ha-falastini be-yisrael" [On the question of the Palestinian minority in Israel]. *Teoria u-Vikoret* 3 (1993): 7–21.

Blackbourn, David and Geoff Eley. *The Peculiarities of German History.* New York: Oxford University Press, 1984.

Blum, Yehuda Z. "Israel and the United Nations: A Retrospective View." In *Israel among the Nations*, Alfred E. Kellermann, Kurt Siehr, and Talia Einhorn, eds., 69–77. The Hague: Kluwer Law International 1998.

———. *For Zion's Sake.* New York: Herzl Press, 1987.

Böhm, Adolf. *Die zionistische Bewegung*, vol. 2. Berlin: Welt-Verlag, 1921.

Borochov, Ber. "The Socialism of Poale Zion Here." In *Class Struggle and the Jewish Nation: Selected Essays in Marxist Zionism*, Mitchell Cohen, ed., 155–62. New Brunswick: Transaction: 1984.

Boyarin, Daniel and Jonathan Boyarin. "Diaspora: Generation and the Ground of Jewish Identity." *Critical Inquiry* 19/4 (1993): 693–725.

Brainin, Reuven. *Hayei Herzl* [The life of Herzl]. New York: Asaph, 1919.

Brechtken, Magnus. *Madagaskar für die Juden: Antisemitische Idee und politische Praxis, 1885–1945.* Munich: Oldenbourg, 1997.

Brenner, Michael. *Prophets of the Past: Interpreters of Jewish History.* Princeton: Princeton University Press 2010.

———. "Warum München nicht zur Hauptstadt des Zionismus wurde—Jüdische Religion und Politik um die Jahrhundertwende." In *Zionistische Utopie—Israelische Realität*, Michael Brenner and Yfaat Weiss, eds., 39–52. Munich: C.H. Beck, 1999.

———, ed. *Geschichte der Juden in Deutschland von 1945 bis zur Gegenwart*, Munich: C.H. Beck, 2012.

Breuer, Isaac. *The Jewish National Home*, Miriam Aumann, trans. Frankfurt a.M.: J. Kaufmann, 1926.

Brown, Benjamin. "Orthodox Judaism." In *The Blackwell Companion to Judaism*, Jacob Neusner and Alan J. Avery-Peck, eds., 311–33. Malden, Mass.: Blackwell, 2003.

Bruder, Edith. *The Black Jews of Africa: History, Religion, Identity.* New York: Oxford University Press, 2008.

Buber, Martin. *Briefwechsel aus sieben Jahrzehnten*, Grete Schäder, ed. Heidelberg: Lambert Schneider, 1972.

Burg, Avraham. *The Holocaust Is Over: We Must Rise from Its Ashes.* New York: Palgrave Macmillan, 2008.

Burstein, Moses. *Self-Government of the Jews in Palestine since 1900.* Tel Aviv: Hapoel Ha-Tsa'ir, 1934.

Campos, Michelle. *Ottoman Brothers: Muslims, Christians, and Jews in Early Twentieth-Century Palestine.* Stanford: Stanford University Press, 2011.

Canguilhem, Georges. *The Normal and the Pathological*, Carolyn Fawcett and Robert S. Cohen, trans. Dordrecht: D. Reidel, 1978.

Caplan, Neil. *Palestine Jewry and the Arab Question, 1917–1925.* London, Totowa, N. J.: Cass, 1978.

Carenen, Caitlin. *The Fervent Embrace: Liberal Protestants, Evangelicals and Israel.* New York: New York University Press, 2012.

Carmel, Erran. "Reflections on How the Israeli High-Tech Sector Success Transformed Israeli Society." In *Reinventing Israel in the Twenty-First Century*, Michael Brenner and Pamela S. Nadell, eds., Detroit: Wayne State University Press, 2018.

Chabon, Michael. *The Yiddish Policemen's Union*, New York: Harper Collins, 2007.

Chazan, Meir. "Mapai and the Arab-Jewish Conflict, 1936–1939." *Israel Studies Forum* 24/2 (2009): 28–51.

Clark, Victoria. *Allies for Armageddon: The Rise of Christian Zionism.* New Haven: Yale University Press, 2007.

Cohen, Hermann. *Deutschtum und Judentum.* Accessed March 3, 2017: http://sammlungen.ub.uni-frankfurt.de/freimann/content/titleinfo /181866.

Cohen, Hillel. *Army of Shadows: Palestinian Collaboration with Zionism, 1917–1948.* Berkeley: University of California Press, 2008.

Cohen, Nir. "From Legalism to Symbolism: Anti-mobility and National Identity in Israel, 1948–1958." *Journal of Historical Geography* 36 (2010): 19–26.

Cohen, Ynon. "Israeli-Born Emigrants: Size, Destinations and Selectivity." *International Journal for Comparative Sociology* 52, 1/2 (2011): 45–62.

Conforti, Yitzhak. "Searching for a Homeland: The Territorial Dimension in the Zionist Movement and the Boundaries of Jewish Nationalism." *Studies in Ethnicity and Nationalism* 14/1 (2014): 36–54.

Crouse, Eric. R. *American Christian Support for Israel: Standing with the Chosen People, 1948–1975*. Lanham, Md.: Lexington Books, 2014.

Dauber, Jeremy. *The Worlds of Sholem Aleichem*. New York: Schocken, 2013.

Dekel-Chen, Jonathan L. *Farming the Red Land: Jewish Agricultural Colonization and Local Soviet Power*. New Haven: Yale University Press, 2005.

DeKoven Ezrahi, Sidra. "The Grapes of Roth: 'Diasporism' Between Shylock and Portnoy." In *Literary Strategies: Jewish Texts and Contexts*, Studies in Contemporary Jewry XII, Ezra Mendelsohn, ed., 148–58. Oxford: Oxford University Press, 1996.

Dershowitz, Alan M. "Israel: The Jew among Nations." In *Israel among the Nations*, Alfred E. Kellermann, Kurt Siehr and Talia Einhorn, eds., 129–36. The Hague: Kluwer Law International, 1998.

Deutscher, Isaac (interview with), "On the Israeli-Arab War." *New Left Review* 1/44 (July/August 1967), 30–45.

Diamond, J. S. *Homeland or Holy Land? The 'Canaanite' Critique of Israel*. Bloomington: Indiana University Press, 1986.

Don-Yehiya, Eliezer and Charles S. Liebman. "The Symbol System of Zionist-Socialism: An Aspect of Israeli Civil Religion." *Modern Judaism* 1/2 (1981): 121–48.

Dowty, Alan. "Much Ado about Little: Achad Ha'am's 'Truth from Eretz Yisrael,' Zionism, and the Arabs." *Israel Studies* 5/2 (2000): 154–81.

Döblin, Alfred. "Jüdische Erneuerung." In *Schriften zu jüdischen Fragen*, Hans Otto Horch, ed., 7–78. Munich: Deutscher Taschenbuchverlag, 1997.

———. "Der allgemeine Territorialismus." In *Schriften zu jüdischen Fragen*, Hans Otto Horch, ed., 348–50. Munich: Deutscher Taschenbuchverlag, 1997.

———. *Briefe*. Heinz Graber, ed. Freiburg i.Br.: Olten, 1970.

Drori, Israel. *Foreign Workers in Israel: Global Perspectives*. Albany: SUNY Press 2009.

Dubnov, Arie M. "Notes on the Zionist Passage to India, or: The Analogical Imagination and Its Boundaries." *Journal of Israeli History* 35/2 (2016): 77–214.

———. *Isaiah Berlin: The Journey of a Jewish Liberal*. London: Palgrave Macmillan, 2012.

Dubnow, Simon. *Buch des Lebens. Erinnerungen und Gedanken. Materialien zur Geschichte meiner Zeit*, vol. 1 (1860–1903), Verena Dohrn, ed. Göttingen: Vandehoeck & Ruprecht, 2004.

———. *Grundlagen des Nationaljudentums*. Berlin: Jüdischer Verlag, 1905.

———. "On Nationalism: Letters on Old and New Judaism." In *Nationalism and History*, Koppel S. Pinson, ed., 73–214. Philadelphia: The Jewish Publication Society of America, 1958.

Elazar, Daniel. *Israel: Building a New Society*. Bloomington: Indiana University Press, 1986.

Elboim-Dror, Rachel. *Ha-mahar shel ha-etmol* [The tomorrow of yesterday]. Jerusalem: Yad Ben-Zvi, 1993.

Eli'ash, Shulamit. "Ha-emda ha-datit, tzionit ve-lo-tzionit, le-tokhnit halukat eretz-yisra'el [The religious position among Zionists and non-Zionists on the partition plan for Eretz Israel], 1937–1938." In *Iyunim be-tokhniyot ha-haluka 1937–1947* [Studies in the Palestine partition plans, 1937–1947]. Isaiah Friedman and Meir Avizohar, eds., 55–74. Kiryat Sdei Boker: Ben-Gurion Research Center, 1984.

Ellenson, David. " 'Jewishness in Israel:' Israel as a Jewish State." In *Essential Israel*, S. Ilan Troen and Rachel Fish, eds., 262–79. Bloomington: Indiana University Press, 2017.

Elon, Amos. *Herzl*. New York: Holt, Rinehart and Winston, 1975.

Englert, Sai. "The Rise and Fall of the Jewish Labour Bund," accessed 26 February 2017: http://isj.org.uk/the-rise-and-fall-of-the-jewish-labour-bund/.

Epstein, Lawrence J. *The Dream of Zion: The Story of the First Zionist Congress*. London: Rowman & Littlefield, 2016.

Falwell, Jerry. *Listen, America!* New York: Doubleday and Company, 1980.

Feige, Michael. *Settling in the Hearts: Jewish Fundamentalism in the Occupied Territories*. Detroit: Wayne State University Press, 2009.

Feigel, Uwe. *Das evangelische Deutschland und Armenien*. Göttingen: Vandenhoeck & Rupprecht, 1989.

Feldestein, Ariel L. "Ben Gurion, Zionism and American Jewry." From *State of Israel, Diaspora, and Jewish Continuity: Essays on the 'Ever-Dying People,'* Simon Rawidowicz, ed., 229–39. Hanover, N. H.: University Press of New England, 1986.

Filiu, Jean-Pierre. "France and the June 1967 War." In *The 1967 Arab-Israeli War: Origins and Consequences*, William Roger Louis and Avi Shlaim, eds., 247–63. New York: Cambridge University Press, 2012.

Fischer, Jens Malte. *Gustav Mahler*, Stewart Spencer, trans. New Haven: Yale University Press, 2011.

———. "Gustav Mahler und das 'Judentum in der Musik.'" In J. M. Fischer, *Jahrhundertdämmerung. Ansichten eines Fin de Siècle*, 131–58. Vienna: Zsolnay, 2000.

Frankel, Jonathan. *Prophecy and Politics: Socialism, Nationalism, and the Russian Jews, 1862–1917*, Cambridge: Cambridge University Press, 1981.

———. "S. M. Dubnov. Historian and Ideologist." In *The Life and Work of S. M. Dubnov*, Sophie Dubnov-Ehrlich, ed., 1–33. Bloomington: Indiana University Press, 1991.

Freiner, Johann. *Herrgott von Wien*. Dresden: Wodni & Lindecke, 1941.

Freud, Sigmund. *The Standard Edition of the Complete Psychological Works*, vol. 4. London: Hogarth Press, 1973.

Friedman, Isaiah. *The Question of Palestine: British-Jewish-Arab Relations, 1914–1918*. 2nd exp. ed. New Brunswick: Transaction Publishers, 1992.

Friedman, Menachem. "The State of Israel as a Theological Dilemma." In *The Israeli State and Society*, Baruch Kimmerling, ed., 165–215. New York: State University of New York Press, 1989.

Fund, Yossef. *Perud o-hishtatfut: Agudat Yisrael mul ha-tzionut u-medinat yisrael* [Separation and participation: Agudat Yisrael in its relationship towards Zionism and the State of Israel]. Jerusalem: Magnes Press, 1999.

Gaissinowitsch, Aba. "Bemerkungen zu Spenglers Auffassung Russlands," PhD diss., University of Vienna, 1924.

Gal, Allon, Athena S. Leoussi, and Anthony D. Smith, eds. *The Call of the Homeland: Diaspora Nationalisms, Past and Present*. Leiden: Brill, 2010.

———. *David Ben-Gurion and the American Alignment for a Jewish State*. Jerusalem: Magnes Press, 1991.

Galnoor, Itzhak. *The Partition of Palestine: Decision Crossroads in the Zionist Movement*. New York: SUNY, 1995.

Gavison, Ruth. "The Controversy over Israel's Bill of Rights." In *Israel Yearbook of Human Rights* 15 (1985): 113–154.

———. *Ha-mahapekha ha-hukatit—te'ur metziuto nevua ha-magshima et atzma* [The legislative revolution: a realistic description of a self-fulfilling prophecy]. Jerusalem: Israel Democracy Institute 1998.

Geiger, Abraham. *Das Judentum und seine Geschichte*. Breslau: Schletter, 1864.

Gelber, Mark. *Stefan Zweig Reconsidered: New Perspectives on his Literary and Biographical Writings*. Tübingen: Max Niemeyer, 2007.

Gelber, Yoav. *Nation and History: Israeli Historiography between Zionism and Post-Zionism*. London: Vallentine Mitchell, 2011.

———. *Palestine 1948: War, Escape and the Emergence of the Palestinian Refugee Problem*. Brighton and Portland: Sussex Academic Press, 2001.

Ghanem, As'ad, Nadim Rouhana, and Oren Yiftachel, "Questioning 'Ethnic Democracy': A Response to Sammy Smooha." *Israel Studies* 3/2 (1998): 253–67.

Gillath, Nurit. "Women and Military Service in Israel 1948–1967." In *Soldatinnen. Gewalt und Geschlecht im Krieg vom Mittelalter bis Heute*, Klaus Latzel, Franka Maubach, and Silke Satjukow, eds., 395–414. Paderborn: Ferdinand Schöningh, 2011.

Gilman, Sander. *Jewish Self-Hatred: Anti-Semitism and the Hidden Language of the Jews*. Baltimore: The John Hopkins University Press, 1986.

Gitelman, Zvi. "A Century of Jewish Politics in Eastern Europe: The Legacy of the Bund and the Zionist Movement." In *The Emergence of Modern Jewish Politics*, Zvi Gitelman, ed., 3–19. Pittsburgh: University of Pittsburgh Press, 2003.

Gitlin, Todd and Liel Leibovitz. *The Chosen Peoples: America, Israel, and the Ordeals of Divine Election*. New York: Simon & Schuster, 2010.

Gold, Dore. *The Tower of Babble: How the United Nations Has Fueled the Global Chaos*, New York: Three Rivers 2004.

Gold, Steven J. *The Israeli Diaspora*. Seattle: University of Washington Press, 2002.

Goldmann, Nahum. "The Creation of Israel." In *The Jewish Paradox*, Goldmann, ed., 88–120. London: Weidenfeld & Nicolson, 1978.

———. *Israel muß umdenken! Die Lage der Juden, 1976*. Reinbek: Rowohlt 1976.

———. "The Road Towards an Unfulfillable Ideal." In *Herzl Year Book* 3:131–43. New York: Herzl Press, 1960.

Goldscheider, Calvin. *Israeli Society in the 21st Century: Immigration, Inequality, and Religious Conflict*. Brandeis University Press: Waltham, MA, 2015.

Goldstein, Yossi. *Ahad Ha-am: biografia* [Ahad Ha-Am: a biography]. Jerusalem: Keter Publishers, 1992.

———. *Ahad ha-am ve-herzl: Ha-ma'avak al ofia ha-politi ve-ha-tarbuti shel ha-tzionut etzel "parshat altneuland"* [Ahad Ha-Am and Herzl: The struggle over the political and cultural profile of Zionism in the "Altneuland Episode"]. Jerusalem: Dinur Center, Salman Shazar Center, 2012.

Gordis, Daniel. *Israel: A Concise History of a Nation Reborn.* New York: Ecco, 2016.

————. *Menachem Begin: The Battle for Israel's Soul.* New York: Schocken, 2014.

Gordon, Aaron David. "Labor." In *Selected Essays,* Frances Burnce, trans., 50–91. New York: League for Labor Palestine, 1938.

Goren, Ilan: *Wo bist Du, Motek? Ein Israeli in Berlin.* Munich: Graf, 2013.

Gorenberg, Gershom. *The Accidental Empire: Israel and the Birth of the Settlements, 1967–1977.* New York: Time Books, 2006.

Gorny, Yosef. *From Binational Society to Jewish State.* Federal Concepts in Zionist Political Thought, 1920–1990, and the Jewish People. Leiden: Brill 2006.

Gribetz, Jonathan. "An Arabic-Zionist Talmud: Shimon Moyal's At-Talmud." *Jewish Social Studies* 17/1 (2010): 1–30.

Grief, Howard. *The Legal Foundation and Borders of Israel under International Law.* Jerusalem: Mazo, 2008.

Grimmeisen, Julie. "Halutzah or Beauty Queen? Images of Women in Early Israeli Society." *Israel Studies* 20/2 (2015): 27–52.

————. "Pionierinnen und Schönheitsköniginnen. Nationale Frauenvorbilder der jungen israelischen Gesellschaft, 1948–1967." PhD diss., Ludwig-Maximilians-University, Munich, 2015.

Grossman, Lawrence. "Transformation Through Crisis: The American Jewish Committee and the Six-Day War." *American Jewish History* 86/1 (1998): 27–54.

Halamish, Aviva. *Mi-bayit le'umi li-medina ba-derekh: ha-yishuv ha-yehudi be-eretz-yisra'el ben milhhamot ha-'olam* [From national home to state in the making: the Jewish settlement in Eretz Israel between the World Wars]. Tel-Aviv: The Open University, 2004.

Halevi, Yossi Klein. *Like Dreamers: The Story of the Israeli Paratroopers Who Reunited Jerusalem and Divided a Nation.* New York: Harper Collins, 2013.

Halkin, Hillel. *Across the Sabbath River: In Search of a Lost Tribe of Israel.* Boston: Houghton Mifflin, 2002.

————. *Jabotinsky. A Life.* New Haven: Yale University Press, 2014.

Halperin, Liora. *Babel in Zion: Jews, Nationalism, and Language Diversity in Palestine, 1920–1948.* New Haven: Yale University Press, 2014.

Halpern, Ben. *The Idea of the Jewish State.* Cambridge, Mass.: Harvard University Press, 1969.

Hamilton, Jill. *God, Guns and Israel: Britain, the First World War and the Jews in the Holy Land.* Stroud: Sutton, 2004.

Handler, Andrew. *Dori: The Life and Times of Theodor Herzl in Budapest (1860–1878).* Tuscaloosa: University of Alabama Press, 1983.

Hazony, Yoram. *The Jewish State: The Struggle for Israel's Soul.* New York: Basic/New Republic Books, 2000.

Heine, Heinrich. "Geständnisse." In *Heinrich Heine. Historisch-kritische Gesamtausgabe der Werke* [Düsseldorfer Ausg.]. Heinrich Windfuhr, ed., 9–58. Hamburg: Hoffmann und Campe, 1982.

Heller, Joseph. *The Birth of Israel: 1945–1949: Ben Gurion and his Critics.* Gainesville: University Press of Florida, 2000.

———. "Emdotey'hem shel Ben-Gurion, Weizman ve-Jabotinsky ba-she'ela ha-aravit." In *Idan Ha-Tzionut*, Yaakov Harris, Jehuda Reinharz and Anita Shapira, eds., 203–41. Jerusalem: The Zalman Shazar Center, 1999–2000.

Heller, Joseph E. *The Zionist Idea.* New York: Schocken, 2nd ed., 1949.

Hertzberg, Arthur. *The Jews in America: Four Centuries of an Uneasy Encounter.* New York: Simon and Schuster, 1989.

———. *The Zionist Idea: A Historical Analysis and Reader.* Garden City/New York: Doubleday and Herzl Press, 1959.

Herzl, Theodor. *Briefe und Tagebücher*, vols. 1–7, Alex Bein, Hermann Greive, Moshe Schaerf, and Julius H. Schoeps, eds. Berlin: Propyläen, 1983–1996.

———. *The Complete Diaries of Theodor Herzl*, vols. 1–5, Raphael Patai, ed.; Harry Zohn, trans. New York: Herzl Press 1960.

———. *The Jewish State. With an Introduction and a Biography.* New York: American Zionist Emergency Council, 1946.

———. *Old-New-Land.* Paula Arnold, trans. Haifa: Haifa Publishing Company, 1960.

Herzog, Hanna. *Interests, Identities, and Institutions in Comparative Politics: Gendering Politics—Women in Israel.* Ann Arbor: University of Michigan Press, 2010.

Hess, Moses. *Rome and Jerusalem: A Study in Jewish Nationalism.* Meyr Waxman, trans. New York: Bloch, 1945.

Hey, Katharina. "Ein Schritt gen Messias: Überlegungen zum Sechs-Tage-Krieg als biographischem Wendepunkt für das jüdische Selbstverständnis in Frankreich." *Münchner Beiträge zur Jüdischen Geschichte und Kultur* 11/1 (2017): 45–56.

Heymann, Michael, ed. *The Uganda Controversy*, vols. 1 and 2. Jerusalem: Institute for Zionist Research, 1970.

Hilbrenner, Anke. *Diaspora-Nationalismus. Zur Geschichtskonstruktion Simon Dubnows*. Göttingen: Vandenhoeck & Ruprecht, 2007.

Hitler, Adolf. *Mein Kampf.* Christian Hartmann, Thomas Vordermayer, Othmar Plöckinger, and Roman Töppel, eds. Munich: Institut für Zeitgeschichte, 2016, vol. 1.

Hodgson, Godfrey. *The Myth of American Exceptionalism*. New Haven: Yale University Press, 2009.

Hoffman, Bruce. *Anonymous Soldiers: The Struggle for Israel, 1917–1947*. New York: Knopf, 2015.

Hofmann, Klaus. "Canaanism." *Middle Eastern Studies* 47/2 (2011): 273–94.

Hyamson, Albert. "British Projects for the Restoration of Jews to Palestine." *American Jewish Historical Society Publications* 26 (1918): 127–64.

Inbari, Motti. *Jewish Fundamentalism and the Temple Mount: Who Will Build the Third Temple?* Albany: SUNY Press, 2009.

———. *Messianic Religious Zionism Confronts Israeli Territorial Compromises*. New York: Cambridge University Press, 2012.

Isaac, Rael Jean. *Israel Divided: Ideological Politics in the Jewish State*. Baltimore: Johns Hopkins University Press, 1976.

Israel Democracy Institute, *Statistical Report on Ultra-Orthodox Society in Israel*, Jerusalem, 2016.

Jabotinsky, Vladimir Ze'ev. *Ba-derekh le-medina* [On the road to statehood]. Jerusalem: Eri Jabotinsky, 1953.

———. *Ekronot manhim li-ve'ayot ha-sha'a* [Guiding principles for the problems of the day], Yosef Nedava, ed. Tel Aviv: Jabotinsky Research Institute, 1961.

———. *Ha-mivta ha-ivri*. Tel Aviv: Ha-sefer, 1930.

———. "Hartza'a al ha-historia ha-yisra'elit" [Lecture on the history of Israel]. In *Uma ve-hevra* [Nation and society], 159–68. Jerusalem: Eri Jabotinsky, 1949.

———. "The Iron Wall." Accessed March 3, 2017: http://en.jabotinsky.org /media/9747/the-iron-wall.pdf.

———. "Ra'ayon ha-yovel" [The idea of the Jubilee Year]. In *Uma ve-hevra*, 173–80. Jerusalem: Eri Jabotinsky, 1949.

———. *Le'umiut liberalit* [Liberal nationalism], vol. 1, Arieh Naor, ed. Tel Aviv: Jabotinsky Institute, 2013.

———. *The War and the Jews*. New York: Dial Press, 1942.

———. *The Jewish War Front*. London: George Allen & Unwin, 1940.

————. *Der Judenstaat*. Vienna: Dr. Heinrich Glanz Verlag, 1938.

Jaffe, Zvi Hirsch, *Ma'amar ha-yahadut ve-ha-tzionut*, n.p. Library of Congress, Hebraic Section, pamphlet collection.

Jamal, Amal. *Arab Minority Nationalism in Israel: The Politics of Indigeneity*. London: Routledge, 2011.

Jörum, Emma Lundgren. *Beyond Syria's Borders: A History of Territorial Disputes in the Middle East*. London: Tauris, 2014

Kallner, Rudolf. *Herzl und Rathenau. Wege jüdischer Existenz an der Wende des 20. Jahrhunderts*. Stuttgart: Klett, 1976.

Kagedan, Allan Laine. *Soviet Zion: The Quest for a Russian Jewish Homeland*. New York: St. Martin's, 1990.

Kaplan, Eran. *The Jewish Radical Right: Revisionist Zionism and Its Ideological Legacy*. Madison: University of Wisconsin Press, 2005.

Kaplan, Zvi Jonathan. "Rabbi Joel Teitelbaum, Zionism, and Hungarian Ultra-Orthodoxy." In *Modern Judaism* 24/2 (2004): 165–78.

Karsh, Ephraim. *Fabricating Israeli History: The 'New Historians'*, 2nd rev. ed. London: Frank Cass, 2000.

Karsh, Efraim and Inari Karsh. *Empires of the Sand: The Struggle for Mastery in the Middle East, 1789–1923*. Cambridge, Mass.: Harvard University Press, 1999.

Katz, David S. *Philo-Semitism and the Readmission of the Jews to England, 1603–1655*. Oxford: Clarendon, 1982.

Katz, Jacob. "The Forerunners of Zionism." In J. Katz, *Essential Papers on Zionism*. Jehuda Reinharz and Anita Shapira, eds., 33–45. New York: New York University Press, 1996.

Katz, Yossi. *Medina ba-derekh* [A state in the making]. Jerusalem: Magnes Press, 2000.

————. *Partner to Partition: The Jewish Agency's Partition Plan in the Mandate Area*. London: Frank Cass, 1998.

Kedar, Nir. "Ben-Gurion's View of the Place of Judaism in Israel." *Journal of Israeli History* 32/2 (2013): 157–74.

————. *Mamlakhtiyut: Ha-tefisa ha-ezrahit shel David Ben-Gurion* [Statism: Ben-Gurion's civic concept]. Jerusalem and Sde Boker: Ben-Gurion Institute, 2009.

Keren, Michael. *The Pen and the Sword: Israeli Intellectuals and the Making of the Nation-State*. Boulder, San Francisco, London: Westview Press, 1989.

Kessler, David. *The Falashas: A Short History of the Ethiopian Jews*. London: Frank Cass, 1996.

Khalidi, Muhammad Ali. "Utopian Zionism or Zionist Proselytism? A Reading of Herzl's *Altneuland*." *Journal of Palestinian Studies* 30/4 (2001): 55–67.

Khalidi, Rashid. *Palestinian Identity: The Construction of Modern National Consciousness.* New York: Columbia University Press, 1997.

Kimmerling, Baruch. *The Invention and Decline of Israeliness: State, Society, and the Military.* Berkeley: Univ. of California Press, 2001.

Kimmerling, Baruch and Joel S. Migdal. *The Palestinian People: A History.* Cambridge: Harvard University Press, 2003.

Klatzkin, Jakob. *Krisis und Entscheidung im Judentum.* Berlin: Jüdischer Verlag, 1921.

Klein, Uta. *Militär und Geschlecht in Israel.* Frankfurt am Main: Campus, 2001.

Koestler, Arthur. *Promise and Fulfilment: Palestine 1917–1949.* New York: MacMillan Company 1949.

Kohn, Hans. "Nationalismus." *Der Jude* 6/11 (1921): 674–86.

Kornberg, Jacques. *Theodor Herzl: From Assimilation to Zionism.* Bloomington: Indiana University Press, 1993.

Kraines, Oscar. *The Impossible Dilemma: Who is a Jew in the State of Israel?* New York: Bloch Publishing Company, 1976.

Kranz, Dani. *Israelis in Berlin. Wie viele sind es und was zieht sie nach Berlin?* Gütersloh: Bertelsmann, 2015.

Kraus, Karl. "Eine Krone für Zion." K. Kraus, *Frühe Schriften. 1892–1900.* J. J. Braakenburg, ed., 1897–1900. Munich: Kösel, 1979, vol. 2.

Kremnitzer, Mordechai and Amir Fuchs, eds. *Ze'ev Jabotinsky on Democracy, Equality, and Individual Rights.* Tel Aviv: Israel Democracy Institute, 2013.

Landau, Asher Felix, ed. *Selected Judgments of the Supreme Court of Israel: Special Volume.* Jerusalem: Ministry of Justice, 1971.

Landau, Jacob M. *The Arab Minority in Israel, 1967–1991: Political Aspects,* Oxford: Clarendon Press, 1993.

Lang, Yossi. "Tzion o Uganda?" Accessed 3, March 2017: http://cms.educa tion.gov.il/NR/rdonlyres/2537B23B-4773-4951-BBC9-AC157DE4E542 /118410/tzion_uganda.doc.

Laqueur, Walter. *A History of Zionism.* London: Weidenfeld and Nicolson, 1972.

The League of Nations. Mandate for Palestine, together with a Note by the Secretary-General relating to its application to the Territory known as Trans-Jordan, under the provisions of Article 25, Cmd. 1785 (1923).

Leibowitz, Yeshayahu. "Forty Years After." In *Judaism, Jewish Values and the Jewish State*, Eliezer Goldman, ed., 241–50. Cambridge, Mass.: Harvard University Press, 1992.

Leibowitz, Yehoshua. *Tora u-mitzvot be-zeman ha-ze*. Tel Aviv: Massada, 1954.

Lessing, Theodor. *Der Jüdische Selbsthaß*. Munich: Matthes & Seitz, 1984.

Levin, Nora. *While Messiah Tarried*. New York: Schocken, 1977.

Lerman, Antony. *The Making and Unmaking of a Zionist*. London: Pluto Press, 2012.

Lichtblau, Albert, ed. *Als hätten wir dazugehört—Österreichisch-jüdische Lebensgeschichten aus der Habsburgermonarchie*. Vienna: Böhlau, 1999.

Liebman, Charles S. "Jewish Fundamentalism and the Israeli Polity." In *Fundamentalism and the State. Remaking Polities, Economics and Militancy*, Martin E. Marty and R. Scott Appleby, eds., 68–87. Chicago and London: University of Chicago Press, 1993.

Lindsey, Hal and Carole C. Carlson, *The Late Great Planet Earth*. Grand Rapids: Zondervan, 1970.

Lipset, Martin Seymour. *American Exceptionalism: A Double Edged Sword*. New York: W.W. Norton, 1996.

Lis, Daniel. "Igbo Jews—Religious Shift: From Igbo Sabbatharians in Nigeria to Igbo Converts to Judaism in Israel." *Chilufim* 11 (2011): 99–124.

———."Israeli Foreign Policy towards the Igbo: The Israeli Factor in Igbo Jewish Identification." In *African Zion: Studies in Black Judaism*, Edith Bruder and Tudor Parfitt, eds., 87–162. Cambridge: Scholars Publishing, 2012.

———. *Jewish Identity among the Igbo of Nigeria: Israel's "Lost Tribe" and the Question of Belonging in the Jewish State*. Trenton: Africa World Press, 2015.

Lis, Daniel, William F. S. Miles, and Tudor Parfitt, eds. *In the Shadow of Moses: New Jewish Movements in Africa and the Diaspora*. Los Angeles: Tsehai Publishers, 2016.

Livnat, Andrea. *Der Prophet des Staates: Theodor Herzl im kollektiven Gedächtnis Israels*. Frankfurt a.M.: Campus, 2011.

Loeffler, James. "Between Zionism and Liberalism: Oscar Janowsky and Diaspora Nationalism in America." *AJS Review* 34/2 (2010): 289–308.

Lustick, Ian. *Arabs in the Jewish State: Israel's Control of a National Minority*. Austin: University of Texas Press, 1980.

———. *For the Land and the Lord: Jewish Fundamentalism in Israel*. New York: Council of Foreign Relations Press, 1988.

Luz, Ehud. *Parallels Meet: Religion and Nationalism in the Early Zionist Movement*. Philadelphia: Jewish Publication Society, 1988.

Mahla, Daniel. "Orthodoxy in the Age of Nationalism: Agudat Yisrael and the Religious Zionist Movement in Germany, Poland and Palestine, 1912–1952." PhD diss., Columbia University, 2014.

Manor, Ehud. *Forward: The Jewish Daily Forward (Forverts) Newspaper: Immigrants, Socialism, and Jewish Politics in New York*. Eastbourne: Sussex Academic Press, 2009.

Maoz, Adia Mendelson. *Multiculturalism in Israel: Literary Perspectives*, West Lafayette: Purdue University Press, 2014, 53–60. Also: https://genius .com/Mahmoud-darwish-identity-card-english-version-annotated.

Masalha, Nur. *Imperial Israel and the Palestinians: The Politics of Expansion*. London: Pluto Press, 2000.

Mattuck, Israel I. *What Are the Jews: Their Significance and Position in the Modern World*. London: Hodder and Stoughton, 1939.

Mazza, Roberto. "Transforming the Holy City: From Communal Clashes to Urban Violence, the Nebi Musa Riots in 1920." In Ulrike Freitag, Nelida Fuccaro, Claudia Ghrawi, and Nora Lafi, eds., *Urban Violence in the Middle East: Changing Cityscapes in the Transition from Empire to Nation State*. New York: Berghahn, 2015, 179–96.

Mendelsohn, Ezra. *Class-Struggle in the Pale*. Cambridge: Cambridge University Press, 1977.

Mendes-Flohr, Paul R. and Jehuda Reinharz, eds. *The Jew in the Modern World: A Documentary History*. New York: Oxford University Press, 2nd ed., 1995.

Meyer, Michael A., ed. *German-Jewish History in Modern Times*. New York: Columbia University Press, 1997, vols. 2 and 3.

Mi'ari, Mahmoud. "Attitudes of Palestinians toward Normalization with Israel." *Journal of Peace Research* 36/3 (1999): 339–48.

Migdal, Joel. *Through the Lens of Israel: Explorations in State and Society*. Albany: State University of New York Press, 2001.

Mintz, Matityahu. "Ber Borokhov." In *Essential Papers on Jews and the Left*, Ezra Mendelsohn, ed., 122–44. New York: New York University Press, 1997.

Mirsky, Yehudah. *Rav Kook: Mystic in a Time of Revolution*. New Haven: Yale University Press, 2014.

Mittleman, Alan L. *Between Kant and Kabbalah: An Introduction to Isaac Breuer's Philosophy of Judaism*. Albany: SUNY Press, 1990.

————. *The Politics of Torah. The Jewish Political Tradition and the Founding of Agudat Israel*. New York: SUNY Press, 1996.

Morahg, Gilead. "A. B. Yehoshua: Fictions of Zion and Diaspora." In *Israeli Writers Consider the "Outsider'*, Leon I. Yudkin, ed., 124–137. London/ Toronto: Associated University ,Press, 1993.

Morgenstern, Matthias. *Von Frankfurt nach Jerusalem: Isaac Breuer und die Geschichte des 'Austrittsstreits' in der deutsch-jüdischen Orthodoxie*. Tübingen: Mohr Siebeck, 1995.

Morris, Benny. *The Birth of the Palestinian Refugee Problem Revisited*. Cambridge: Cambridge University Press, 2004.

————. *Israel's Border Wars, 1949–1956*. New York: Oxford University Press, 1997.

Moyn, Samuel. "Fantasies of Federalism," *Dissent* 62/1 (2015): 145–51.

Mulvey, Paul. *The Political Life of Josiah C. Wedgwood: Land, Liberty and Empire, 1872–1943*. Woodbridge: Royal Historical Society, 2010.

Myers David M. *Between Jew and Arab: The Lost Voice of Simon Rawidowicz*. Waltham: Brandeis University Press, 2008.

Naor, Arye. "Ha-mitve ha-hukati shel Ze'ev Jabotinsky le-medina ha-yehudit be-eretz yisrael" [Ze'ev Jabotinsky's outline of a constitution for a Jewish state in the land of Israel]. In *Ish ba-sa'ar: Masot u-mehkarim al Ze'ev Jabotinsky*, Pinhas Ginosar and Avi Bareli, eds., 51–92. Be'er Sheva: The Ben-Gurion Research Center for the Study of Israel and Zionism, 2004.

Navon, Itzhak. "Preface." In David Ben-Gurion, *Like Stars and Dust: Essays from Israel's Government Year Book*, 3–4. Sede Boqer: Ben Gurion Research Center, 1997.

Near, Henry, ed. *The Kibbutz Movement*, vols. 1 and 2. Oxford: Vallentine Mitchell, 1992–1997.

Nevo, Eshkol, *Neuland*. London: Vintage, 2016.

Nirenberg, David. *Anti-Judaism: The History of a Way of Thinking*. New York: W.W. Norton, 2013.

Novak, David. *Zionism and Religion—A New Theory*. New York: Cambridge University Press, 2015.

Novick, Peter. *The Holocaust in American Life*. Boston: Houghton Mifflin, 1999.

Ohana, David. *Meshihiut u-mamlakhtiut: Ben-Gurion ve-ha-intelektualim* [Messianism and statism: Ben-Gurion and the intellectuals]. Sde Boker: The Ben-Gurion Research Institute, 2003.

Oren, Michael B. *Six Days of War: June 1967 and the Making of the Modern Middle East*. Oxford: Oxford University Press, 2002.

Oren, Tasha G. *Demon in the Box: Jews, Arabs, Politics, and Culture in the Making of Israeli Television*. New Brunswick: Rutgers University Press, 2004.

Oz, Amos. *In the Land of Israel*. San Diego: Harcourt Brace, 1993.

Oz-Salzberger, Fania. "Democratic First, Jewish Second: A Rationale." In *The Israeli Nation-State: Political, Constitutional and Cultural Challenges*, Fania Oz-Salzberger and Yedidia Z. Stern, eds., 66–77. Brighton, Mass.: Academic Studies Press, 2014.

Palestine Royal Commission Report (Peel Report), accessed March 3, 2017: http://unispal.un.org/pdfs/Cmd5479.pdf.

Parfitt, Tudor. *Black Jews in Africa and the Americas*. Cambridge, Mass.: Harvard University Press, 2013.

———. *Journey to the Vanished City: In Search for a Lost Tribe of Israel*. New York: St. Martin's, 1992.

———. *Operation Moses: The Story of the Exodus of the Falasha Jews from Ethiopia*. New York: Stein and Day, 1985.

———. "What Will the Worldwide Explosion of New Israelite Communities and Judaizing Movements Mean for the Jewish State?" In *Reinventing Israel in the Twenty-First Century*, Michael Brenner and Pamela S. Nadell, eds. Detroit: Wayne State University Press, 2018.

Parfitt, Tudor, and Natenel Fisher, eds. *Becoming Jewish: New Jews and Emerging Jewish Communities in a Globalized World*. Newcastle upon Tyne: Cambridge Scholars Publishing, 2016

Parfitt, Tudor, and Netanel Fisher, eds. *New Jews and Emerging Jewish Communities in a Globalized World*. Newcastle upon Tyne: Cambridge Scholars Publishing, 2016.

Pawel, Ernst. *The Labyrinth of Exile: A Life of Theodor Herzl*. New York: Farrar, Straus & Giroux, 1989.

Peled, Yoav. *Class and Ethnicity in the Pale: The Political Economy of the Jewish Workers' Nationalism in Late Imperial Russia*. London: St. Martin's Press, 1989.

Peleg, Ilan. "Israel's Constitutional Order and Kulturkampf: The Role of Ben-Gurion." In *Israel Studies* 3/1 (1998): 230–50.

Peleg, Yaron. *Directed by God: Jewishness in Contemporary Israeli Film and Television*. Austin: University of Texas Press, 2016.

Penslar, Derek J. "Historians, Herzl, and the Palestinian Arabs: Myth and

Counter-Myth." In Penslar, *Israel in History: The Jewish State in Comparative Perspective*, 52–61. Abingdon: Routledge, 2007.

———. "Is Zionism a Colonial Movement?" In Penslar, *Israel in History: The Jewish State in Comparative Perspective*, 90–111. Abingdon: Routledge, 2007.

———. *Jews and the Military*. Princeton: Princeton University Press, 2013.

Peres, Shimon. *The Imaginary Voyage: With Theodor Herzl in Israel*. New York: Arcade 1999.

Peres, Shimon, with Aryeh Naor. *The New Middle East*. New York: Henry Holt and Company, 1993.

Peri, Yoram. *Yad ish be-ahiv: Rezah Rabin u-milhemet ha-tarbut be'yisrael* [Brothers at war: Rabin's assassination and the cultural wars in Israel]. Tel Aviv: Bavel, 2005.

Peters, Joel. *Israel and Africa: The Problematic Friendship*. London: British Academic Press, 1992.

Pew Research Center, *Israel's Religiously Divided Society*, Washington DC, 2016.

Pianko, Noam. *Zionism and the Roads Not Taken: Rawidowicz, Kaplan, Kohn*. Bloomington: Indiana University Press, 2010.

Pinsker, Leo. "Auto-Emancipation." In Pinsker, *Road to Freedom*. Westport, Conn.: Greenwood Press, 1975.

Pinto, Diana. *Israel Has Moved*. Cambridge Mass.: Harvard University Press, 2013.

Rabinovici, Doron and Natan Sznaider. *Herzl Reloaded. Kein Märchen*. Berlin: Suhrkamp Verlag 2016.

Rabinovich, Itamar. *Yitzhak Rabin: Soldier, Leader, Statesmen*. New Haven: Yale University Press, 2017.

Rabinovitch, Simon. *Jewish Rights, National Rites: Nationalism and Autonomy in Late Imperial Russia*. Stanford: Stanford University Press, 2014.

———. *Jews and Diaspora Nationalism: Writings on Jewish Peoplehood in Europe and the United States*. Waltham, Mass.: Brandeis University Press, 2012.

Ram, Uri. *The Globalization of Israel: McWorld in Tel Aviv, Jihad in Jerusalem*. New York: Routledge, 2008.

Rathenau, Walther. "Höre Israel!" In W. Rathenau, *Impressionen*, 1–21. Leipzig: Hirzl, 2nd ed., 1902.

———. "Staat und Judentum. Eine Polemik." In W. Rathenau, *Gesammelte Schriften* 1: *Zur Kritik der Zeit. Mahnung und Warnung*, 188–89. Berlin: S. Fischer, 1918.

Ratzabi, Shalom. *Between Zionism and Judaism: The Radical Circle in Brit Schalom*. Leiden: Brill, 2002.

Ravitzky, Aviezer. *Messianism, Zionism, and Jewish Religious Radicalism*. Chicago: University of Chicago Press, 1996.

Rawidowicz, Simon. "Excerpts from a Correspondence between David Ben-Gurion and Simon Rawidowicz." In *State of Israel, Diaspora, and Jewish Continuity: Essays on the 'Ever-Dying People'*, Simon Rawidowicz, ed., 194–204. Hanover N.H.: University Press of New England, 1986.

———. "Israel: The People, the State." In *State of Israel, Diaspora, and Jewish Continuity: Essays on the 'Ever-Dying People,'* Rawidowicz, ed., 182–93. Hanover, NH: University Press of New England, 1986.

———. Rawidowicz, Simon. "Jerusalem and Babylon." In *State of Israel, Diaspora, and Jewish Continuity: Essays on the 'Ever-Dying People'*, Simon Rawidowicz, 229–239. Hanover NH: University Press of New England, 1986.

Rayner, John D. *A Jewish Understanding of the World*. Oxford: Berghahn, 1998.

Raz-Krakotzkin, Amnon. "Galut mitoh ribonut: Le-vikoret shlilat ha-galut ba-tarbut ha-yisraelit [Exile within sovereignty: on the theory of the negation of exile in Israeli culture]." In *Teoria u-Vikoret* 4 (1994): 6–23.

Rebhun, Uzi and Lilach Lev Ari. *American Israelis: Migration, Transnationalism, and Diasporic Identity*. Leiden: Brill, 2010.

Regev, Motti and Edwin Seroussi. *Popular Music and National Culture in Israel*. Berkeley: University of California Press, 2004.

Reinharz, Jehuda and Itamar Rabinovich, eds. *Israel in the Middle East: Documents and Readings on Society, Politics, and Foreign Relations, 1948 to the Present*. Lebanon, N.H.: University Press of New England, 2008.

Reinharz, Jehuda. *Chaim Weizmann: The Making of a Statesman*. New York: Oxford University Press, 1993.

———. *Chaim Weizmann: The Making of a Zionist Leader*. New York: Oxford University Press, 1985.

Reitter, Paul. *On the Origins of Jewish Self-Hatred*. Princeton: Princeton University Press, 2012.

Rekhess, Elie. "The Arab Minority in Israel: Reconsidering the 1948 Paradigm." *Israel Studies* 19 (2014): 187–217.

———. "Identity Dilemmas of the Palestinian-Arabs in Israel and the October–November 2015 Violence." In *Reinventing Israel in the Twenty-First Century*, Michael Brenner and Pamela S. Nadell, eds. Detroit: Wayne State University Press, 2018.

————. "Resurgent Islam in Israel." In *Asian and African Studies* 27 (1993): 189–206.

Renton, James. "Flawed Foundations: The Balfour Declaration and the Palestine Mandate." In *Britain, Palestine and Empire: The Mandate Years*, Rory Miller, ed., 15–39. Farnham: Ashgate, 2010.

Reuveni, Gideon. "Sports and the Militarization of Jewish Society." In *Emancipation through Muscle*, Michael Brenner and Reuveni Gideon, eds., 44–61. University of Nebraska Press: Lincoln and London, 2006.

Robinson, Shira. *Citizen Strangers: Palestinians and the Birth of Israel's Liberal Settler State*. Stanford University Press, 2013.

Rodinson, Maxime. *Israel: A Colonial Settler State?* New York: Monad Press, 1973.

Rose, Jacqueline. *The Question of Zion*. Princeton University Press, 2005.

Rose, N. A. *The Gentile Zionists: Study in Anglo-Zionist Diplomacy, 1929–1939*. Abingdon: Routledge, 1973.

Rosenfeld, Alvin. *Progressive Jewish Thought and Antisemitism*. New York: American Jewish Committee, 2006.

Roth, Philip, *Operation Shylock*. New York: Simon and Schuster, 1993.

Rouhana, Nadim N. *Palestinian Citizens in an Ethnic Jewish State: Identities in Conflict*. New Haven: Yale University Press, 1997.

Rouhana, Nadim N. and Areej Sabbagh-Khoury. "Palestinian Citizenship in Israel: A Settler Colonial Perspective." In *Contemporary Israel: New Insights and Scholarship*, Frederick Greenspahn, ed., 32–61. New York: New York University Press 2016.

Rovner, Adam. *In the Shadow of Zion: Promised Lands before Israel*. New York: New York University Press, 2014.

Rozen, Orit. *The Rise of the Individual in 1950s Israel: A Challenge to Collectivism*. Waltham: Brandeis University Press, 2011.

Rubin, Gil Shalom. "The Future of the Jews: Planning for the Postwar Jewish World." Ph.D. diss., Columbia University, 2017.

Rubinstein, Amnon and Medina, Barak. *Ha-mishpat ha-konstitutsyoni shel medinat yisrael*, 2 vols., Jerusalem: 5th ed.,1996.

Rubinstein, Elyakim. "The Declaration of Independence as a Basic Document of the State of Israel." *Israel Studies* 3 (1998): 195–210.

Rynhold, Jonathan. *The Arab-Israeli Conflict in American Political Culture*. Cambridge: Cambridge University Press, 2015.

Sagiv, Assaf. "George Steiner's Jewish Problem (followed by G. Steiner's response)." In *The Wounds of Possibility: Essays on George Steiner*, Gil Soeiro, ed., 194–214. Newcastle: Cambridge Scholars Publishing, 2012.

Said, Edward. "An Ideology of Difference." *Critical Inquiry* 12/1 (1985): 38–58.

Salzberger, Eli. "The Law of Politics and the Politics of Law: The Changing Relationships Between the Political Branches and the Legal Institutions in Israel." In *Reinventing Israel in the Twenty-First Century*, Michael Brenner and Pamela S. Nadell, eds. Detroit: Wayne State University Press, 2018.

Sand, Shlomo. *The Invention of the Jewish People.* London: Verso, 2009.

———. *The Invention of the Land of Israel.* London, Verso, 2012.

Saposnik, Arieh B. *Becoming Hebrew: The Creation of a Jewish National Culture in Ottoman Palestine.* New York: Oxford University Press, 2008.

———. "Wailing Walls and Iron Walls: The Western Wall as Sacred Symbol in Zionist National Iconography." *The American Historical Review* 120/5 (2015): 1653–1681.

Salkin, Jeffrey K., ed. *A Dream of Zion: American Jews Reflect Why Israel Matters to Them.* Woodstock, VT: Jewish Lights, 2007.

Salmon, Joseph. *Im ta'iru ye-im te'oreru: Ortodoksia bi-metzarey ha-le'umiut* [Do not provoke providence: Orthodoxy in the grip of nationalism]. Jerusalem: The Zalman Shazar Center, 2006.

———. *Religion and Zionism: First Encounters.* Jerusalem: Magnes Press, 2002.

Schneer, Jonathan. *The Balfour Declaration: The Origins of the Arab-Israeli Conflict.* New York: Random House, 2010.

Schorske, Carl E. *Fin-de-Siècle Vienna: Politics and Culture.* New York: Alfred Knopf, 1980.

Schulte, Christoph. *Psychopathologie des fin de siècle: Der Kulturkritiker, Arzt und Zionist Max Nordau.* Frankfurt a.M.: Fischer, 1997.

Segal, Alan F. *Rebecca's Children: Judaism and Christianity in the Roman World.* Boston: Harvard University Press, 1986.

Segev, Tom. *1949: The First Israelis.* New York: Free Press, 1986.

———. *1967: Israel, the War, and the Year that Transformed the Middle East.* New York: Metropolitan Books, 2007.

———. *One Palestine Complete: Jews and Arabs under the British Mandate.* New York: Holt, 2000.

Seltzer, Robert. *Simon Dubnow's "New Judaism": Diaspora Nationalism and the World History of the Jews.* Leiden: Brill, 2014.

Semel, Nava. *Isra-Isle.* Jessica Cohen, trans. Simsbury, Conn.: Mandel Vilar Press, 2016.

Senor, Dan and Singer, Paul. *Start-up Nation: The Story of Israel's Economic Miracle*. New York: Twelve, 2009.

Shafat, Gershon. *Gush emunim: Hasipur me-ahorey ha-klayim* [Gush Emunim: The story behind the scenes]. Bet El: Bet El Publications, 1995.

Shafir, Gershon. *Land, Labor, and the Origins of the Israeli-Palestinian Conflict, 1882–1914*. Cambridge: Cambridge University Press, 1989.

Shahar, Yoram. "Early Drafts of the Israeli Declaration of Independence." In *Iyunei mishpat* 26 (2002): 523–600.

———. "Jefferson Goes East: The American Origins of the Israeli Declaration of Independence." *Theoretical Inquiries in Law* 10/2 (2009): 589–618.

Shapira, Anita. "Ben Gurion and the Bible: The Forging of an Historical Narrative?" *Middle Eastern Studies* 33/4 (1997): 645–74.

———. *Israel: A History*. Waltham, Mass.: Brandeis University Press, 2012.

———. *Land and Power: The Zionist Resort to Force, 1881–1948*. New York: Oxford University Press 1992

———. *Yosef Haim Brenner: A Life*. Stanford: Stanford University Press, 2014.

Shavit, Ari. *My Promised Land*. New York: Spiegel & Grau, 2013.

Shavit, Yaacov. *Jabotinsky and the Revisionist Movement, 1925–1948*. London: Frank Cass, 1988.

———. *Me-Ivri 'ad kena'ani* [From Hebrew to Canaanite]. Jerusalem: Domino, 1984.

———. *The New Hebrew Nation: A Study in Israeli Heresy and Fantasy*. London: Frank Cass, 1987.

Shechtman, Joseph B. *Rebel and Statesman: The Life and Times of Vladimir Jabotinsky*, vol. 1. New York: Eschel Books, 1959.

Shelef, Nadav G. *Evolving Nationalism: Homeland, Identity, and Religion in Israel, 1925–2005*. Ithaca: Cornell University Press, 2010.

———. "From 'Both Banks of the Jordan' to the 'Whole Land of Israel': Ideological Change in Revisionist Zionism." In *Israel Studies* 9/1 (2004): 125–148.

Shilo, Margalit. "The Double or Multiple Image of the New Hebrew Woman." *Nashim* 1 (1998): 73–94.

Shilon, Avi. *Menachem Begin: A Life*. New Haven: Yale University Press, 2012.

Shimoni, Gideon. *The Zionist Ideology*. Waltham: Brandeis University Press, 1995.

Shimoni, Gideon and Robert S. Wistrich, eds. *Theodor Herzl: Visionary of the Jewish State*. Jerusalem and New York: Herzl Press, 1999.

Shindler, Colin. *The Rise of the Israeli Right: From Odessa to Hebron*. Cambridge: Cambridge University Press, 2015

Shohat, Ella. *Israeli Cinema: East/West and the Politics of Representation*. Austin: University of Texas Press, 1989.

Shoshani, Reuven. "Ha-basis ha-metodologi shel heker idiologiut: Makhshavato ha-medinit ve-ha-tarbutit shel Zeev Jabotinsky ke-dugma [The Methodological Basis of a Study on Ideology: Zeev Jabotinsky's Thoughts about State and Culture as an Example]." PhD diss., Hebrew University of Jerusalem, 1992.

Shumsky, Dimitry. *Beyond the Nation State: The Zionist Political Imagination from Pinsker to Ben-Gurion*. New Haven: Yale University Press, 2018.

―――. "Brith Shalom's Uniqueness Reconsidered: Hans Kohn and Autonomist Zionist." *Jewish History* 25/3–4 (2011): 339–53.

―――. "Leon Pinsker and 'Autoemanciation!'" *Jewish Social Studies* 18/1 (2011): 33–62.

―――. "Tzionut be-merkavot kefulot: Ha-im haya Dubnov lo-tzioni? [Zionism in Quotation Marks: Was Dubnov a non- Zionist?]." *Zion* 77/3 (2012): 369–84.

―――. "Tzionu u-medinut ha-le'um: Ha'aracha me-hadash" [Zionism and Nationality Politics: A Reappraisal]. *Zion* 77/2 (2012): 223–54.

Siegemund, Anja. "Utopia in Palästina? Deutsche und Prager Zionisten und ihre Idee der Verständigung mit den Arabern, bis zur Gründung des Staates Israel." PhD diss., Ludwig-Maximilians-University Munich, 2005.

Smith, Frederick Edwin. *The World in 2030 A.D.* London : Hodder & Stoughton, 1930.

Smooha, Sammy. *Arabs and Jews in Israel: Conflicting and Shared Attitudes in a Divided Society*. Boulder: Westview, 1989.

―――. "Ethnic Democracy: Israel as an Archetype." *Israel Studies* 2/2 (1997): 198–241.

―――. "Is Israel Western?" In *Comparing Modernities: Pluralism versus Homogeneity: Essays in Homage to Shmuel N. Eisenstadt*, Eliezer Ben-Rafael and Yitzhak Sternberg, eds., 413–42. Leiden: Brill, 2005.

Snir, Reuven. "Double Exclusion and the Search for Inessential Solidarities: The Experience of Iraqi Jews as Heralding a New Concept of Identity and Belonging." In *Israeli Identity: Between Orient and Occident*, David Tal, ed., 140–60. London: Routledge, 2013.

Sokolow, Nahum. *History of Zionism*, vol I. London: Longmans, Green and Co., 1919.

Spector, Stephen. *Evangelicals and Israel: The Story of American Christian Zionism.* Oxford: Oxford University Press, 2009.

Sprinzak, Ehud. "The Genesis of Zionist Fundamentalism: the Case of Gush Emunim." *Orim* 3/1 (1987): 8–27.

———. "Three Models of Religious Violence: The Case of Jewish Fundamentalism in Israel." In: *Fundamentalism and the State*, Martin E. Marty and R. Scott Appleby, eds., 462–90. Chicago: The University of Chicago Press, 1993

Stanislawski, Michael. "A Jewish Monk? A Legal and Ideological Analysis of the Origins of the 'Who is a Jew' Controversy in Israel." In *Text and Context. Essays in Modern Jewish History and Historiography in Honor of Ismar Schorsch*, Eli Lederhendler and Jack Wertheimer, eds., 547–77. New York: The Jewish Theological Seminary, 2005.

———. *Zionism and the Fin-de-Siecle: Cosmopolitanism and Nationalism from Nordau to Jabotinsky.* Berkeley: University of California Press, 2001.

Staples, Amy L. S. "The Birth of Development: How the World Bank, Food and Agriculture Organization and the World Health Organization Changed the World, 1945–1965." *American Historical Review* 112/5 (2007): 1513–14.

Stein, Joshua. *Our Great Solicitor: Josiah G. Wedgwood and the Jews.* Susquehanna University Press, 1992.

Steinberg, Isaac Nahum. *Australia—An Unpromised Land: In Search of a New Home.* London: Viktor Gollancz, 1948.

Steiner, George. "Our Homeland, the Text." In Steiner, *No Passion Spent: Essays, 1978–1995*, 304–27. New Haven: Yale University Press 1996.

Stern, Fritz. "The Burden of Success: Reflections on German Jewry." In Stern, *Dreams and Illusions: The Drama of German History*, 97–113. New York: Alfred A. Knopf, 1987.

Stern, Yedidia "Israel: A Jewish Democracy." In *Essential Israel: Essays for the 21st Century*, S. Ilan Troen and Rachel S. Fish, eds., 182–200. Bloomington: Indiana University Press, 2017.

———."Religion, State and the Jewish Identity Crisis in Israel." Unpublished working paper of the Center for Middle East Policy at the Brookings Institution, Washington DC: 2016.

Sternberger, Ilse. *Princes without a Home: Modern Zionism and the Strange Fate of Theodor Herzl's Children, 1900–1945.* San Francisco: International Scholars Publications, 1994.

Strum, Philippa. "The Road Not Taken: Constitutional Non-Decision Making in 1948–1950 and Its Impact on Civil Liberties in the Israeli Political Culture." In *Israel: The First Decade of Independence*, Ilan Troen and Noah Lucas, eds., 83–104. New York: SUNY Press, 1995.

Tal, Alon. *The Land is Full: Addressing Overpopulation in Israel*. New Haven: Yale University Press, 2016.

Talmon, Jacob L. *The Six Day War—in Historical Perspective: Reflections on Jewish Statehood*. Rehovot: Yad Haim Weizmann, 1971.

Tobias, Henry. *The Jewish Bund in Russia: From its Origins to 1905*. Stanford: Stanford University Press, 1972.

Troen, Ilan S. "Conclusion: Imagination and Reality in the Imagination of Israel's Future." In *Contemporary Israel: New Insights and Scholarship*, Frederick E. Greenspahn, ed., 261–82. New York: New York University Press 2016.

Troy, Gil. "Israel in World Opinion." In *Essential Israel: Essays for the 21st Century*, S. Ilan Troen and Rachel S. Fish, eds., 151–81. Bloomington: Indiana University Press, 2017.

Udelson, Joseph H. *Dreamer of the Ghetto: The Life and Works of Israel Zangwill*. Tuscaloosa: University of Alabama Press, 1990.

Unna, Moshe. "Oz ve-shalom" [Strength and Peace]. In *Staat und Religion in Israel*, Karlheinz Schneider, ed., 75–89. Berlin: Deutsch-Israelischer Arbeitskreis für Frieden im Nahen Osten, 1984.

Villa, Chaim Ya'akov (Eugenio): *Eretz Yehuda. Tossefet le-pitaron she'elat ha-yehudim* [Land of Judah. An Addition to the Solution of the Jewish Question]. Buenos Aires, 1939, Hebrew Pamphlet Collection, Library of Congress.

Vital, David. *The Origins of Zionism*. Oxford: Clarendon Press, 1975.

Volkov, Shulamit. *Walther Rathenau: Weimar's Fallen Statesman*. New Haven: Yale University Press, 2012.

Wahrhaftig, Zerah. *Huka le'yisrael: Dat u-medina* [A constitution for Israel: religion and state], Jerusalem: Mesilot, 1988.

Walzer, Michael, Menachem Lorberbaum, and Noam Zohar, eds. *The Jewish Political Tradition*, vol. II: *Membership*. New Haven: Yale University Press, 2006.

Wasserstein, Bernard. *Herbert Samuel: A Political Life*. Oxford: Clarendon Press, 1992.

Wattad, Mohammed S. "A Vision of Citizenship: Arabs in a Jewish & Democratic State." In *Global Governance, Human Rights and Develop-*

ment, Manoj Kumar Sinha, ed., 185–207. New Delhi: Satyam Law International, 2009.

Waxman, Dov. "Israel's Other Palestinian Problem: The Future Vision Documents and the Demands of the Palestinian Minority in Israel." *Israel Affairs* 19/1 (2013): 214–29.

Weber, Timothy P. "American Evangelicals and Israel: A Complicated Alliance." In *Studies in Contemporary Jewry* 24, Jonathan Frankel and Ezra Mendelsohn, eds., 141–57. New York: Oxford University Press, 2010.

Weil, Shalva. "Lost Israelites from North-East India: Re-Traditionalisation and Conversion among the Shinlung from the Indo-Burmese Borderlands." *The Anthropologist* 6/3 (2004): 219–33.

Weinberg, David H. *Between Tradition and Modernity: Haim Zhitlowski, Simon Dubnow, Ahad Ha-Am, and the Shaping of Modern Jewish Identity.* New York: Holmes and Meyer, 1996.

Weiss, Yfaat. *A Confiscated Memory: Wadi Salib and Haifa's Lost Heritage.* New York: Columbia University Press, 2011.

Weitz, Yehiam, ed. *Beyn hason le-revisia: Mea shenot historiografia tzionit* [Between vision and revision: a hundred years of Zionist historiography]. Jerusalem: Salman Shazar, 1996.

———. *Ha-tza'ad ha-rishon le-khes ha-shilton: Tenu'at ha-herut, 1949–1955* [The first step to power: the Herut Movement, 1949–1955]. Jerusalem: Yad Ben Zvi, 2007.

———."The Herut Movement and the Kasztner Trial." *Holocaust and Genocide Studies* 8/3 (1994): 349–71.

Woodward, C. Vann. "The Comparability of American History." In *The Comparative Approach to American History*, C. Vann Woodward, ed. Oxford: Oxford University Press 1997, 2nd ed.

Wolfe, Alan. *At Home in Exile: Why Diaspora Is Good for the Jews.* Boston: Beacon Press, 2014.

Wróbel Bloom, Magdalena M., *Social Networks and the Jewish Migration between Poland and Palestine, 1924–1928.* Bern: Peter Lang, 2016.

Wyman, Mark. "Emigrants Returning: The Evolution of Tradition." In *Emigrant Homecomings: The Return Movement of Emigrants, 1600–2000.* Marjory Harper, ed., 16–31. Manchester: Manchester University Press, 2005.

Yacobi, Haim. " 'Let Me Go to the City': African Asylum Seekers, Racialization and the Politics of Space in Israel." *Journal of Refugee Studies* 24/1 (2010): 1–22.

Yakobson, Alexander. "Jewish Peoplehood and the Jewish State, How Unique?—A Comparative Survey." *Israel Studies* 13/2 (2008): 1–27.

Yehoshua, A. B. *Ha-kir ve-ha-har* [The wall and the mountain]. Tel Aviv: Zmora Bitan, 1989.

———. "The Holocaust as Junction." In Yehoshua, *Between Right and Right*, 1–19. New York: Doubleday & Co., 1981.

Yehudai, Ori. "Forth from Zion: Jewish Emigration from Palestine and Israel, 1945–1960." Ph.D. diss., University of Chicago 2013.

Yerushalmi, Yosef H. *Freud's Moses: Judaism Terminable and Interminable.* New Haven: Yale University Press, 1991.

Zadoff, Noam. "From Mishmar Haʿemek to Elon Moreh: Moshe Shamir and the Socialist Roots of Gush Emuni." In *Reinventing Israel in the Twenty-First Century*, Michael Brenner and Pamela S. Nadell, eds. Detroit: Wayne State University Press 2018.

Zahra, Tara. *The Great Departure: Emigration from Eastern Europe and the Making of the Free World.* New York: W.W Norton & Company, 2016.

Zangwill, Israel. "A Land of Refuge." In *Speeches, Articles and Letters of Israel Zangwill*, Maurice Simon, ed., 234–61. London: Soncino, 1937.

Zentralbüro der Zionistischen Organisation, *Stenographisches Protokoll der Verhandlungen des V. Zionisten-Kongresses in Basel.* Vienna: Erez Israel Verlag, 1901.{or Eretz?}

Zentralbüro der Zionistischen Organisation. *Der XII. Zionisten-Kongress Karlsbad 1.–14. September 1921.* Berlin: Jüdischer Verlag, 1922.

Zertal, Edith. "From the People's Hall to the Wailing Wall." In *Representations* 69 (2000): 96–126.

Zerubavel, Yael. *Recovered Roots: Collective Memory and the Making of Israeli National Tradition.* Chicago: The University of Chicago Press, 1995.

Zimmerman, Joshua D. *Poles, Jews, and the Politics of Nationality.* Madison: Wisconsin University Press, 2004.

Zipperstein, Steven J. *Elusive Prophet: Ahad Ha'am and the origins of Zionism.* Berkeley: University of California Press, 1993.

Ziv, Guy. *Why Hawks Become Doves: Shimon Peres and Foreign Policy Change in Israel.* New York: SUNY Press, 2014.

Zweig, Stefan. *World of Yesterday.* Lincoln: University of Nebraska Press, 1964.

INDEX

Page numbers in italics refer to illustrations.

antisemitism: Ahad Ha'am's view of, 67, 69; Ben-Gurion's youthful experience of, 154; Bund's militance against, 42; Herzl criticized for capitulating to, 33; Herzl's early experiences of, 28–29; Herzl's Old New Land as haven from, 64; Herzl's play about self-criticism and, 29; Holocaust as culmination of, 239; Jabotinsky's Zionism in response to, 108; of Karl Lueger, 24–26; otherness and, 3–4; Pinsker on disease of, 39; of Rathenau though Jewish, 20; recently increasing in Europe, 233, 314n16; recrudescence of, often as anti-Zionism, 287; in right-wing regimes in Europe of 1920s and 30s, 13; rise of political Zionism and, 173; rising in Europe at end of nineteenth century, 18; rising in Herzl's Vienna, 34; Soviet plans to eliminate, 131–32; Steiner on Jewish state as indispensable response to, 244; targeting Mahler, 24

anusim (descendants of forcibly-baptized Jews), 260

apartheid state, Rabin's warning of, 216

Arab population. *See* Palestinian Arab population of Israel; Palestinian Arabs of pre-state Palestine

Arafat, Yassir, 228

Argentina, Jewish state in: envisioned by Herzl, 30, 40, 127; envisioned by Pinsker, 40; in fictional *Neuland*, 250–53, 251

army: *Haganah* (pre-state army), 101, 141; Jewish army demanded by Jabotinsky, 110, 117, 301n71. *See also* Israeli army (*Tzahal*)

Artson, Bradley Shavit, 145

Ashkenazi Jews: condescension toward Middle Eastern Jews, 181; as vast majority of pre-state immigrants, 99

Asia: emerging Jewish groups in, 261, 262–63, 263; German-speaking Jews' view of, 70–71; guest workers in Israel from, 263

assimilation: Buber on risk of national version of, 192; Herzl on Jews remaining in diaspora and, 39; Herzl's early belief in, 28; Herzl's model viewed as, 12, 69; Rathenau's argument for, 19, 20–23

assimilationism: Dubnow's fierce rejection of, 48–49; radical, 11, 19, 20–23

Auerbach, Jerold, 7

Australia, advocates for Jewish territory in, 13, 133, 135

Autoemancipation! (Pinsker), 39, 46

autonomism, 11, 19, 39–40, 44, 47, 48–49; outlawed in Soviet Union, 130

autonomy solution for Jews in Palestine, 12, 90–104

Avichail, Elyahu, 262

Avishai, Bernard, 266, 282

Avner, Yehuda, 208

Avnery, Uri, 178, 306n67

Avni, Yoav, 253

Bachar, Jacques, 63, 64

Baghdad, Jewish population of 1930s in, 99–100

Balfour, Arthur, 89, 102

Balfour Declaration: Arab population of Palestine and, 95–97; British retreat from, in 1939, 109, 124–25; Christian evangelicals' view of, 221; Jabotinsky's insistence that British honor, 109; Jewish immigration and land acquisition subsequent to, 99; mentioned in Israel's Declaration of Independence, 147; "national home" in, 12, 89–92, 123; national loyalties of Jews in Europe and, 97; resolution of First Zionist Congress and, 36, 89; statement of, 89; Twentieth Zionist

Ben-Gurion's request for definition of a Jew and, 14, 161–65; Bnei Menashe of India and, 262–63; Burg's call for cancellation of, 248; case of Brother Daniel and, 167; conversion outside of Israel and, 307n68; guaranteeing Jewish majority, 171; Igbo of Nigeria and, 259; non-Jewish family members of Jews from former Soviet Union and, 264; Ratosh's call for abolition of, 179. *See also* immigration to Israel

laws, 148–49; on marriage and divorce, 103, 148, 150, 282. *See also halakha* (Jewish religious law)

League of Nations Mandate over Palestine. *See* British Mandate over Palestine

Lebanon, and Six-Day War, 188

Lebanon War of early 1980s, 236, 276

Leibovitz, Liel, 6–7

Leibowitz, Yeshayahu, 192, 196–97

Lemba, 259, 260

Lenin's government, 126, 130, 134

Levin, Itzhak, 150

Levinas, Emmanuel, 190

Levinger, Moshe, 214

Lewinsky, Elchanan Leeb, 63

Libya, Jewish immigrants to Israel from, 181

Liessin, Abraham, 45

light unto the nations: Ben-Gurion's vision of, 140, 157; biblical call for, 9; Brit Shalom members' belief in, 106; Canaanites' plan in conflict with, 179; Israel as materialization of, 14; as religious concept underlying Herzl's thought, 86. *See also* model society

Likud party: Begin and, 207; Mizrahi Jews helping to empower, 211; Moshe Shamir in, 195; settler movement and, 217

Lilienblum, Moshe Leib, 46

Lindsey, Hal, 220

Listen America (Falwell), 220

Littwak, David: in Herzl's *Old New Land*, 59–60, 61, 63, 295n29; Nevo's fictional evocation of, 252

Lloyd George, David, 90, 94

lost tribes of Israel: Africans and Asians claiming descent from, 16, 231, 258, 259, 261, 262–63; Black Hebrews in North America and, 260; early Israeli committee to search for, 262; legends of, 316n69; little historical credibility of, 262

Lovers of Zion (Hibbat Zion, *Hovevei Zion*) movement, 40, 46, 67

Luban, Chaim Zelig, 128

Lubavitch, 82

Lubavitcher Rebbe (Shalom Dov Baer Schneersohn), 84

Lubavitcher Rebbe (Menachem Mendel Schneerson) visited by Begin, 207, 208

Lueger, Karl, 24–26, 33–34; photo of, 25

Madagascar: group claiming Jewish descent, 259; as option of Nazis and Polish nationalists, 132

Madrid Middle East Peace Conference, 224

Magnes, Judah Leib, 125, 126

Mahla, Daniel, 85

Mahler, Gustav, 23–24, 26

Maimon, Yehuda Leib, 163

Mann, Thomas, 134

Mapai (Social Democratic) party: absence of constitution and, 147; resistance to introduction of television, 184

Mapam party, 196

Margalit, Avishai, 168

al-Mar'I, Sami, 276

Marmorek, Alexander, 34, 295n29

Marmorek, Oskar, 33–34, 61

marriage and divorce laws, 103, 148, 150, 282

gions conquered from, 88; First Zionist Congress and, 36; Palestinian Arab aspirations and, 81

Oz, Amos, 193, 202–3, 204

Oz-Salzberger, Fania, 234, 284

Pale of Settlement: plan of resettlement to Crimea from, 131; supporters of the Bund in, 43

Palestine: autonomy solution for, 12, 90–104; concepts for future Jewish society in, 12–13; emerging Jewish society of, 99–104; immigration waves to (Aliyah), 40, 101, 232; Jabotinsky's model constitution for, 114, 115–16; land acquisition advancing Zionist cause in, 36, 96, 99; resolution of First Zionist Congress and, 36; in Sykes-Picot agreement of 1916, 88; uncertain borders after British conquest, 94–95. See also Balfour Declaration; British Mandate over Palestine; immigration of Jews to Palestine; one-state solution; partition of Palestine; two-state solution

Palestinian Arab population of Israel, 170–76; Christian evangelicals' disdain for, 221; consisting of 150,000 left in Israel after 1949, 175–76; declining Israeli acceptance of equality for, 278; educated segment fighting for their equality, 276–77; expanded by Six-Day War, 14, 188, 275–76; future state of Israel envisioned by, 272, 279–80; growing anger at being second-class citizens, 174–75, 277; as growing minority, 267, 275; growing radicalization of, 15, 278–79; latent period in national consciousness of, 175–76; laws retroactively sanctioning property seizure from, 172; merging of parties for 2015 Israeli elections, 279; Muslim, Christian, and

secular, 272–73; negotiation with Sadat over autonomy for, 223–24; New Historians on flight/expulsion of 1948/49, 248; not recognizing Israel's right to exist, 174, 282–83, 285; Peres on necessity of reconciliation with, 15, 227; resistance to treatment as minority, 170–71; right-wing attacks on, 217–18; rising prominence of, 275–80; schools of, 268; seen as threat to the state, 173, 276; settler movement and, 173, 216; sharing some culture with Jews of Arab countries, 211; solidarity with Palestinians beyond the Green Line, 276, 277; status in the Jewish state, 171–73; Yehoshua on continuous conflict with, 193

Palestinian Arabs of pre-state Palestine: Ahad Ha'am's warning of conflict with, 67, 69; Balfour Declaration and, 95–96; Borochov's naïve and paternalistic view of, 76; fled or driven out by end of war in 1949, 141, 172, 248, 279; guard protecting Jewish farmers against, 78; Herzl's vision of Jewish state and, 54–55, 60, 63, 65, 81; Jabotinsky's condescension toward, 108; Jabotinsky's policies toward, 110–12, 115–16, 123–24; Jabotinsky's vision of full equality for, 12, 111, 112, 114, 124; national movement beginning among, 80–81; one-state and two-state solutions and, 105; otherness of Jews among, 80; rejecting any partition plans, 123; resisting Jewish immigration to Palestine, 96–97, 117; violence of 1920/21 between Jews and, 90, 96; violence of 1936-1939 against Yishuv by, 117; Zionist attempts to deal with leadership of, 97

Palestinization, 173, 276, 277